AF335254

Legacies of Modernism

Studies in European Culture and History

edited by

Eric D. Weitz and Jack Zipes
University of Minnesota

Since the fall of the Berlin Wall and the collapse of communism, the very meaning of Europe has been opened up and is in the process of being redefined. European states and societies are wrestling with the expansion of NATO and the European Union and with new streams of immigration, while a renewed and reinvigorated cultural engagement has emerged between the East and West. But the fast-paced transformations of the last fifteen years also have deeper historical roots. The reconfiguring of contemporary Europe is entwined with the cataclysmic events of the twentieth century, two world wars and the Holocaust, and with the processes of modernity that, since the eighteenth century, have shaped Europe and its engagement with the rest of the world.

Studies in European Culture and History is dedicated to publishing books that explore major issues in Europe's past and present from a wide variety of disciplinary perspectives. The works in the series are interdisciplinary; they focus on culture and society and deal with significant developments in Western and Eastern Europe from the eighteenth century to the present within a social historical context. With its broad span of topics, geography, and chronology, the series aims to publish the most interesting and innovative work on modern Europe.

Published by Palgrave Macmillan:

Fascism and Neofascism: Critical Writings on the Radical Right in Europe
by Eric Weitz

Fictive Theories: Towards a Deconstructive and Utopian Political Imagination
by Susan McManus

German-Jewish Literature in the Wake of the Holocaust: Grete Weil, Ruth Klüger, and the Politics of Address
by Pascale Bos

Turkish Turn in Contemporary German Literature: Toward a New Critical Grammar of Migration
by Leslie Adelson

Terror and the Sublime in Art and Critical Theory: From Auschwitz to Hiroshima to September 11
by Gene Ray

Transformations of the New Germany
edited by Ruth Starkman

Caught by Politics: Hitler Exiles and American Visual Culture
edited by Sabine Eckmann and Lutz Koepnick

Legacies of Modernism: Art and Politics in Northern Europe, 1890–1950
edited by Patrizia C. McBride, Richard W. McCormick, and Monika Žagar

Legacies of Modernism

Art and Politics in Northern Europe, 1890–1950

Edited By

Patrizia C. McBride,
Richard W. McCormick, and
Monika Žagar

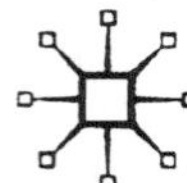

LEGACIES OF MODERNISM

First published in 2007 by
PALGRAVE MACMILLAN™
175 Fifth Avenue, New York, N.Y. 10010 and
Houndmills, Basingstoke, Hampshire, England RG21 6XS
Companies and representatives throughout the world.

PALGRAVE MACMILLAN is the global academic imprint of the Palgrave Macmillan division of St. Martin's Press, LLC and of Palgrave Macmillan Ltd. Macmillan® is a registered trademark in the United States, United Kingdom and other countries. Palgrave is a registered trademark in the European Union and other countries.

ISBN-13: 978–1–4039–7323–8
ISBN-10: 1–4039–7323–7

Library of Congress Cataloging-in-Publication Data

Legacies of modernism : art and politics in northern Europe, 1890–1950 / edited by Patrizia C. McBride, Richard W. McCormick and Monika Žagar.
p. cm. —(Studies in European culture and history)
Based on papers presented at a conference held Spring 2002, University of Minnesota.
Includes bibliographical references and index.
Contents: High, low, and other : the politics of music — Modernism/ Antimodernism, race and eugenics in Scandinavia — Science, technology, and German modernism — Architecture and urban planning in Weimar modernity — The politics of visual culture : Weimar, exile, and postwar — The politics of visual culture in the Third Reich — Modernist politics now : critiques of liberalism.

ISBN 1–4039–7323–7 (alk. paper)
1. Arts—Political aspects—Europe, Northern—History—19th century—Congresses. 2. Arts—Political aspects—Europe, Northern—History—20th century—Congresses. 3. Modernism (Aesthetics)—Europe, Northern—Congress. I. McBride, Patrizia C. II. McCormick, Richard W., 1951– III. Žagar, Monika.

NX180.P64L44 2007
700.94'09034—dc22 2006051384

A catalogue record for this book is available from the British Library.

Design by Newgen Imaging Systems (P) Ltd., Chennai, India.

First edition: February 2007

10 9 8 7 6 5 4 3 2 1

Printed in the United States of America.

Contents

Section III Science, Technology, and German Modernism

Section IV Architecture and Urban Planning in Weimar Modernity

Section V The Politics of Visual Culture: Weimar, Exile, and Postwar

Section VI The Politics of Visual Culture in the Third Reich

Section VII Modernist Politics Now: Critiques of Liberalism

List of Figures

Acknowledgments

This volume is based on papers presented at a conference organized in Spring 2002 by the Department of German, Scandinavian and Dutch at the University of Minnesota, titled "After the Decline of the 'Master Narrative': Rethinking Modernism. Art and Politics in Germany and Scandinavia, 1890–1950." Generous funding for the conference was provided by the Department of German, Scandinavian and Dutch; the Center for German and European Studies; the Center for Scandinavian Studies; the CLA Scholarly Events Fund; the Humanities Institute; the European Studies Consortium; the Norwegian Ministry of Culture; and the Max Kade Foundation. We also want to thank the Ph.D. candidates at Minnesota who worked as research assistants for us: we thank Nicole Grewling for her work on the index and Brechtje Beuker for her research assistance, and we give special thanks to Alison Guenther-Pal, who first lent her invaluable organizational skills to the conference in 2002 and then went on to do such fine work for us as an editorial assistant for this volume. For the cover photo, Meister in Wachs (Masters in Wax, 1928/29) by Umbo (Otto Umbehr), we thank Phyllis Umbehr of the Gallery Kicken, Berlin, as well as Anna Kröger and Maria Makela. For assistance with the other illustrations we thank the Art Institute of Chicago, Sabine Hake, Linda Schulte-Sasse, and (once again) Alison Guenther-Pal. We also thank Maria Makela and Tom Haakenson for their valiant efforts on behalf of illustrations we were not able to use.

Notes on the Contributors

Thomas O. Haakenson is a doctoral candidate in the Department of Cultural Studies and Comparative Literature at the University of Minnesota, Twin Cities. He is the recipient of fellowships from the U.S. Fulbright Program and the Social Science Research Council. He is is working on his dissertation on visual culture in the early-twentieth-century Berlin.

Sabine Hake is the Texas Chair of German Literature and Culture in the Department of Germanic Studies at the University of Texas at Austin. She is the author of *German National Cinema* (2002, published in German in 2004 as *Film in Deutschland: Geschichte und Geschichten ab 1895*), *Popular Cinema of the Third Reich* (2001), *The Cinema's Third Machine: German Writings on Film 1907–1933* (1993), *Passions and Deceptions: The Early Films of Ernst Lubitsch* (1992), as well as of numerous articles on German film and Weimar culture. Her current book project deals with urban architecture and mass utopia in Weimar Berlin.

Poul Houe is Professor of Scandinavian languages and literature at the University of Minnesota. He has written widely on the nineteenth- and twentieth- century Scandinavian and European literature, including such authors as Sören Kierkegaard, Georg Brandes, Henrik Ibsen, and August Strindberg; his next book, a collection of essays on Hans Christian Andersen, will appear in Danish this fall. A regular contributor of critiques on American and Scandinavian culture to Scandinavian newspapers and magazines, he has lectured at numerous conferences and universities in North America and Europe.

Lutz Koepnick is Professor of German, Film and Media Studies at Washington University in St. Louis. He received his Ph.D. from Stanford University in 1994. He is the author of *The Dark Mirror: German Cinema between Hitler and Hollywood* (University of California Press, 2002); *Walter Benjamin and the Aesthetics of Power* (The University of Nebraska Press, 1999), for which he received the MLA's Scaglione Prize for Studies in Germanic Languages and Literatures in 2000; and of *Nothungs*

Modernität: Wagners Ring und die Poesie der Politik im neunzehnten Jahrhundert (Wilhelm Fink Verlag, 1994). His current book project is entitled, *Framing Attention: Windows on Modern German Culture*. He is also the coeditor of *Sound Matters: Essays on the Acoustics of German Culture* (Berghahn Books, 2004), of *Caught by Politics: Hitler Exiles and American Visual Culture* (forthcoming, Palgrave Macmillian) and of *Between the Local and the Global: Re-Visiting the Sites of Postwar German Cinema* (forthcoming, University of Michigan Press).

Maria Makela teaches Art History in the Department of Visual Studies at California College of the Arts. She has written articles and books widely on nineteenth- and twentieth- century German culture, and is the author of *The Munich Secession. Art and Artists in Turn-of-the-Century Munich* and coauthor of *The Photomontages of Hannah Höch*. She is currently coediting an anthology on Max Beckmann and researching a book on rayon.

Patrizia C. McBride is Associate Professor of German at the University of Minnesota, Twin Cities. Her fields of interest include the relationship between literature, philosophy, and political theory, theories of modernity, literary modernism, and Austrian literature and culture. She is the author of *The Void of Ethics: Robert Musil and the Experience of Modernity* (Northwestern University Press, 2006) and of articles on J.M.R. Lenz, Adolf Loos, Jörg Haider, Hermann Broch, and Kurt Schwitters.

Richard W. McCormick is Professor of German at the University of Minnesota, where his research and teaching are focused primarily on German cinema. He is the author of *Politics of the Self: Feminism and the Postmodern in West German Literature and Film* (Princeton University Press, 1991) and *Gender and Sexuality in Weimar Modernity: Film, Literature, and "New Objectivity"* (Palgrave, 2001); he coedited the anthologies *Gender and German Cinema: Feminist Interventions* (Berg, 1993) and *German Essays on Film* (Continuum, 2004).

Andreas Michel is Associate Professor of German and European Studies at Rose-Hulman Institute of Technology. His research focus is on Modern European Intellectual History. His publications include essays on aesthetic modernism, in particular on Carl Einstein, postmodernism, and the philosophy of technology.

Chantal Mouffe is Professor of Political Theory at the Centre for the Study of Democracy at the University of Westminster in London. She has taught and researched in many universities in Europe, North America, and South America and is a member of the Collège International de Philosophie in Paris. She is the editor of *Gramsci and Marxist Theory* (Routledge and Kegan Paul, 1979), *Dimensions of Radical Democracy. Pluralism, Citizenship, Community*

(Verso, 1992) *Deconstruction and Pragmatism* (Routledge, 1996) and *The Challenge of Carl Schmitt* (Verso, 1999); the coauthor, with Ernesto Laclau, of *Hegemony and Socialist Strategy. Towards a Radical Democratic Politics* (Verso, 1985) and the author of *The Return of the Political* (Verso, 1993), *The Democratic Paradox* (Verso, 2000), and *On the Political* (Routledge, 2005).

Carl Niekerk is Associate Professor of German at the University of Illinois, Urbana-Champaign. He is a specialist in modern German literature and culture, and is currently working on a book-length manuscript titled "Reading Mahler: About the Literature, Philosophy, and Paintings in Mahler's Music."

William Rasch is Professor and Chair of the Department of Germanic Studies at Indiana University. He is the author of *Niklas Luhmann's Modernity: The Paradoxes of Differentiation* and *Sovereignty and Its Discontents: On the Primacy of Conflict and the Structure of the Political* (translated into German as *Konflikt als Beruf: Die Grenzen des Politischen*). He has edited a collection of essays by Luhmann called *Theories of Distinction: Redescribing the Descriptions of Modernity* and is coeditor (with Wilfried Wilms) of a volume of critical essays called *Bombs Away: Representing the Air War over Europe and Japan*.

Matthew Rohn is Associate Professor of Art History at St. Olaf College, Northfield, Minnesota. Author of *Visual Dynamics in Jackson Pollock's Abstractions* and contributing author to the *The Prints of Frank Stella, a Catalogue Raisonné 1967–1982*, Rohn has written a variety of articles on modern art, the history of modern art criticism and the intellectual history of American modern culture.

Nils Roll-Hansen is Professor of History and the Philosophy of Science in the Department of Philosophy, the History of Ideas and Art, and Classical Languages at the University of Oslo. His fields of interest include history and the philosophy of biology. He has published works on the history of classical genetics, eugenics, plant breeding, and environmental science, as well as on the interaction of science and politics and on reductionism in biology. He is a co-editor with Gunnar Broberg of *Eugenics and the Modern State* (1997), and the author of *The Lysenko Effect: The Politics of Science* (2005).

Linda Schulte-Sasse is Professor of German Studies at Macalester College. Her research interests include cinema of the Third Reich, American political discourses, and horror cinema. She is author of *Entertaining the Third Reich: Illusions of Nazi Cinema* (Duke University Press, 1996), and is completing a monograph on Dario Argento.

Janet Ward is Associate Professor of History at the University of Nevada Las Vegas. She researches and teaches urban studies, visual culture, European modernity, memory studies, and Holocaust representation. Her book, *Weimar Surfaces: Urban Visual Culture in 1920s Germany*, was published in 2001 with the University of California Press. Her current book project is entitled *Berlin Borders: Building the Post-Wall Metropolis.*

Marc A. Weiner is Professor of Germanic Studies, Adjunct Professor of Comparative Literature, Communication and Culture (Film Studies), and Cultural Studies at Indiana University, Bloomington. His interests include nineteenth- and early-twentieth -century literary and cultural studies of Europe; German and Austrian music; German intellectual history; the Frankfurt School; histories of racial and sexual iconography; German-Jewish relations; Fin-de-Siècle Vienna; and the German film. Recent Publications include: *Antisemitische Fantasien: Die Musikdramen Richard Wagners* Trans. Henning Thies (Berlin, Henschel Verlag, 2000.) German translation of *Richard Wagner and the Anti-Semitic Imagination* (Lincoln, Nebraska: University of Nebraska P, 1997) (winner of the Eugen F. Kayden national book award for best book in the humanities); "Weimar Film, Hollywood Opera: German Cultural History and Modern American Practice," *The Harold Jantz Memorial Lecture* (Oberlin, Oberlin College P, 2001); "Why Does Hollywood Like Opera?" *In between Opera and Cinema*, edited by Jeongwon Joe and Rose Theresa (New York: Garland, 2001), 75–91; "Über Wagner sprechen: Ideologie und Methodenstreit." *In Richard Wagner im dritten Reich*, edited by Jörn Rüsen and Saul Friedländer (Munich, Beck, 2000), 339–59; "In Search of Politics and Music." *Music and Letters* 81, no.1 (February 2000): 65–72; "Opera and the Discourse of Decadence: From Wagner to AIDS." *In Perennial Decay: The Aesthetics and Politics of Decadence in the Modern Era*, edited by Liz Constable, Dennis Denhishoff, and Matthew Potolsky (Philadelphia, University of Pennsylvania Press, 1999), 119–41.

Monika Žagar is Associate Professor of Scandinavian at the University of Minnesota, Twin Cities where she lectures on a variety of subjects within the field of Scandinavian literature and culture. She has a Ph.D. in Scandinavian Studies from the University of California, Berkeley. She has published a number of articles on various authors as well as a book on Dag Solstad: Ideological Clowns: Dag Solstad – From Modernism to Politics (2002). She has served on the editorial board for the Encylopedia of Contemporary Scandinavia; currently she is writing a book on Knut Hamsun.

Introduction: The Future's Past—Modernism, Critique, and the Political

Patrizia C. McBride

The story of how modernism came under fire from postmodern aesthetic practices in the 1960s and 1970s has often been told. At stake was the possibility of redefining the critical and political potential of art beyond categories that had governed aesthetic discourse for centuries. These included the aesthetic concepts of autonomy, representation, temporality, and narrativity, as well as epistemological categories such as a stable self and self-transparent consciousness, linear time and teleological history, or universal morality and self-determining reason. The first wave of critics that read the rise of new artistic and philosophical discourses in Europe and North America as evidence of the end of modernity and the exhaustion of modernism soon found itself faced with intractable conceptual and methodological problems, however. Indeed, early endeavors to define postmodernism in contradistinction to modernism foundered on the conspicuous persistence of modernist concerns in postmodern art and literature. As it soon became clear, the attempt to demarcate epochal caesurae—postmodernism versus modernism, postmodernity versus modernity—remained caught in modes of temporalization and categorization that reproduced the problem rather than offering a solution. Perhaps the most glaring deficit of these early attempts was their failure to grasp the most fruitful tendency within postmodern thought, namely, its paradoxical sense of continuity and rupture with regard to the past; in particular, with regard to its modernist past.[1]

In briefly revisiting this (hi)story, I offer a partial account of the ways in which the postmodern debates fostered an expanded understanding of art's critical potential. What interests me most in this endeavor is the possibility of translating the heightened sensitivity of postmodernism to historical continuity and rupture into a springboard for redefining the critical impetus of art in our day. My admittedly selective discussion of a specific set of philosophical and aesthetic issues is not intended to provide a comprehensive account of the postmodern debates, but rather to stake out a number of questions that suggest the continued relevance of the modernist constellation for our day.

The critical impulse of modernism has been traditionally located in its self-understanding as a critique of modernity. Modernity in this context is broadly defined as a confluence of social and economic processes harnessed by an ideology of progress, secularization, and emancipation, whose mature formulation surfaced in the Enlightenment. According to this narrative, modernity is haunted by an acute sense of crisis, which grows out of the awareness that the modern period had conspicuously strayed from the goals and values that secured its legitimation. It is this crisis that modernism articulates. This account portrays modernism as the aesthetic and cultural sensibility that castigated modernity for its failure to redeem its highest promises, namely, emancipation, justice, and economic equality. This flattering conceptualization of a recurrent modernist self-stylization is complicated by several blind spots, however. According to Jean-François Lyotard, modernism registered the epochal transformation in Western practices of knowledge, which dispensed with the external legitimation of traditional master-narratives—the life of the spirit as grasped by speculative reason or the emancipation of a humanity endowed with inalienable rights. Yet it did so in a nostalgic fashion, and this is what sets it apart from postmodernism. In other words, according to Lyotard, the limitation for modernism lies in the fact that its critique becomes mingled with a nostalgia for what is (about to be) lost, a desire for what it is impelled to reject as impossible (79–81). Other postmodernist critiques, informed by the perspectives of feminism, queer theory, or postcolonial studies, have offered their own commentaries on this nostalgia, noting how it often fed into the modernists' own generalizing and conspicuously undiscriminating master-narratives. In claiming to give voice to the plights of the "modern subject" threatened by the logic of modernization, for instance, modernists often did little more than recount the alienation of white, male, bourgeois subjectivity, unwittingly exposing its troubling proclivity to mistake itself for the default, and thus universal prototype of humanity.[2]

This is not the place to rehearse the long list of criticisms of which modernism became a target and that, to be fair, often constituted a repudiation not of the modernist tradition per se, but rather of the domesticated and highly selective version of high modernism that scholars in the United States and Germany elevated to a safe cultural norm in order to buttress the deeply conservative academic and cultural environment of the 1950s and 1960s. Suffice it to say that critics generally refrained from concluding that such blind spots irremediably tainted the critical impulse of modernism. After all, this conclusion would have flown in the face of the series of modernist returns within postmodern critical practices. For the more attentive observers the question rather became how to negotiate the historical caesura symptomatically expressed in the postmodern debates. At stake was the perceived need to (re)define the critical and political potential of art in the years spanning the 1970s to the mid 1980s, when several countries in Western Europe witnessed the failure of the student movement and its coda of terrorism and disenchantment, which were accompanied by the conservative retrenchments of the Reagan-Thatcher era.

As Andreas Huyssen perceptively put it in an important essay on postmodernism, "in the age of late capitalism, [the crisis of modernism] is a new crisis of art's relationship to society."[3] Huyssen's aim in this essay was not so much to defend modernism as to rescue postmodernism from the charge of being apolitical or, worse yet, affirmative of a status quo defined by the unholy alliance of political neoconservatism and multinational capitalism. If postmodernism looked arbitrary or light-weight to some contemporary critics, he maintained, this was because it was measured against criteria of critical engagement schooled on the most austere version of high modernism and formulated at times of extreme crisis (totalitarianism as the backdrop for Adorno's high modernism and Lukács' realism, the Cold War for Clement Greenberg's and the New Critics' version of high modernism) (Huyssen, *Great Divide* 197). These criteria were no longer adequate for evaluating the critical potential of art in the1980s because the critical interventions of postmodernism unfolded in a field of ambivalent and multiply coded meanings that could not be grasped by means of the dichotomizing categories forged on the "classical accounts of modernism," namely, "progress vs. reaction, left vs. right, present vs. past, modernism vs. realism, abstraction vs. representation, avant-garde vs. Kitsch" (Huyssen, *Great Divide* 217). As Huyssen added in a later essay cowritten with David Bathrick, these neat polarities were not at all inherent in the modernist tradition they sought to describe, but rather represented highly selective categories deployed in the postwar period to contain the heterogeneity of modernist practices and thereby purge them of their ambivalence. The result was a sanitized, politically tenable, and morally exemplary version of high modernism.

Huyssen's achievement lies in having shown that the presumably monolithic discourse of modernism in Germany and the United States was a projection of conservative critics and of a specific historical constellation in the immediate postwar period and in having highlighted the plurality of genealogies that make up the modernist tradition. If the postmodern debates marked the erosion of the categories traditionally deployed in describing the critical interventions of modernism and postmodernism alike, then the end of the Cold War and the ensuing radicalization of fundamentalisms of various kinds dealt established discourses on the critical role of the artist and the intellectual a further blow, for they produced a weakening of the very categories that had sustained Cold War political discourse: liberalism, democracy, rational consensus, equality, and human rights. In analyzing these changes in unified Germany, Huyssen has noted that the fall of the Berlin Wall and the process of unification marked "the end of the unquestioned role in West German intellectual life of the left-liberal consensus" (*Twilight Memories* 45). At the same time, they helped to test the limits of distinctions such as left and right, progressive and conservative, and democracy and illiberalism. In the immediate aftermath of 1989, many of the critical interventions of intellectuals and artists concerning Germany's unification and its new role in the international arena exposed the ideological parochialism and historical myopia of traditional intellectual discourse, revealing the need for a "redefinition of the role of intellectuals, writers, and artists in the new Germany" (Huyssen, *Twilight Memories* 42).

This redefinition is underway, not only in Germany, but also throughout Europe and North America. One may well argue that established aesthetic concepts, cultural norms, and the very categories of classical political discourse have become more porous at the beginning of a new millennium marked by the complex interplay of political regionalisms and economic globalization. Given this situation, what can a rereading of modernism offer us today and how should one approach this task? At issue is the need for an analytical framework suited for articulating the perception of both unsettling proximity and utter remoteness that modernism evokes as a circumscribed constellation of aesthetic and philosophical issues—the dispersion of subjectivity and the crisis of artistic expression, the differentiation of life spheres and the relativization of structures of knowledge, the instability of the real and the contingency of the ethical. These concerns are both intimately connected to contemporary debates, irrevocably cut off from our present by a series of historical caesurae nested in the folds of interlocking political, economic, social, and technological developments. It is precisely this befuddling sense of modernism's concomitant closeness and remoteness that seems to defy all attempts at portraying its relation to our contemporary perspective in terms of a linear sequence of discrete historical phenomena. But if modernism appears both irreducibly past and tremendously present, what is the analytical value of this observation and how is one to translate it into productive categories of analysis?

Hal Foster has confronted this issue head-on in his investigation of the relation between the historical avant-garde and the neo–avant-garde movements of the 1960s and 1970s. Writing ten years after Huyssen's essay on postmodernism, Foster is also intent on (re)defining the critical potential of art in a "post-age" that finds itself at a loss as it tries to discriminate between genuine aesthetic innovation and effect-seeking "anything goes," between selfless artistic engagement and self-enamored stylization, between ironic critique of art's commodification and opportunistic exploitation of an overheated art market. Starting from Peter Bürger's momentous conceptualization of avant-garde art, Foster takes issue with the teleological notions of time and historical unfolding that prompted Bürger to view the historical avant-garde as the sole bearer of a critical and aesthetic project, which the neo–avant-garde could only ape and betray. Freud's concept of *Nachträglichkeit*, or deferred action, provides Foster with a tool for productively complicating the linearity of Bürger's account. Drawing on Lacan's reading of Freud, Foster likens history to the structure of subjectivity as "a relay of anticipations and reconstructions of traumatic events" (*Return* 29). In this model, traumatic events are not endowed with fixed meanings that unfold chronologically from the point of occurrence. Rather, the structure of trauma is such that it requires other, later events to serve as triggers for a resurfacing of the traumatic event. It is this process of repeated resurfacing that plays out as trauma. To the extent that trauma is constitutive for the structure of subjectivity, this complex temporal interplay makes up the very fabric of the subject. In Foster's words, "one event is only registered through another that recodes it; we come to be who we are only in deferred action (*Nachträglichkeit*)" (*Return* 29).

The appeal of reading history in terms of traumatic subjectivity lies for Foster in the possibility of overcoming "any simple schema of before and after, cause and effect, origin and repetition" (*Return* 29). There is no sense of an origin or inception of meaning; rather, meaning is assigned and reassigned in a complex exchange among different temporal triggers. What emerges when one extends this temporal structure to the relations between the historical and the neo avant-gardes is "a complex relation of anticipation and reconstruction" (Foster, *Return* 13). This interplay allows Foster to amend Bürger's thesis about the presumably fraudulent practices of the neo–avant-garde. Far from seeing the neo–avant-garde as opportunistically mimicking its historical forerunner, this perspective portrays it as that "which comprehends and enacts" the project of the historical avant-garde (Foster, *Return* 20)—a comprehension and enaction that have nothing to do with closure and completion, or with the better vision presumably gained in hindsight. "The avant-garde returns from the future" (Foster, *Return* 29): this oxymoron well captures the paradoxical temporality entailed in the relation of mutual implication Foster is describing. For the anticipation that the historical avant-garde represents is itself part of the backward projection (or reconstruction) operated by the neo–avant-garde.

Thus Foster's model makes it possible to grasp the relation between the two "objects" in a temporally open-ended, nonhierarchical fashion, which takes into account the critical investment of the observer whose observations establish this very relation. If the aesthetic and critical practices at the onset of the twentieth century and in the aftermath of World War II can illuminate each other outside of any relation of cause and effect or origin and derivation, it is because, in keeping with the analogy of trauma, they are activated by analogous triggers.

I am interested in examining what it might mean to "reconstruct the modernist past" from today's vantage point, or, to paraphrase another of Foster's formulations, to what extent we can argue that "modernism returns from the future." The issue is whether there is something like a traumatic constellation that might prompt us to appropriate the heterogeneous tradition of modernism as a productive symptom of our day in a self-aware act of temporal inversion. I do not intend to offer yet another metanarrative, the likes of which were often simultaneously longed for and undermined within the modernist tradition, but I argue that what returns from "our future" in the modernist constellation is an awareness about the insufficiencies of established ways of thinking the human, of conceptualizing individual and collective experience, as well as an anxiety about the disastrous effects that could ensue if the admittedly inadequate categories currently being deployed were to be dismissed. This anxiety arises from confrontation with a series of historical traumas, of events that defy the experiential and interpretive categories available to individuals and collectives: World War I and the rise of totalitarianism for European modernism; the war in the Balkans, the destruction of the World Trade Center, or the genocides perpetrated in Africa in full view of a complacent international community for our present. In pointing to a traumatic constellation in which both the modernists and our present possibly share, my intention is not to draw historical parallels between distinct sets of horrific events, much less learn edifying lessons from the past. Rather I am concerned with acknowledging that modernism first registered the utter bankruptcy of a discourse on the human that had harnessed Western culture for centuries and that it openly confronted the challenges, the risks, and the temptations entailed in moving beyond this discourse. I believe that our time faces challenges not unlike those that shaped the modernist constellation. These challenges are at the heart of the temporal interplay of anticipation and reconstruction that allows us to claim that modernism returns from the future. The issue then becomes understanding the nature of this return and how it interacts with our present.

Walter Benjamin's essay "Experience and Poverty" represents a paradigmatic example for the modernist discourse to which I am referring and can help specify the significance of its return for the twenty-first century. Written in 1933, the essay offers itself as a commentary on an epoch ominously framed by two historical cataclysms in Germany, namely, the carnage of World War I and the affirmation of National Socialism. Benjamin starts by noting how, at the onset of the twentieth century, technology and its applications in all realms of life so deeply transformed individual and collective existence that a radical disconnect began separating everyday experience from customary ways of making sense of it. "We have given up one portion of the human heritage after another" ("Experience" 735), Benjamin remarks, for this heritage appears to be of little use in dealing with the present; indeed, received modes of interpreting existence seem utterly obsolete. The sentiment voiced by Benjamin can easily be fitted into a discourse concerning the erosion of Western cultural and metaphysical signposts—the self, the community of men, reason, history, and freedom—that reaches back to Nietzsche. Yet Benjamin's text fails to reinforce the nostalgia for lost points of reference that marks, for instance, the discourse of cultural pessimism of contemporaries like Thomas Mann, Rainer Maria Rilke, or Hugo von Hofmannsthal. The impossibility of drawing on inherited interpretive categories for understanding experience has resulted in an utter "poverty of experience," Benjamin concedes, but this is not as negative a condition as the formulation seems to suggest. In fact, this experiential paucity inspired contemporaries such as Adolf Loos, Paul Klee, Paul Scheerbart, and Cubist painters to reject "the traditional, solemn, noble image of man festooned with all the sacrificial offerings of the past" and to embrace a radical new vision freed from good old humanist crutches such as "humanlikeness" (Benjamin, "Experience" 733). The artificial language in which these artists communicate enables them to imagine and shape a future that is not held hostage by inherited experiential modes.

Key to the efforts of the artists Benjamin celebrates is a "new, positive concept of barbarism," which they have embraced. The barbarian is an individual who lacks the interpretive categories that would allow him to turn his bare existence into meaningful experience. This poverty of experience forces him "to start from scratch [. . .], to begin with a little and build up further, looking neither left nor right" (Benjamin, "Experience" 732). This enterprise appears at once exhilarating and frightening, for also inscribed in the term "barbarian" is an awareness of the violence and disruption that could be unleashed by such an undertaking. For the barbarian stands outside civilization as its inassimilable other. His relation to civilization is marked by an antagonism lined with potential violence. It is nonetheless apparent that for Benjamin the poverty of experience that characterizes his age leaves no choice but to explore barbarism. There is no point in instilling new life into the moribund ideas of experience and humanity that have historically underpinned the civilization of the West, for those ideas have been discredited by the disruption of World War I. Unfolding further the metaphor of the barbarian, one can argue that Benjamin's text registers the degree to which Western civilization had already become porous to the barbarian "outside" against which it had defined itself for centuries—the contemporary violence of the National Socialist regime constituting an ominous seal to this process. Within this frame, Benjamin's positive concept of barbarism points to the need for boldly investigating the "outside" to current notions of humanity—an outside that had already powerfully infiltrated modern life—in order to imagine more adequate modes of individual and collective experience.

One can argue that in the contemporary Western world the sense of rupture described by Benjamin is more acute than ever. If the end of the Cold War prompted early enthusiasts to prophesy the imminent triumph of the Western model of liberal democracy and of its underlying vision of enlightened and compassionate humanity,[4] one can claim that the discrepancy between this hopeful vision and the reality of resurgent religious, ethnic, and national fundamentalisms on the old continent and elsewhere has become ever more conspicuous at the dawn of the twenty-first century. For many, this awareness is compounded by the belief that the post–Cold War world of economic globalization and information revolution is being threatened by a presumably obstreperous and insufficiently enlightened Islam. I would like to suggest that the traumatic horizon we share with modernism might be found precisely in this sense of disconnect, as well as in the perception of an imperative to inspect the "barbarian" outside to current notions of individual and collective experience. In this perception fear about the ruinous consequences that might ensue if one were to abandon old constructs and beliefs holds the balance with awareness that failure to scrutinize the old notions is already producing calamitous effects.

Benjamin's positive notion of barbarism recalls the radical interrogation that is at the heart of the ethos championed by Michel Foucault in "What is Enlightenment?" Foucault's discussion is relevant in this context because it outlines the two ends of a field of tension in which the Western discourse on the human has unfolded at least since the eighteenth century. On the one hand there is the Enlightenment ethos of modernity, an attitude driven by an exhilarating critique of the historical "limits that are imposed on us" and by the "experiment with the possibility of going beyond them" (Foucault, *Reader* 50). At issue is a constant reinvention of the parameters of what it means to be human whose quintessentially modern site is art, as Foucault maintains in pointing to Baudelaire's heroic self-stylization. At the other end of the spectrum there is a desire, sometimes as strong as a compulsion, to ground this critique in some stable notions of "man" or the community of "men,"[5] which in the West has issued in various forms of humanism. Foucault is adamant about not conflating the two. Humanism, he notes, is a variable set of themes and values that "has always been obliged to lean on certain conceptions of man borrowed from religion, science, or politics." Unlike the inherently self-transcending reflection that defines the Enlightenment, humanism operates within a circular field of ideological legitimation, for it "serves to color and to justify the conceptions of man to which it is, after all, obliged to take recourse" (Foucault, *Reader* 44). That is to say, the Enlightenment ideal of radical interrogation of historical practices and constructs is antithetical to the circular operation of ideological stabilization through which humanism at once borrows from and lends legitimation to presumably desirable notions of the human. Taking Foucault's remarks to their logical conclusion, one could argue that the ethos of the Enlightenment is of necessity a critique of humanism anytime the advantages of the stable constructs humanism can provide are exceeded by their disadvantages—for instance, their inability to offer a viable framework for interpreting experience, which is at the heart of Benjamin's dispute with late-nineteenth-century humanism.

And yet the restraint with which Foucault addresses the issue of humanism in this text is remarkable for a thinker who had explored it time and again as a powerful tool of subjugation in his genealogical inquiries into entwinement of discourse, knowledge, and power in Western culture. While it is clear that his sympathies here lie with the imaginative critique Foucault associates with the Enlightenment, his appeal for an investigation of the historical links between humanism and Enlightenment suggests that he is nonetheless inclined to grant humanism a legitimate role in the field of tension that has historically defined the Western discourse on the human. If Foucault is willing to come to terms with humanism, it is because humanism both expresses and fulfills a basic need for ideological stabilization, for providing a shared framework for individual and collective experience. At the same time, the ethos of the Enlightenment is needed to curb the humanist propensity for disguising a contingent, historical model of the human in terms of essential, universal, suprahistorical truths. Thus the modern condition Foucault probingly describes in his praise of the Enlightenment appears founded in a paradox. On the one hand there is the need for a stable framework of desirable humanness to ground meaningful action and political life; on the other hand there is the imperative to constantly scrutinize the available paradigm(s) of desirable humanity in order to allow for their outside to gain expression and for competing models to surface. Enlightenment emerges in this context as the historical inquiry into the possibility of a critique that retains its claim to ground political action while drawing on models of humanness that are admittedly time-bound, contingent, and mutually competing.[6] The quest that Benjamin saw triggered by the contemporary disconnect between experience and available models of interpretation becomes for Foucault the condition of possibility for modernity's Enlightenment. Thus, when the modernist Baudelaire proposes a notion of beauty consigned to the ability to see that the "lasting" is not beyond or behind the "ephemeral," it is rather nested deep inside it: what is at stake for Foucault is not just a new historical concept of the beautiful, but rather the ability of art to embody the ethos of modernity and to stake out a field of meaningful action for the present (Foucault, *Reader* 39–42).

The operation of temporal inversion through which modernism returns from the future, I argue, enables the contemporary critic to rethink the familiar trope of a "death of the subject" so as to also view it as the collapse of the self-assured subjectivity of nineteenth-century humanism. The relevance of the modernist ethos for the current century lies in its difficult negotiation of humanist stabilization and Enlightenment critique. This negotiation offers a broad framework for the writings collected in this volume, which are based on papers presented at a conference held by the Department of German, Scandinavian and Dutch at the University of Minnesota in 2002. The cultural and geographical focus for the volume lies in Northern Europe, with a special emphasis on Germany and Scandinavia.

Section one is dedicated to the politics of music in the tension between high and popular culture. Marc Weiner's contribution explores the anxieties underlying the binary oppositions that structure the modernist perception of music. In focusing on the ultraconservative composer Hans Pfitzner, Weiner analyzes his best known opera, *Palestrina*, as expressing Pfitzner's anxieties about the instabilities of these binaries, especially the one opposing written and performed text. Such anxieties, Weiner suggests, cannot be simply accounted for in terms of Pfitzner's extreme right-wing ideology, but rather cut across the political spectrum of the modernist reflection on music. In further complicating the political assessment of the modernist musical imagination, Weiner stresses that Pfitzner's aesthetic practice often contradicts the fears expressed in his theoretical work, thus mitigating the very binaries he set out to reinforce. Carl Niekerk's chapter examines Gustav Mahler's musical practice from the perspective of a complex, cultural border crossing. In drawing on the Dutch reception of the composer at the beginning of the twentieth century, Niekerk reconstructs Mahler's paradoxical articulation of German and Jewish identities through such sources as Richard Wagner's music and Julius Langbehn's *Rembrandt as Educator*.

The writings in section two articulate the multiple intersections of the discourses on art, culture, and race that negotiated the humanist legacy in Scandinavia. Poul Houe examines the 1882 novel *Germanernes Lærling* (GL;

The Teutons' Apprentice) by Danish writer Karl Gjellerup as paradigmatic for the aporias of the modernist movement in Nordic literature. Houe traces Gjellerup's move away from naturalism and embrace of a secularized religiosity inflected with neo-Romantic mysticism as symptoms of a humanist resistance to the modern movement. Gjellerup's ambivalent stance, so Houe, succeeded in problematizing both the discourse of humanism and the practice of modernism. Along similar lines, Monika Žagar reads Knut Hamsun's novel *Ringen sluttet* (The Ring is Closed, 1936) as expressing the predicament of humanist subjectivity in modernity. As Žagar argues, the novel casts its protagonist Abel Brodersen in the deeply oxymoronic and racially overdetermined position of the "white negro" to at once denounce the modern domestication of eccentric humanity and express modernity's impossible quest for authenticity. Nils Roll-Hansen reconstructs the intellectual and scientific roots of the eugenics movement in Scandinavia through a comparison with Nazi Germany. In focusing on the practice of sterilization, Roll-Hansen traces the complex relation between science, technology, and politics in pre– and post–World War II Scandinavia in order to offer a meditation on the political role of science in our day.

Section three examines the modernist negotiation of the human in the fields of the life sciences and technology. Andreas Michel questions received wisdom on the illiberal turn taken by German scientific discourse in the first decades of the twentieth century. In examining the cultural writings of German engineers, Michel shows how their attempt at reconciling technology and culture did not always lend credit to the theory of a fascist-leaning, "reactionary modernism," that Jeffrey Herf articulated in his influential study. Thomas Haakenson focuses on the category of "immediate visual perception" articulated within the life sciences in late-nineteenth-century Germany and inscribed in the organization of Rudolf Virchow's pathbreaking Museum of Medical Pathology in Berlin. According to Haakenson, this discourse forms a backdrop for Hannah Höch's photomontages, which visually turned the new scientific standard of perception on its head in order to critique its surreptitious domestication of the human.

Section four focuses on the modernist contribution to architecture and urban planning. Sabine Hake undertakes a reevaluation of the utopian imaginary of the architectural avant-garde by drawing on Ludwig Hilberseimer's 1928 proposal for an office and business complex in Berlin's Friedrichstadt. According to Hake, Hilberseimer's never-realized, hyper rationalistic design belies a fear of the chaotic space of the city, while at the same time exemplifying the avant-garde's propensity for aesthetic solutions that suppressed the socioeconomic and cultural divisions of Weimar Germany. Janet Ward also scrutinizes the visual imaginary of the architectural avant-garde to raise the question about the democratic potential of urban architecture in our day. In her chapter, the multicoded trope of the tower of Babel serves as a catalyst for reflections on the expressionist tower, the urban skyscraper, and the missing Twin Tower silhouette of the World Trade Center.

Sections five and six are dedicated to the exploration of visual culture, especially film and painting. Maria Makela probes the political valences of the postexpressionist, representational visual styles associated with New Objectivity. Makela pleads for an analysis that refrains from typecasting the style and its practitioners as either left or right wing. As she argues, New Objectivity "meant different things at different times even within the career of a single artist," as demonstrated by Rudolf Schlichter's tortuous trajectory from left-wing intellectual to Nazi sympathizer to Nazi critic. Richard McCormick's section sets out to question conventional wisdom regarding the expressionist roots of the American film noir. In reviewing the American career of three prominent émigré directors, Fritz Lang, Georg Pabst, and Billy Wilder, McCormick shows how their influence on Hollywood's film noir owes more to the sardonic realism of New Objectivity than to the late-Romantic irrationalism commonly associated with expressionism. Matthew Rohn examines the post–World War II reception of German modernism through the lens of the most influential art critic in the United States, Clement Greenberg. Rohn reconstructs the early Cold War framework that led Greenberg to revise his early endorsement of Germanic modernist painting in favor of a French modernism untainted by National Socialism and Marxism. Lutz Koepnick's chapter examines the architecture of Hitler's Alpine retreat at Berghof as emblematic for the paradoxical principle governing much of National Socialist visual culture, namely, its endeavor to engage the modern so as to escape from it. As Koepnick shows, the cinematic, visual space construed by the Berghof deploys radical strategies of spatial modernization in order to neutralize "the multiplicity of modern embodied vision" and "to lodge seductive equations of power and sight directly in the beholders' senses." In the final section, Koepnick discusses two installations by Marcel Odenbach, which offer a keen commentary on the manipulation of sight performed by the architecture of the Berghof. Linda Schulte-Sasse investigates the symbolic doubling of art and life within the gender economy of two Nazi feature films, *Venus Before the Court* (1941) and *Freed Hands* (1939). While both movies ostensibly celebrate high art and modern patriarchy as true paths to women's liberation, this very message is undercut by the low-brow, kitschy nature of the entertainment film favored by the German film industry in the Third Reich, as it is explicitly foregrounded by the farcical elements of the 1939 movie.

The writings in the final section interrogate the potential for our day of the critique of liberalism articulated by the prominent political theorist and Nazi ideologue Carl Schmitt. Chantal Mouffe draws on Schmitt to analyze the limits of the Western model of liberal democracy. The liberal postulates of rational communication and consensus, so Mouffe's Schmittian argument, fail to grant expression to the existential antagonisms that underlie political life. According to Mouffe, the resurgent fundamentalisms of the post–Cold War period can be seen as the radicalization of antagonisms, which liberalism invisibilizes rather than confronting. Finally, William Rasch reconstructs Schmitt's polemics against the liberal argument through which the United States sought to legitimize its newly gained hegemony in the world politics of the interwar period. Rasch shows how Schmitt's main charge, according to which liberalism's celebrated rule of law does not overcome, but rather surreptitiously naturalizes the preliberal concept of sovereignty, serves well to articulate the limits of the liberal claims that continue to authorize U.S. foreign policy today.

Notes

1. For an account of the postmodern debates in aesthetics, philosophy, and social theory, see Calinescu 1987; Huyssen 1986; Bauman 1991; and Sheppard 2000. For attempts at delimiting postmodernist from modernist practices see Ihab Hassan's and Umberto Eco's typological models; for accounts that see in postmodernism not a qualitative change, but rather a radicalization of modernist concerns and practices, Lyotard, "Answering the Question: What Is Postmodernism" (in *The Postmodern Condition*) is instructive. See also Art Berman's account of modernism as modernity's bad consciousness in chapter one of his *Preface to Modernism*. As Richard Sheppard has noted, the great accomplishment of the postmodern debates lies in having established a connection between modernism as an aesthetic sensibility and modernity as a social and economic process, and in having raised anew the question of the critical role of art in modernity. Pivotal essays in this regard were Jürgen Habermas' "Modernity Versus Postmodernity" (1980; trans. 1981) and Fredric Jameson's "Postmodernism or the Cultural Logic of Late Capitalism" (1984; reprinted in *Postmodernism, or the Cultural Logic of Late Capitalism*).
2. See the arguments made by Linda Hutcheon in *The Politics of Postmodernism*.
3. See Huyssen's essay "Mapping the Postmodern," from 1984, reprinted in *After the Great Divide* 178–221, here 218.
4. See for instance Francis Fukujama's *The End of History*.
5. I purposely retain the gendered formulation deployed by Foucault as symptomatic of the mechanisms of exclusion that inform the generalizing and universalizing labels of humanism.
6. As Hubert Dreyfus and Paul Rabinow have argued, in his reading of Kant Foucault pursued a notion of maturity—that is, a model of humanness worth striving for—that is no longer grounded in presumably atemporal laws and metaphysical truths about the human, but instead derives its legitimation precisely from self-referential reflection on its historicity and contingency. Dreyfus and Rabinow 118.

Section I

High, Low, and Other: The Politics of Music

Hans Pfitzner and the Anxiety of Nostalgic Modernism

Marc A. Weiner

The perception of sound unfolds in the modernist imagination across a trajectory of polar oppositions that are legacies of long-standing musical traditions. Already in the nineteenth century, Wagner's juxtaposition of German versus non-German aesthetic practice formed a conceptual nexus, a structure of thought, that reappears in the works of Nietzsche, with its polarization of northern and southern art, and in the reflections on music in the writings of a host of celebrated German and Austrian authors of the early twentieth century, such as Hauptmann, Dauthendey, Schnitzler, Werfel, Hesse, and Thomas Mann, and of course in the critical reflections of Theodor Adorno.

The perception of music through a conceptual structure that opposes one category against another by no means vanished as the Frankfurt School was superseded by its postmodernist followers, for Adorno's polarizations find their structural parallel in the recent work of Peter Sloterdijk, who—in an essay entitled "Where are we when we hear music?" (*Wo sind wir, wenn wir Musik hören?*)—has argued that our entire musical experience can be segregated into two categories that are nonetheless intimately, dialectically related: into a kind of music that is outward-directed, recalling for Sloterdijk the post-Lapsarian experience of birth, and the kind of music that expresses a yearning for a return to stasis, to rest, to the fluidity of preconsciousness, or to the timeless tranquility of the womb:

> Prior to individuation, we hear in an anticipatory fashion—that is, fetal hearing anticipates the world as a noise- and sound-totality [*Geräusch- und Klangtotalität*], which is always in the process of developing; it listens ecstatically in the darkness toward the world of sound, usually oriented in a mundane or worldly fashion [*meist weltwärts orientiert*]. . . . After the formation of the subject, we hear backwards—the ear wants to undo the world as a noise-totality, longs to return to the archaic euphonious state of the pre-worldly interior, it activates the memory of a euphonic stillness-as-being

> [*Enstase*], which accompanies us like an afterglow from Paradise. One could say that the individuated or unhappy ear strives inexorably from the real world back to a space of the inmost a-cosmic reminiscences.
>
> Understood in this way, music was always the connection between two tendencies, which created two dialectically related gestures. One leads out of a positive nothingness, out of the world-less, interior, uterus-familiar [*aus dem Schoßhaften*] toward the world into the manifestation, the open scene, the world arena—the other, out of the fullness, the dissonance, the overburdened back into the world-less, the free, the interiorized. The music of the coming-into-the-world is a Will to Power as sound, which emerges along the lines of a continuum from within and which desires itself like an irrepressible life gesture; the music of retreat, however, after the dissolution of the continuum, strives to return to the a-cosmic condition of hovering [*in den akosmischen Schwebezustand*], in which the damaged life, as an Unwill to Power, collects and heals itself (Sloterdijk, "Wo sind wir" 301; see also "Poetik der Entbindung" and "Die sokratische Maieutik").[1]

This last observation brings to light something that I feel informs other oppositions in the modernist perception of sound as well, namely, an anxiety that helps to account for the rigidity of these polarized extremes. Just as the move out into the world is fraught with danger, so the desire for a return to the warmth of stasis may prove a utopian fantasy, something in danger of never being regained. Though this is seldom articulated as such, a good deal of the work on musical modernism implicitly concerns the psychological investment, the anxiety behind its pervasive polarized motifs of a loss of control and a recurrent nostalgia that typifies the modernist musical imagination. On the one hand, music emerges here as a sign of insurrectionary, libidinal forces usually associated with leftist politics (that is, "outward-directed music"; this is certainly how it appears in the works of Thomas Mann), and on the other, it can also be associated with something that is more familiar and more comforting, with the status quo and a longing for tradition, as something more conservative. Of course, this bifurcated model (juxtaposing interiority and stasis with exteriority and teleological development) is so simplistic as to prove ultimately difficult to apply to a host of aesthetic objects and projects in the modernist age, but nonetheless, if Sloterdijk is right, both the outward or future-oriented and the introspective or nostalgic trajectories of Western music are based on an originary cataclysmic event, one that scars the perception of music forever, and it is this repressed event that may help to account for the pervasive psychological investment in musical polarities that shows up repeatedly in this period. This perception of music as scarred transcends both its manifestation as an art perceived as volatile or threatening and one that functions as a hallmark of tradition.

The work of Hans Pfitzner (1869–1949)—that most cantankerous of conservative musical modernists and in his day rivaled for the title of preeminent German composer only by Richard Strauss (Mahler-Werfel 25, 164)—constitutes an example of the modernist musical imagination affiliated not solely with music as a sign of leftist insurrectionary forces, but quite the opposite, with avowed indebtedness to venerated musical traditions that constitute for Pfitzner the longed-for status quo, the pre-Lapsarian point of rest so threatened by the outward-directed forces of change in the modern world. The fact that Pfitzner's fame was so extensive, and yet so temporally circumscribed, makes him a figure particularly revealing of his time.[2] While his work is located at the far end of the right-wing of the political spectrum, it also reveals an anxiety that collapses the polarizations of musical modernism, and hence those found on both sides of the political experience.

Pfitzner's work, like that of his great model, Wagner, unfolds according to a cognitive system that views the world in terms of binary oppositions, so that a given aesthetic practice is defined for him by another kind of art that it rejects. The rigid, thematic oppositions in Pfitzner's reflections on music that define the sociopolitical world of early-twentieth-century Germany are well known: left-wing foreigners, internationalists, Bolsheviks, and Jews form one wing of a cultural climate vilified by those with whom Pfitzner identifies: German nationalists faithful to—and longing for—the political hegemony and a set of values of the Wilhelminian Empire. These binarisms are informed by other tropes as well, such as the feminine versus the masculine, the popular versus the more esoteric, the public versus the private spheres, the masses versus the individual, the ephemeral versus the legitimate, and the insurrectionary versus the law-abiding citizen. Pfitzner abhors the influx into Germany in the postwar years of foreign cultural production—such as jazz, boxing, the circus, and film—and the experimental and innovative musical practices of the New Vienna School of Schönberg, Berg, and Webern, as well as that of his contemporaries Werner Egk, Carl Orff, Ernst Křenek, and Ferruccio Busoni, all of them representing for him a disrespect for the proven superiority of German musical tradition manifested in the works of Beethoven, E.T.A. Hoffmann, Schumann, and above all Wagner, whose sole representative and legitimate heir Pfitzner believed himself to be (Adamy 41–85; Skouenborg 9–17; Weiner, *Undertones* 35–71).

What interests me more is another binarism that has received far less attention in the recent discussion of Pfitzner, namely the opposition within his essays and music dramas of signifier and signified, of the material of representation and the transcendental or suprasensible realm to which it alludes—an opposition and a preoccupation that directly link Pfitzner to

Wagner and to the German idealist tradition—because that opposition makes clear the tremendous anxiety underlying virtually all of the other oppositions just mentioned, an anxiety that these rigid, polarized structures will collapse, thus making impossible a return to tradition as the guarantor of identity, of (to refer once again to Sloterdijk's model) stasis as repose (examples of the discussion of Pfitzner within the last twenty-five years can be found in Adamy; Williamson; Vogel; and the 2001 special issue of *The Musical Quarterly* devoted to the composer). The opposition of music as conceptual form and sounding presence harbors within it a fear that the place of repose, the pre-Lapsarian point, the "afterglow from Paradise" that is necessarily superior to every specific, and therefore ephemeral quotidian experience, can never be perfectly achieved, leaving the conscious subject, the "unhappy ear" awash in the flow toward "the world arena."

Pfitzner was primarily concerned with what he believed to be the development of an irreverent, capricious, and willful approach to the performance, and especially the staging, of musical-dramatic works in the opera houses of early twentieth-century Germany, manifested most blatantly perhaps in the experimental stagings of the Kroll Oper in Berlin. In response to the changing cultural scene in early twentieth-century Europe, with its growing cosmopolitanism and experimentation, Pfitzner sought to establish guidelines for controlling the means by which an artwork could be interpreted, both by those who mediate its reception (such as directors and performers) and by the public at large. In his published writings from 1905 to 1929—*Stage Tradition* (*Bühnentradition*), *The Futurist Danger* (*Futuristengefahr*), *The New Aesthetics of Musical Impotence* (*Die neue Ästhetik der musikalischen Impotenz*), and above all in his lengthy aesthetic treatise *Work and Performance* (*Werk und Wiedergabe*)—part diatribe and part instruction manual in the art of stage production as faithful reproduction—Pfitzner argued for universally applicable, normative guidelines, or even rules, that would guarantee the superiority of German music, of music structurally based on an original idea (or *Einfall*), and of the execution of such music precisely as its composer had imagined it (cf. Behne; Ermen; Osthoff).

Virtually all of his polemical writing is based upon an anxiety concerning the written word and the written signs of musical notation, upon which he is dependent but views with great skepticism. Pfitzner's dilemma is that, as an opera composer, he is dependent on the intervention of third parties to interpret and execute the written instructions of his works, and for that reason he opens *Werk und Wiedergabe* (1929) with a section on different genres distinguished by the degree to which they are subject to such mediation. He distinguishes between those works that rely on signs, or "Aufzeichnungen," and those dependent on sensual representation, or "Sinnlichkeit." He therefore places the visual arts in a category of works that requires no further mediation once completed, and he makes the same claim for *written* works as well. I would like to quote a passage from his discussion of literary works, because it reveals some remarkable assumptions regarding signification:

> In a written book, everything that is sensual is drawn into that which is rational. . . . For that reason this art is initially grasped through a cognitive activity, in this case through that of reading. This corresponds to looking at a painting or its figures; between creator and recipient there is no need of an intermediary link; one doesn't require reproduction through a third party. (Pfitzner, *Werk und Wiedergabe* 4)

In addition to the split between ratio and the corporeal—and with it the implied fear of sensuality—the passage is interesting because it shows that Pfitzner denigrates and disavows the *mediating function* of the written text, viewing it instead as a transparent and universally available phenomenon that circumvents or bypasses signification as mediation. Implicitly, the materiality of writing as signifier recedes in favor of its postulated capacity for transparency. Pfitzner relies on what he presents as an *unequivocal* property of the written sign, which allows for direct communication between the artist/creator/author and the recipient. Indeed, throughout the treatise the written word appears untroubled and privileged, the problem lying not with multiple possibilities of its interpretation, but with those who *choose* to disregard the written word because they believe they are not bound by the wishes of its author (whether librettist, composer, or both).

Something of the sort was already implied in Pfitzner's debate with the music critic Paul Bekker, who, in his popular book on Beethoven from 1911, had interpreted Beethoven's works as conveying a series of "programs," "images," and "poetic ideas" that Bekker believed should be accessible to a wide and untrained audience. In *Die neue Ästhetik der musikalischen Impotenz* (1919), Pfitzner characteristically responded to Bekker as follows:

> He who does not understand that a Beethoven theme is to be enjoyed *directly*, as a world unto itself, indivisible, untranslatable, he who has a need to dissect, describe, or to interpret it, to chop it up into its component parts, . . . [that person] doesn't know what music is. (Pfitzner, *Die neue Ästhetik* 155) (Italics added)

The key here is the notion that meaning can and should be conveyed in a direct and apparently unmediated fashion that bypasses the processes of signification, and with them all the aesthetic practices associated for Pfitzner with the inferior vagaries of art in the modern public sphere. The entire 350-page argument of *Werk und Wiedergabe*, too, constitutes a diatribe against actors, singers, conductors, set designers, and directors who fail to follow the composer's transparent credo.

And yet, Pfitzner's theoretical reflections actually reveal a fear of the instability of extreme polarizations, for the vituperative affect of loss, violence, and impending annihilation everywhere apparent in his writings discloses a concern over the possibility that the binarisms upon which his view of aesthetic practices is based are in danger of collapsing. For while *Werk und Wiedergabe* argues for a fidelity to the written word tantamount to devotion, Pfitzner bases this argument on the vilified—because feared—*distinction* between sign and signified. Already in his polemical text *Futuristengefahr* (1917)—a debate with Ferruccio Busoni—anxiety over the instability of the sign is made clear when Pfitzner states:

> *precisely because* an exactitude, an absolute faithfulness is *not* possible, precisely for this reason we have a profound duty, indeed we might even call it the First Commandment of reproduction, to strive for faithfulness with all the strength we can muster. This Commandment appears to me to be artistically so self-evident that actually I would like it treated as a moral issue. (Pfitzner, *Futuristengefahr* 206) (Italics in the original)

The anxiety at the heart of this passage is typical, and what is more, it reemerges not solely here and elsewhere in Pfitzner's theoretical writings, but in his *aesthetic* practice as well. For while the work for which he is best remembered today, the "musical legend" *Palestrina* (1917) is most often associated with the theme of inspiration, it can also be interpreted in conjunction with Pfitzner's theories regarding the veneration of the written word as a vehicle of authorial intention and his despair over the degree of its reliability—over what happens to the work in the afterlife of the finished composition. (It is no coincidence that the music drama emerged temporally contiguous with the Busoni polemic.) In this sense, the music drama is a cipher for the vagaries of aesthetic practice in the irreverent, volatile, and outwardly directed modern age. The nostalgia and despair at the heart of the work are discernible behind, and overwhelm, its many thematic polarizations.

Palestrina depicts a moment of crisis in the life of the composer of the Counter Reformation, Giovanni Pierluigi Palestrina, who is portrayed as the last representative of a vanishing and glorious tradition of sacred music, superceded and threatened by newer and inferior schools of composition (cf. Toller). In this respect, he is unabashedly a representative of Pfitzner as the last, and beleaguered, representative of a specifically German musical tradition overwhelmed by the fads of musical internationalism, jazz, and atonality in the modern age. The central plot device constitutes a decree from Pope Pius IV that, owing to new practices of polyphonic vocal writing that obscure the sacred text, all liturgical music since the Middle Ages will be burned, unless an exemplary mass can be produced that demonstrates that the word of God can be heard even in a polyphonic setting. Palestrina's friend, Cardinal Borromeo, beseeches the composer to undertake this task, explaining that the "new [textual and musical] vagaries, monstrous to the ear" (*Die neuen Irrungen, unhold dem Ohre*) are eating away at the traditions that Palestrina reveres and represents (Pfitzner, *Palestrina* 12). Borromeo explains that in recent polyphonic compositions, new texts have been added to traditional sacred music, which, as he says, "makes the true text unintelligible" (Pfitzner, *Palestrina* 13). Such practice forms an allegory of bad *Wiedergabe*, making it clear that the status and life of the artwork following its composition is a mere postexistence, always in danger, and always inferior to the original and nostalgically privileged event of its creation. The new compositions, then, resemble the work of the modern-day directors Pfitzner so despised, with their willful and irreverent approach to the texts of musical-dramatic tradition.

But Palestrina refuses to write the mass, and is then visited by the spirits of nine former composers, followed by a scene in which a chorus of angels dictates to him the exalted mass as Act I comes to a close. The moment of inspiration—which constitutes, ironically, a dramatic representation of *un*mediated art—is couched in musical themes that will later reappear in contexts important for an understanding of the work's portrayal of aesthetic reception (Pfitzner, *Palestrina: Klavier-Auszug* 148–49).

Palestrina's paradigmatic mass is presented in three manifestations: initially, in its primal, originary state as it unfolds through the spontaneous inspiration vouchsafed by the angels, and then twice again in two distinct, though related kinds of reception. First, at the conclusion to Act I, after Palestrina has collapsed at his desk and scattered the pages of the newly dictated mass on the floor, it is read by his student, Silla, and by his son, Ighino, when the boys come in for their morning music lesson. When Silla and Ighino read the mass, the orchestra quietly invokes in instrumental form the vocal lines that had been sung by the angels (Pfitzner, *Palestrina: Klavier-Auszug* 167–68).

This second manifestation of the mass unfolds in the brass as the boys imagine its sounds in the interior, private act of obviously adequate reading; we are shown that this is an example of silent and authentic reception, if not *Wiedergabe* (it is, after all, *not* identical to the vocal lines of the scene of the mass, with its Latin text), then at least a "renewed presence" (*Wiedergegenwärtigkeit*) that both underscores its difference from the originary event and, at the same time, the possibility of authentic exegesis. The mass is again read and interpreted when it is performed, between Acts II and III, for the pope, who then in the final Act visits Palestrina personally, recalls the experience of listening to the work (this is its third manifestation), and extols the composer as the "Fürst der Musik aller Zeiten"—the "prince of music for all time" (Pfitzner, *Palestrina* 54), after which the drama comes to a close.

In the "Miraculous Night" (*Wundernacht*) of Act I, we have a performance that is disavowed and presented instead as unmediated and transparent, or as a nonperformance. In Act III, we have a nonperformance representing and recalling a performance (located between Acts II and III), and between them there is the boys' reading at the conclusion of Act I, the position of which between these extremes highlights its ambiguous function. The dramatic conceit is that we hear what Palestrina hears as the voices of the angels dictate to him their holy music. We are not subject to a public mediation, but are privileged by our private, interior, and superior reception, an experience that places the uniformity of a standardized individual response above the uncontrollable vagaries and heterogeneity of a public performance dictated by a mediating agent.

Our privileged hearing distinguishes our experience from that of the pope, who must rely on the work's execution through gifted singers. For this reason, Pfitzner does not stage this mediated performance, but only the pope's recollection of it. When the papal choir boasts about their successful singing of Palestrina's mass, they are portrayed as vain and obviously inferior to their angelic counterparts from Act I (Pfitzner, *Palestrina* 53). Their performance is deemed successful only insofar as it faithfully reveals the original text, and thus we may interpret this event, despite its necessarily inferior status when compared to the angelic representation of a pure aesthetic experience, as an allegory, again, of good *Wiedergabe*. But that still means that even the best reproduction falls short of the ideal, Platonic essence it evokes. The violin lines accompanying the pope's vocal material, like those heard in the horns when Silla and Ighino read the mass at the conclusion to Act I, echo the musical material of Palestrina and the angels (Pfitzner, *Palestrina: Klavier-Auszug* 351–53). So Pfitzner wants it both ways: the scene recalls good reception, but this is a reception that is based on performance, which at worst is a falsification or distortion, and at best a reproduction, second-best to the original work. Therefore, the status of the mass as a temporally and materially determined accomplishment is both reinforced through the banality of the singers and also partially disavowed when the pope recalls its performance. It is characterized as an interior communication with the godly creator who transcribed it (Palestrina) and with God, that is, ironically, as *un*mediated. The materiality of the transcription is effaced—through it the pope directly hears the voices of the angels—and yet it recalls the postangelic music of a mediation through reading that had been staged at the end of Act I. Through these musical-dramatic manifestations, Pfitzner's work articulates an ambivalence about its own reception not unlike the anxiety at the heart of *Werk und Wiedergabe* and emphasizes his dependence on the very thing he feared.

One could examine this ambivalence as a reaction to a reliance on a concept of interiority and its necessary compromise in the act of public performance, a tension that informs the political opposition of the citizen as monad and the public sphere as the arena of collectivity. Or, to put it differently (and to once again recall Sloterdijk), this ambivalence informs the work's longing for interiority and its fear that such a safe haven will forever be threatened by the outwardly directed forces of change in the irreverent and dangerous place of music in the modern public sphere. This would help to account for the structure of *Palestrina*, which juxtaposes the interior world of the composer in Acts I and III—both are set in his home—and the political turmoil of Act II, which portrays a meeting of the Council of Trent, during which the mass is only briefly mentioned, and obviously not appreciated, as one item among many on the political agenda. The realm of politics is that of the outwardly directed, post-Lapsarian musical experience, "the world as a noise-totality," while the monad seeks to retreat into the safety of an interiority that is increasingly womb-like, "the archaic euphonious state of the pre-worldly interior," an interiority that is forever longed for, but in danger of vanishing into the realm of unrealized utopia (Sloterdijk, "Wo sind wir?" 301). During the first manifestation of the mass by means of a chorus representing angels, Palestrina clearly distinguishes between an interior, private realm of godly inspiration and the mundane, earthly realm that will receive the finished work when he exclaims:

> I have been raised to
> Overwhelming joy!
> *Worldly* success lies far below.
> Blessed I send my thankful glance
> Toward heaven,
> *Inwardly* praising
> Love's eternal power,
> Which has brought peace to me. (Pfitzner, *Palestrina* 23) (Italics added)

Here, the emphasis lies on the interiority of the event (*innig* zu loben), and Pfitzner's dramaturgy essentially collapses the distinction between the interior experience of inspiration and its external manifestation, or execution. If we read this text through the lens of Sloterdijk's psychology of music, the perception of acoustical space from the confines of a guarded interior seamlessly conflates with the nostalgia at the heart of *Palestrina*'s conservative desire for a return to the status quo as a time, and a locus, of safety.

There are a number of ways Pfitzner's work contradicts his theory, which is not unusual for an artist—this was often the case with his forerunner

Wagner—and the tensions between his theoretical reflections and aesthetic practice serve to underscore even further the tendency for his insistent polarizations to break down or to edge toward collapse. Many commentators have noted that Pfitzner's music is far more experimental than his theory would lead one to believe. In his review of *Palestrina* at the Frankfurt Opera, for example, Adorno remarked on the work's innovative employment of timbre, or "Klang," as an imaginative compositional device, and others have recognized in such works as the Goethe-Lied "An den Mond" and the C-sharp minor String Quartet an employment of sonic material that so expands tonal expectations that it both recalls Debussy's pentatonic scales and at times virtually borders on the very atonality Pfitzner abhorred in the New Vienna School (Adorno, "Pfitzner's *Palestrina*" 35; Skouenborg 143, 151; on the quartet see Vogel 97; on the Goethe song see Williamson 234–37).

The binarisms at work throughout Pfitzner's thought, with its distrust of signification as the plaything of irreverent and often leftist, internationally inclined, and sometimes Jewish intellectuals, brings Pfitzner's body of work close to that of a host of conservative thinkers of the modernist period, from Hofmannsthal and George at the start of the century (Williams 6–20; Norton passim), to Jünger and Riefenstahl during the development of proto-fascist and fascist modernism. As Russell Berman has argued, one of the fundamental principles of fascist aesthetics is its polarization of the written word and image, a polarization that denigrates the former as associated with rationalism and parliamentary politics and privileges the latter as a vehicle for immediate, sensate, and collective reception, so that the emphasis on form suggests a suspicion of the vagaries of the hermeneutics of literate culture and implies that the sensual impressions of image are more reliable (99–103, 109–17).

On the other hand, Pfitzner's ambiguity and his distinctions between written and performed text, as well as the tensions between his avowed polarizations and their mitigated repercussions in his aesthetic practice, would suggest that his work by no means fits neatly into such a bifurcated cognitive structure. And surprisingly, if one finds Berman's model persuasive, this ambiguity on Pfitzner's part would make him ill-fitted to the fascism with which he is historically, that is, manifestly connected. Despite his opportunistic association with the National Socialist movement in the 1930s (Kater 144–82) (during which his cantata *From the German Soul—Von deutscher Seele*—was performed in a ceremony welcoming Goebbels to Berlin, Pfitzner was made a *Reichskultursenator*, Pfitzner "Festspiele" were organized as a celebration of German art under the auspices of the Nazi Party, and the movement banned the very kind of art Pfitzner so abhorred—from jazz to dodecaphony), the integrity of his aesthetic practice might allow us to view his work in a far more favorable light than such a model as Berman's would cast on a contemporary figure such as Jünger. While Pfitzner distinguishes between spirit, the written word, and third-party intermediaries necessary for performance, the fascist modernists purportedly view Pfitzner's second level of signification, the written word, with the same degree of skepticism that Pfitzner directed against the vagaries of contemporary performance and staging practice. For unlike the National Socialists, Pfitzner's aesthetics emerges from an extreme anxiety concerning the inferiority of the hermeneutic abilities of those around him and a pervasive longing for a return to a moment located somewhere in the past, including the moment of creation of his own works of art, and manifested in a variety of other superior German works as well. This distinction may partially mitigate a comparison of Pfitzner with the National Socialists that his historical position and biography would otherwise justify. Such unyielding arrogance and cultural nostalgia, such outward and inward movements of the imagination, recur throughout not only Pfitzner's work, but that of his leftist modernist contemporaries as well, betraying a widespread reliance on bifurcated conceptual models that recur across the political spectrum, and in this respect, Pfitzner is a symptomatic figure. This description of Pfitzner could equally apply, for example, to the work of his strangest of bedfellows, Theodor W. Adorno. Where would we place him in Sloterdijk's categories of psychic-sonic perception? One has only to think of Adorno's notoriously reactionary writings on jazz and film—the very cultural production of the modern age that Pfitzner so abhorred—to discern a similar effect of despair and a fear of annihilation that are everywhere apparent in Pfitzner's writings (Adorno, "Abschied vom Jazz," "Jazz," "Über Jazz," "Zeitlose Mode: Zum Jazz;" Weiner, "*Urwaldmusik*" 483–85). I choose to compare Pfitzner and Adorno precisely because one would think of them as so diametrically opposed, owing to their distinctive political (not to mention ethnic) affiliations. The point is not simply that they shared a distaste for specific cultural works deemed foreign, but rather, that the similar affect that accompanied their thought demonstrates the pervasive nature of the tension between the outwardly directed music of which Sloterdijk speaks and the nostalgia that constitutes its despairing alternative. For Adorno's polarized categories (of E, or "ernste [serious]" and U, or "Unterhaltungs- [low-brow or trivial] Musik," for example) also reveal an anxiety that one may be overwhelmed by the libidinal forces of outwardly directed change, even as one recognizes the futility of searching for a lost and purportedly superior past (*Einleitung* 199–218). Adorno's nostalgia is readily apparent, though it is never explicit, and it is a key to his historical and cultural moment (Subotnik 17–18, 21–22; Thomas, passim). No wonder the authentic artwork retreats from the inferior public sphere in both

Pfitzner's and Adorno's thought. The contours of the artworks they deem superior may be vastly different, but the affect—which locates the subject in Sloterdijk's despairing "afterglow from Paradise"—that accompanies both of them and the works they mutually reject is not. It is a signature of the modernist imagination.

Notes

1. All translations are my own.
2. Pfitzner was championed—and later vilified—by Thomas Mann (Abendroth 222), despised by Bertolt Brecht (Lucchesi 94, 283) and Georg Kaiser (Kaiser 113), and made note of in the reflections of a number of prominent thinkers in the early twentieth century, including Musil (Musil, *Tagebücher* 481–82; *Tagebücher: Anmerkungen* 309–10) and Schnitzler (Schnitzler 179).

Mahler, Rembrandt, and the Dark Side of German Culture

Carl Niekerk

Musicologists have lately argued that Gustav Mahler is a composer with great affinity to the avant-garde. This argument is based on the observation that the principles underlying Mahler's compositions bear great resemblance to those of the so-called *Second Vienna School.* This section tries to develop the same argument from a Cultural Studies perspective by focusing on the philosophical, political, and aesthetic debates dominating the discourse about German culture in the first decade of the twentieth century. Peter Bürger has defined the historical avant-garde as the moment in Western art when artists no longer pursued one ideal form of art, but instead started experimenting with all available existing artistic forms (*Theorie* 23). Theodor Adorno, in his long and problematic essay on Mahler, thinks that at the core of Mahler's music there is indeed an overreliance on older musical materials and forms (*Mahler* 126). Adorno sees this as something negative in that it ties Mahler's work to outlived ideologies, but, as I show in the following, Mahler's use of tradition also has a critical and emancipatory side.

According to Peter Bürger, in the historical avant-garde the work of art enters a stage of self-reflection and also of self-criticism regarding its functioning in society (*Theorie* 28). In a highly specialized society in which art has become something abstract, accessible to only a small number of consumers, the avant-garde wants to reinvest art with a critical and political potential. Self-reflection in Mahler takes on the form of a critical adoption of the German cultural tradition, and in particular of the imprint that Wagner's aesthetic and political writings have left on the German cultural landscape. While Mahler is, on the one hand, in awe of the formal innovations underlying Wagner's work, he cannot but feel highly uncomfortable with its anti-Semitic undertones. In spite of the fact that Mahler's concept of culture is indebted to Romanticism and to a concomitant view of culture as a conversation among great men—his interest in Rembrandt, to be discussed in detail later, is a case in point—his cultural agenda nevertheless approaches the ideal of the historical avant-garde.

In addition to Mahler's experimentation with inherited musical forms and materials and the element of self-reflection in his work, there is a third aspect of his oeuvre that brings him into proximity with the historical avant-garde. Bürger points to the ambiguous relationship the avant-garde work of art has to politics and to reality outside the realm of aesthetics. On the one hand, the avant-garde acknowledges the autonomy of art and the split between art and society; on the other hand, its ambition is to bridge the gap between art and the outside world and to bring art back to the people by associating itself with a progressive political agenda.[1] In the following, I argue that there is, particularly in Mahler's later compositions, a polemical and critical impetus that self-consciously attempts to construct alternative traditions. In his later compositions—in the following I mainly discuss the *Seventh Symphony*, but similar observations can be made about the *Eighth* and *Das Lied von der Erde*—Mahler develops and articulates a progressive notion of alterity that gradually moves to the core of his work. Mahler articulates, I argue, an increasing interest in the margins of German culture.

Dutch culture can be understood, in part, as a margin of German culture. With that remark I do not mean to idealize Dutch culture; fin de siècle Dutch culture was not particularly progressive or experimental.[2] Its importance for Mahler lies not in the fact that it presents an important alternative national tradition or another canon as a point of orientation, but rather in its ability to represent alternative aspects of German culture—to function as a margin of German culture. There existed a lively interest in German culture in the Netherlands around 1900, as well as a curiosity about French and English culture. Rather than conceiving of Dutch culture from the standpoint of a strong national tradition, it might be more productive to see it as a culture of margins, as a border zone where different identities meet. This would explain a certain skepticism in the Netherlands toward the nationalistic and often conservative tendencies underlying the national cultures surrounding it. It is precisely this skepticism that, I would argue, attracted Mahler to the Netherlands. It is interesting to note that Mahler apparently spoke quite openly about his Jewishness to his Dutch contacts (Nikkels 331), and in other respects as well he was quite outspoken while in the Netherlands. At a dinner party hosted by the affluent benefactors of the Concertgebouw, Mahler—often said to have conventional literary taste—created quite a stir by forcefully defending Multatuli, the Dutch author of *Max Havelaar*, a novel highly critical of colonialism (Micheels, "Gustav Mahler" 25, 33).

Mahler visited Amsterdam four times (in 1903, 1904, 1906, and 1909), mostly to rehearse and conduct his own music with the still very new Concertgebouw orchestra. Two figures were particularly important for him at this point. Mahler's main contact in Amsterdam was Willem Mengelberg (1871–1951), the young but internationally quite famous conductor who was to lead the Concertgebouw for half a century, from 1895 to 1945. Mahler also developed a close relationship with Alphons Diepenbrock (1862–1921), a classics teacher, private tutor, part-time composer and conductor, strongly influenced by Wagner and Nietzsche. It is clear that Mahler could discuss his music and intellectual interests on a very sophisticated level with these men. But above all, in Amsterdam Mahler found a conductor and an orchestra excited about performing his music and willing to use unconventional means to foster interest in it.

Rembrandt

According to Willem Mengelberg, Mahler's *Seventh Symphony* was meant at least partially as an acoustic representation of Rembrandt's *Night Watch*. In Mengelberg's copy of the second movement of the score of the *Seventh* the following note can be found: "Strict march. 'Night Watch' Rembrandt. Left, right, left, right. Suggest olden times' " (De la Grange, *Triumph* 852). Mahler had seen Rembrandt's *Night Watch* during his first visit to Amsterdam in late 1903 (Micheels, "Gustav Mahler" 25); he started composing the second movement of the *Seventh*, the first of two *Nachtmusiken*, half a year later in the summer of 1904 (De la Grange, *Triumph* 842). During his second visit in October 1904 he went by Rembrandt's house and was clearly very impressed (De la Grange, *Triumph* 370). During these visits, Amsterdam was preparing for a celebration of the 300th anniversary of Rembrandt's birth (1606/1906). As part of the planned festivities, four Dutch composers were asked to write music based on Rembrandt's etchings. Mahler's friends Willem Mengelberg and Alphons Diepenbrock were among them (Zwart 205).

Mengelberg's annotation concerning Rembrandt can no doubt be traced to conversations between himself and Mahler. It is impossible to discuss Rembrandt reception in the German-speaking countries around 1900 without acknowledging Julius Langbehn's extremely popular book *Rembrandt als Erzieher (Rembrandt as Educator)* (1890). This book was a bestseller in the 1890s; it went through 72 prints in just three years (1890–92).[3] Langbehn was a conservative critic and a cultural pessimist, strongly influenced by Nietzsche. At the beginning of his project he observes that

Germany is in a state of cultural decline; a renewal of German society, however, is possible via a return to its roots, and in particular to a tradition personified by Rembrandt. It is easy to read and dismiss *Rembrandt als Erzieher* as an example of conservative, elitist, ultranationalistic, imperialistic, anti-intellectual, antidemocratic, and at times deeply racist and anti-Semitic cultural criticism. This is all very true. But in accordance with the goals of the conference on which this volume is based—thinking beyond master narratives, looking beyond simple dichotomies such as "left/right"—I propose bracketing Langbehn's political intentions, and instead I want to focus on his cultural criticism.

In *Rembrandt als Erzieher*, Langbehn attacks the modern world in which sciences, mechanical thinking, and over-specialization dominate (103). In particular, Langbehn criticizes the lack of individualism (3ff.) among his German contemporaries, even though this is part of the essence of Germanness. He is convinced that art will save the Germans (Langbehn 99). A new synthesis is necessary, and the personification of this new synthesis is Rembrandt and the tradition for which he stands. It is part of Langbehn's paradoxical argumentation that he demands more individualism from German art while attempting to create a new collective consciousness (Hein 71). It is important to distinguish between such critical-deconstructive and reconstructive impulses in Langbehn's text. But why is Rembrandt of such essential importance for Langbehn? Rembrandt is for Langbehn the most individual of all German artists (9); "ein hoher Grad von Unregelmäßigkeit Verschobenheit Eigenartigkeit" (a high degree of irregularity displacement singularity) characterizes his work (12). This is the critical Langbehn speaking. From a return to the tradition represented by Rembrandt, Langbehn expects what he once calls "die Schaffung neuer geistiger Werte" (the creation of new spiritual values)(268). More specifically, he hopes for a deepening of German national consciousness beyond everyday politics: "Früher war man kosmopolitisch, jetzt sollte man kunstpolitisch sein; eben diese Kunstpolitik könnte das ideale Gegengewicht gegen die oft so trivialen Interessen der jeweiligen Tagespolitik bilden" (Langbehn 269).

Langbehn's alternative reconstruction of the German cultural tradition has Romantic roots. The idea that art compensates for the disappointments of political life—elements of this idea of Langbehn were adapted by Thomas Mann in his *Betrachtungen eines Unpolitischen* (*Reflections of a Non-Political Man*) (Hein 61, 91–102)—can of course be traced back to Romanticism. In many respects, Langbehn's program is fairly typical for conservative turn-of-the-century cultural criticism. However, this should not make us overlook the fact that, in terms of cultural memory, his text does contain a rather radical move; Langbehn wants to locate the center of

German culture outside Germany. He discusses the problem that Rembrandt is Dutch and not German early in his text (Langbehn 9). But he sees this as a purely political matter; "innerlich"—one could say: in spirit—Rembrandt belongs to the Germans. Rembrandt figures as an alternative for the dominant cultural discourse that goes back to Winckelmann (Langbehn 30ff.), is continued by Goethe—although Langbehn also tries to align Goethe with Rembrandt—and Schiller, and is dominated by the "foreign" and therefore "false" (Langbehn 33) ideals projected on ancient Greece.

It is highly interesting that Langbehn, in the process of his decentering and then recentering of the German cultural tradition, also mentions Rembrandt's interest in Jews:

> Eigenthümlich genug zeigt sich endlich die Vornehmheit Rembrandt's in—seiner Vorliebe für die Juden; hier begegnen sich seine lokale und seine vornehme Gesinnung, sein Blick in die Nähe und sein Blick in die Höhe. Er hatte diese M[e]nschengattung täglich vor Augen; denn er wohnte in der Judenbreitstraße zu Amsterdam; die Keime solcher künstlerischen und geistigen Besonderheiten liegen oft näher zur Hand, als man meint [. . .] Ein echter und altgläubiger Jude hat unverkennbar etwas Vornehmes an sich; er gehört zu jener uralten sittlichen und geistigen Aristokratie, von der die meisten modernen Juden abgewichen sind; in dieser Hinsicht fühlte Lord Beaconsfield also halbwegs richtig, als er sie für den ältesten Adel der Welt erklärte. Rembrandt's Juden waren echte Juden; die nichts Anderes sein wollten als Juden; und die also Charakter hatten. Von fast allen heutigen Juden gilt das Gegentheil; sie wollen Deutsche Engländer Franzosen u.s.w. sein; und werden dadurch nur charakterlos. [. . .] diese, wie sie heute sind, würde er verabscheut oder nie begriffen haben. (43)[4]

The similarity between Rembrandt and Spinoza—the radical Enlightenment thinker who also gets Langbehn's respect—is also relevant here (Langbehn 52ff.). *For a moment,* Langbehn makes Rembrandt's Jews the ultimate representatives of an ideal German culture. One could read the quoted passage as a statement that their legacy could be, and maybe, even should be, part of German culture. Later, Langbehn does give something of a foundation, albeit a problematic foundation, to this idea when he discusses contemporary racial theory. "Blutmischung" is responsible for undermining Prussia's natural conservatism and for the progressive politics that threaten to destroy Bismarck's national program (Langbehn 134ff.). But Langbehn also defends "racial mixing." He uses Venice as an example of how the racial profile of one people can improve by mixing with other races. Ideally the new racial mix will unify the best traits of the races that contributed to it (Langbehn 136f.).

In the end though Langbehn's text remains an anti-Semitic pamphlet. Toward the end in a section added later, he makes the Jews explicitly responsible for Germany's decline (Langbehn 347).[5] I by no means wish to trivialize the extremely intolerant racist and anti-Semitic agenda underlying Langbehn's book. He not only falls back on the anti-Semitic stereotypes of his time; he actively helped to create these stereotypes. This is also clear in the passage cited earlier, in which positive deliberations are followed by observations that immediately revoke the revolutionary potential of the earlier statements. Langbehn's position here is not unlike that of Herder, who also respected the ancient Jews but was highly critical of his Jewish contemporaries (Berghahn 195–205). This is a pattern one finds again and again in *Rembrandt als Erzieher*. Langbehn's seemingly rather radical interpretations serve, in the end, to fortify an extremely normative model of German culture.

The Seventh Symphony

It may very well be the critical potential of Rembrandt's paintings—the potential to reconstruct another German tradition on their basis, extrapolated by Langbehn—that explains Mahler's interest in Rembrandt. I have no evidence that Mahler had read Langbehn, but it is highly likely when one considers the extreme popularity of *Rembrandt als Erzieher*, Mahler's own well-developed intellectual curiosity, and his well-documented interest in Rembrandt (Walter 104). We also know that Mahler's close friend and intellectual companion, Siegfried (Salomo) Lipiner, admired Rembrandt (Nathorp 7). If one accepts the hypothesis that Mahler was familiar with Langbehn's text, however, it is worth emphasizing that Mahler does not reconstruct Langbehn's arguments, but rather rereads Langbehn. Mahler was interested in the critical and deconstructive side of Langbehn's program, not its nationalistic or reconstructive aspects.

Rembrandt als Erzieher is pervaded by a highly rhetorical use of images of light and darkness. It is literally the dark side of German culture, represented by Rembrandt's paintings (Langbehn 44, 290f.), which for Langbehn is a desirable alternative to the German fixation on the lightness of Greece (44). Interestingly, darkness and light also play an important role in Mahler's *Seventh*. For instance, Mahler's symphony contains not one but two *Nachtmusiken* (the second and fourth movements). The first *Nachtmusik*, the second movement, was in fact the first section Mahler composed for the *Seventh*. But the Adagio, the first movement of the *Seventh*, also is meant to evoke a nocturnal atmosphere, as is clear from the notes in Mengelberg's score based on conversations with Mahler (De la Grange, *Triumph* 854–55). Diepenbrock even speaks of the "nocturnal atmosphere" in the first *four* movements of Mahler's symphony (Nikkels 331). All of this could of course still be considered coincidental; the fact that images of darkness and light have a constitutive function for Rembrandt's visual compositions is apparent even when one merely examines his work superficially.

But there is more. At two places in *Rembrandt als Erzieher*, Langbehn offers an explicit musical program, including a critique of Wagner. Music is part of the nationalistic cultural program Langbehn envisions; he has a very specific ideal of "Rembrandtian" music. In the section entitled "Musikalisches" (Musical Matters) (Langbehn 22f.), Langbehn calls the Adagio "das speziell deutsche Musiktempo" (the specifically German musical tempo) (22). Mahler begins his symphony with an Adagio—something unique among his compositions. In fact, the first four movements of the *Seventh* are characterized by slow tempi. In his later symphonies (in particular the *Ninth* and the unfinished *Tenth*) Mahler in general tends to privilege slower movements. Langbehn's call for a "German" Adagio is followed by speculations about how one form of art (painting) can be translated into another form (music). Here, too, Rembrandt seems to help out: "in Rembrandt's Gemälde scheint etwas von dem leisen Rauschen des Meeres hineinzutönen, das seine Heimath umspült" (in Rembrandt's painting, something of the soft rush of the sea surrounding his homeland seems to resound) (Langbehn 22). The first movement of the *Seventh* starts with the sound of water.[6] The dark colors of Rembrandt's paintings have their equivalent in the melancholic nature of the musical ideal Langbehn envisions. Langbehn mentions "zartverschwiegene weltabgekehrte deutsche Anmuth" (soft and reticent, withdrawn German grace) (22) as an alternative to the superficial lightness of southern European music. One could think of the chamber music atmosphere of the two *Nachtmusiken* as an example for such *Anmuth* (grace).

To understand Mahler's affinity with the musical ideal that Langbehn sketches in his text, it helps to look at the second section of *Rembrandt als Erzieher* that deals with music (276ff.). This section on Wagner is remarkably critical of the composer. This can no doubt be explained through Langbehn's biographical connection with Nietzsche,[7] although Nietzsche does not figure prominently in *Rembrandt als Erzieher*. Langbehn questions how long Wagner's music will dominate the German musical landscape. He criticizes Wagner's lack of modesty; Wagner's music knows no rest. Wagner is interested only in superficial effects; his music is characterized by nervousness (Langbehn 276f.). His music is not even German and has more in common with Meyerbeer than he himself wants to admit (Langbehn 277f.). Langbehn then formulates an alternative musical ideal: "nach ihm wird die Musik, wenn sie überhaupt fortschreiten will, zur höchsten Intimität zurückkehren müssen" (after him music, if it wants to progress, will have to return to the highest intimacy) (ibid.). At the beginning of the book Langbehn states that the "Ueberkultur" typical of German music and art is worse than "Unkultur" (3). Germans are obsessed with "culture," but their concept of art is essentially superficial. Wagner caters to these superficial needs.

All this may help us to understand the controversial final movement, the Rondo-Finale, of Mahler's *Seventh Symphony*. This movement has been criticized because of its "pompous attitude" and "superficial splendor" (Revers 377); it has been characterized as typical "Kapellmeistermusik" (De la Grange, *Triumph* 881). In particular, the juxtaposition of the Leitmotiv of Wagner's *Meistersinger* with a theme from Léhar's *Lustige Witwe* has stupefied critics (Revers 377–78). Musicologists have claimed that this must be an intentional play on the tradition of an "affirmatory finale" (Revers 377), but are at a loss to explain what Mahler may have intended. Langbehn's cultural criticism may be of help here. Mahler is articulating his frustration with contemporary audiences who loved the operas of Wagner and Léhar, but despised Mahler's own far more demanding symphonies. In the last movement of the *Seventh*, Mahler makes fun of his audiences' need for "Ueberkultur"; that is, of their intense but superficial interest in things cultural. Interpreted in this way, through the lens of Langbehn, the *Seventh Symphony* is a comment on the decline of art, but is at the same time the product of competing paradigms of art; the superficiality of the finale follows the intimacy of the middle movements. Mahler's avant-gardist eclecticism—the use of materials from heterogeneous sources—has a critical function in the *Seventh*. It explains the many contradictions that characterize this work. Mahler is interested in a rereading of the German cultural tradition, in finding alternatives, and in a moment of alterity within that tradition.

Amsterdam around 1939

Thus far, I have made an argument in favor of the importance of Mahler's interest in the margins of German culture. I now want to focus on his impact on the Dutch cultural scene, which may tell us something about Mahler's music and especially about the political implications of the notion of alterity in his last works. In particular, the case of Mahler's friend and colleague Willem Mengelberg demonstrates the ambiguous status that the supposed autonomy of the work of art and its nevertheless concomitant political ambitions have in avant-garde aesthetics (Murphy 26ff.). As already stated, the avant-garde on the one hand presupposes that the work of art is autonomous; freedom from everyday life is a necessary condition for the avant-garde work of art. On the other hand, the avant-garde wants to destroy the barriers between art and life in order to come to a new synthesis between the two. The paradoxical nature of the avant-garde's concept of autonomous art becomes particularly clear when we look at the movement's political ambitions. For the avant-garde has political ambitions, even though it does not articulate these ambitions in the content of its works but rather trusts that formal innovations will eventually have an impact on politics.

After Mahler's death in 1911, Mengelberg kept the composer's memory alive by performing his music, also during times in which the interest in Mahler was fading. Between 1911 and 1919, Mengelberg conducted 106 concerts featuring works by Mahler (Micheels, " 'Sterben' " 38). In 1920, at a festival organized to celebrate his twenty-fifth year at the Concertgebouw, he and "his" Concertgebouw orchestra performed all nine symphonies and the *Lied von der Erde*. But Mengelberg kept the interest in Mahler's music alive after 1920 as well. In the 1930s, interest in Mahler had waned in England and the United States and his works could no longer be performed in Germany after 1933 and in Austria after 1938. When the bust of Mahler made by Rodin, kept at the Wiener Staatsoper after the *Anschluss*, was returned to Alma Mahler, its rightful owner, she wrote a letter to the administration of the Concertgebouw donating it to them.[8] There was no place anywhere else for Mahler as a cultural icon. Still, Mengelberg kept performing his works frequently.

In the last season (1939/40) before the German occupation of the Netherlands in May 1940, Mengelberg had scheduled the *Lieder eines fahrenden Gesellen*, the *Fourth Symphony* and the *Lied von der Erde*. Recordings of these performances have survived. This fact is significant for the history of performance practice, because Mengelberg and Mahler worked very closely on improving Mahler's scores and there are good reasons to believe that Mengelberg's style of performing comes very close to Mahler's ideals (see Kropfinger 111–75). In contrast to Bruno Walter's "balanced" performances of Mahler's scores, Mengelberg takes great liberties and, in particular, emphasizes contrasts, dissonances, and the heterogeneity of the music. One could say that Mengelberg has a very avant-gardist approach to Mahler.

Mengelberg was not a courageous man. As someone of German descent, he had worked for a long time in a country that, especially after the end of World War I, had become increasingly critical of the Germans. There is no doubt that Mengelberg was a high-profile collaborator during World War II. He performed frequently in Germany and Austria. He became a member of the *Kulturkammer*, dismissed the Jewish members of the Concertgebouw (although he let them borrow instruments for the newly founded Jewish symphony orchestra), and he turned the Concertgebouw into a National Socialist theater (people referred to it at the time as "the brown house on the

Van-Baerle-street") (van Amerongen and Bregstein 11). It has often been said that Mengelberg was naive or simply stupid for doing such things, and this may be true. Since the second volume of Mengelberg's biography that will cover the years 1920–51 has not yet been published, however, it is very difficult to form a complete picture of his activities during this period.

In part, Mengelberg's actions can be understood better in the context of his aesthetic philosophy and its emphasis on the autonomy of art vis-à-vis society. When sixteen Jewish members of the Concertgebouworkest were dismissed in 1941 upon National Socialist orders, Mengelberg protested by arguing that this would be detrimental to the quality of the Concertgebouw orchestra (three members were permitted to stay temporarily) (van Amerongen and Bregstein 139). Mengelberg insisted on performing Mahler's *First Symphony* during the 1940/41 season under German occupation; here he certainly did something of which he knew the authorities would not approve. But what is the purpose of this "stubbornness"? What is its effect? If anything, Mengelberg's acts demonstrate the limits of the avant-garde's aesthetic program, and in particular of its ambition to change society through formal innovations of the work of art. A direct connection between Mahler's music and society is hard to imagine. Nevertheless, in some of his programmatic statements of the late 1930s, Mengelberg suggests the existence of a real connection between music and the outside world:

> Ik ben een kunstenaar en een kunstenaar moet zich niet met politiek bezighouden. Als ik zeg politiek, dan moet men er tegenwoordig ook helaas bij zeggen: rassen. De kunst is in het algemeen, evenals de zon, geschapen [. . .] om alle mensen van alle rassen van de gehele wereld te beschijnen. Politieke overtuiging of staatsvorm raken mij niet wanneer ik een dirigeerstok opneem [. . .].[9]

In this fragment, Mengelberg explicitly emphasizes the autonomy of art. Of course, it is questionable whether he sees the Nazis' racism as a "political" issue and not as a crime against humanity or as a general humanitarian concern. But he argues that in spite of the autonomy of art, music does have a function for society. It can bring people of all races and nations together. Less than a year after this interview, on March 14, 1938, Mengelberg conducted a concert in Aachen to celebrate Austria's annexation by the Third Reich—an event that indeed brought two nations together as is noted in a speech accompanying the concert.[10]

The late 1930s mark the definitive end of the avant-garde's effort to reform German culture, and Mahler's work, for a moment, made this end visible. On October 5, 1939, Mengelberg had fallen ill and was replaced as conductor at the last moment by Carl Schuricht for a performance of

Mahler's *Lied von der Erde*. During a quiet moment toward the end of the final movement of *Das Lied*, a woman stood up, walked to the conductor and said, with a noticeable Dutch accent, "Deutschland über alles, Herr Schuricht" (Germany above all, Mr. Schuricht). A recording of the incident has survived. One can speculate about the precise intentions behind this action, but it can be read as an attempt to repress the existence of a critical dimension in Mahler's music, a dimension closely connected to a notion of alterity that is, as I hope to have demonstrated, an integral part of Mahler's aesthetic program. Ironically, the failure of the attempt to reform German culture from within could only be articulated in its margins.

Notes

1. See Bürger, *Theorie* 67–73; Murphy 27ff. The fact that this "progressive" connection in Mahler's work was recognized at the time is clear from the socialist reception of the *Eighth Symphony* in Vienna in the 1920s (see Painter 144ff.).
2. An overview of fin-de-siècle Dutch literature and culture can be found in Kemperink. She shows that Dutch literature and culture at the turn of the century is strongly influenced by biological-evolutionary models in the style of Darwin, Spencer, Haeckel, and Lamarck. Anti-Jewish stereotypes are fairly common (ibid. 31, 87–93).
3. Public attention to Langbehn's book later faded, but the book remained an object of fascination for a few (Stern 146). I thank Meike Werner (Vanderbilt University) for sharing her knowledge of Julius Langbehn and the literature on Langbehn with me.
4. "Strangely enough, Rembrandt's nobility shows itself, in the end, in—his love for the Jews; here his local and noble attitude, his view of what is close and what is high, meet. He saw this species of mankind every day, because he lived in the Jodenbreestraat in Amsterdam; the kernel of such artistic and intellectual particularities is often closer at hand than one would expect [. . .] A real and religious Jew in the old sense has unmistakably something noble about him; he belongs to that centuries-old moral and spiritual aristocracy from which most modern Jews have strayed away; in this respect Lord Beaconsfield was halfway right when he declared them the oldest aristocracy on earth. Rembrandt's Jews were real Jews who wanted to be nothing but Jews, and who also had character. For almost all Jews today one has to say the opposite; they want to be Germans, Englishmen, Frenchmen etc., and because of that only lose their character. [. . .] Jews as they are today he would have loathed or never understood." (Langbehn 43).
5. See Stern 146 and Behrendt 102f. According to Behrendt, the first edition of *Rembrandt als Erzieher* could be characterized as "undecided" (unentschieden) in relation to its portrayal of Jews; in subsequent editions, anti-Semitic elements become increasingly prominent. This phenomenon was already noted at the time, for instance in an article in the anti-Semitic *Deutsch-Soziale Blätter. Organ der deutsch-sozialen Partei* (Das Rembrandt-Buch über das Judentum; see also Puschner 56, 304).
6. See Mahler's letter to his wife Alma, No. 303.

7. During the winter 1889–90, Langbehn acted as Nietzsche's guardian after his collapse (Stern 143).
8. See Wouthuysen 108–13. Wouthuysen gives a fascinating reconstruction of the history of this bust. It survived World War II in the Dutch consulate in Vienna and was—mistakenly, since it was now property of the *Concertgebouw*—returned to the *Wiener Staatsoper* after the war. When in 1947 the *Concertgebouw* tried to claim the bust, it was told the bust could not be found. On May 16, 1948, a festive reinstatement of Mahler's bust in the presence of Bruno Walter took place in the *Wiener Staatsoper*. According to the board of the *Wiener Philharmoniker*, however, the original bust was still lost, but the orchestra had located another copy of Rodin's work at an exhibition and that copy was officially reinstated. Alma Mahler later claimed that this second copy of the bust had been in the possession of her family.
9. "I am an artist, and an artist should not be concerned with politics. When I say politics, nowadays one unfortunately has to add: race. Art is in general, like the sun, created [. . .] to shine on all people from all races in the whole world. Political conviction or organization of state don't bother me when I pick up the baton [. . .]." Interview with Willem Mengelberg from May 1937, cited in van Amerongen and Bregstein 139.
10. Sources are contradictory about the issue of whether it was Mengelberg or someone else who addressed the audience (cf. van Amerongen and Bregstein 144f.).

Section II

Modernism/Antimodernism, Race and Eugenics in Scandinavia

The Resistance to Modernism in Karl Gjellerup's *Germanernes Lærling* (1882)

Paul Houe

I

The modern breakthrough in Nordic literature was ushered in by the Danish critic Georg Brandes (1842–1927), who began delivering his landmark lectures on the main currents in European literature in 1871. For all its complexity his movement came to be associated—polemically or programmatically—with simplistic catchword versions of naturalism and positivism; and thanks to its affront to the Danish national liberals and their cultural and clerical establishment, the breakthrough's ideological tenor was generally seen as a soulless materialistic rationalism: "If you insist on talking about a naturalistic form of religion, it must be an optimistic faith in progress, by which perfection will once be arrived at" (Andersen 19).[1]

As it turned out, this secularized religion proved to be the Achilles' heal of the modern breakthrough. During the 1870s and 1880s, realistic prose—with analogues in painting and sculpture—ran its course and exhausted its mixed illusions of radical politics and scientific objectivity. By 1890 its potential had degenerated into bone-dry writing techniques and disillusionment about political and democratic institutions. Yet, what paved the way for a shift in tastes and artistic performance toward spiritual subjectivity and musical poetry was in no small part modernism's indelible religious vein, previously tied down to the rational doctrine of progress but now liberated as neoromantic and symbolist visions of nature and soul.

The modern had altered its focus and agenda, and while still a secular endeavor compared to clerical doctrines, its religious potential now came out in the form of principal and practical correspondences between souls and landscapes, and interiors and exteriors. The political residue amongst the new generation of artists notwithstanding, their overall artistic and intellectual schemes must be viewed as super- or pan-naturalistic designs beyond the political deadlock of the epoch and the public mudslinging of the day.

Some of these authors were aristocratic idealists who redirected the naturalist impulses forwarded by Brandes, to whom several remained indebted. Rather than engaging the general public and the common weal, they employed his lessons to bestow divine authority on their own creative genius. And Brandes followed suit. In Nietzsche, whom he introduced to Scandinavia and the rest of Europe, he found resonance for his own aristocratic radicalism and growing preoccupation with history's exceptional movers and shakers. In so doing he echoed the neoromantics themselves as they reached for transcendental heights and values without believing, as both romantics and Christian idealists had done, that such heights and values were essentially meaningful.

The writer who began his career as an ardent if belated follower of the young Georg Brandes, yet changed his mind and became a dubious source of inspiration for the symbolist generation as well as for the entire *Jugendstil* of the fin de siècle was the Danish author Karl Gjellerup (1857–1919), whose artistic trajectory even traversed the cultural and epochal divisions with which he was most readily associated. A displaced anachronist and intellectual borderliner, Gjellerup, who was to share the 1917 Nobel Prize for literature, was solidly homesteaded in classical German culture before he actually added decades of physical residency in Dresden to his cross-cultural credentials and spiritual exile from Danish national and cultural life.

I have argued elsewhere that Gjellerup's writing from the outset—and in spite of its clamoring efforts to be modern—is pregnant with a much different spiritual synergy; and in a recent literary biography I outline a connection between the author's roots in classical idealism, claims to modern realism, and future engagement with Buddhism.[2]

Religious proclivities at odds with contemporary theology are key to Gjellerup's attachment to and break away from the modern project. But is the latter disposition necessarily less modern than the former? Is the resistance to modernism not a modernistic gesture in itself? None of his texts is better suited to furnish an answer than the novel *Germanernes Lærling* (GL; The Teutons' Apprentice), published in 1882. At the time, the author was still under the influence of Brandesian realism, but the influence was retreating into a busy intersection of alternative modes of narration. As I turn to probing the resulting process of hybridization, my objective is to query why modernism appears so irresistible even to its opponents, and why the humanistic resistance it provokes merely takes both humanism and modernism to new problematic levels.

II

An *epochaltypisch* novel, GL negotiates its conflictual themes on the basis of historical verisimilitude and strives for its own outlook within the context of representational schemes. Its societal backdrop is the political stalemate and democratic paralysis caused by the constitutional struggle between Denmark's ruling aristocracy and the electoral majority of yeoman farmers. During the last decades of the nineteenth century, political life in the small country was under the thumb of the landed gentry and its urban allies among top church officials, military officers, and conservative civil servants; and the mindset of progressive intellectuals was inflicted increasingly with bouts of despondence.

In its opening chapter GL's protagonist, the young teacher Niels Hjorth, sides cavalierly with the reactionaries and speaks up against their democratic challenger during the 1872 parliamentary election, whereas in the last chapter Hjorth himself is a serious candidate for the 1877 democratic ticket. In both elections the aristocrats are defeated, but because the elections are for the rather powerless lower house of parliament, the result is inconsequential. The inadequate democratic constitution allows for emergency rule under provisional state budgets approved by an upper house majority only. Yet while Hjorth appears to have merely committed himself to an exercise in growing political futility, his personal development holds the promise of intellectual maturation in the midst of societal dreariness.

The relative disconnect between political misfortune and personal opportunity is suggested from the outset, when Hjorth's personal—and then political—friend Jessen has just lost the election for the aristocratic party. The outcome was no fly in Hjorth's ointment, though, for with due respect to his nation's political destiny, he experiences national identity in a spiritual rather than a narrowly political sense. With his roots in northern Schleswig, the border province between Denmark and Germany, his sentiments are at once profoundly Danish and beholden to German culture. Provincial with a vengeance, his feelings are, all the same, aspiring to the spiritual realm of the eagle, whereas the island province of Zealand, where he actually practices his calling as a teacher and even plans for a family with his fiancée Kristine, is the pedestrian, materialistic land of the crow.

Kristine's indolence and bodily preoccupations are disturbing instances of reality at odds with Hjorth's idealism. But no less disturbing are the official representatives of idealism at whose bosom he seeks solace. Pastor Krarup displays an embarrassingly ample supply of eternal truths, while land agent Ravn is a more prosaic hypocrite and moralist. Himself a subservient agent of the gentry, Ravn wields sufficient influence to command the submission of Hjorth's friend Mr. Jessen, Ravn's clerk and underling and the gentry's political errand boy, whose free-thinking rationalism is unwelcome among his superiors. The fact that the same theology of agnosticism is both recommended to and accepted by Hjorth for self-examination is yet another indicator that he too is precariously out of sync with the baser mores and ways of the local higher-ups. An idealist in exile from the so-called real world, he purports to make a virtue of necessity and envisions a future for himself as a Lutheran parson and not simply a downtrodden village schoolteacher.

Unlike his fiancée, Hjorth is not a social climber, and his reach for the ministry is not driven by ambition. His calling has higher, if undefined, idealistic goals, and education for the ministry is but a phase in his life. Even so, it leads to adversarial contact with yet another pillar of the established power structure. Professor Petersen of the University's Divinity School is a pedantic eclectic, bent on compiling knowledge, *Bildung*, and faith for the ultimate Lutheran symbiosis.[3] Hjorth's encounter with this authority figure turns his own vaguely articulated religious skepticism into a Germanstyle of Bible criticism, and soon a conglomerate of spiritual inclinations begins to emerge. While his waxing animosity toward conventional theology and Christendom is further aggravated by Kristine's vulgar superficiality, he finds in Georg Brandes's naturalism not an incentive for likeminded godless pursuits but a challenge so offensive as to actually endow Christianity with respectable gravity. The antitheological Hjorth turns antirealistic as well, or at least realistic in a German sense and with marked qualifications. Aided by German Bible critics, his faith in scriptural doctrine begins to yield to higher aesthetic and classical values.

In his effort to keep these heterogeneous forces in balance, Hjorth is drawn to and absorbed by the atmosphere in Lessing's *Nathan*. Written on the border of orthodox faith in God and enlightened faith in Man, this textual paragon of moral rationalism and rationalistic morality prefigures the gap between free-thinking men and conventional Christians that was to open during the modern breakthrough more than a hundred years later. The gospel of Lessing sustains Niels Hjorth in his move away from church and altar, a move that is edged with images of dead theological erudition on the one hand, and short-lived attempts at impressionism and social Darwinism, on the other. The light at the end of the narrative tunnel—and of narrative time—is virtue, and Hjorth is further propelled in this direction by an illicit encounter between his fiancée and land agent Ravn. The tryst between the two, both of easy virtue, throws the serious virtue of GL's protagonist into favorable relief as it surrounds his journey of life with images of lustful nature and animalistic orgasm attributable to his two counterparts.

Within GL's narrative taxonomy, theological doctrine and plain sexuality are both consigned to the fall, whereas Hjorth's existential path approaches

Schiller's humanistic idealism. Yet, though headed for a long-awaited equilibrium, the path offers no position of rest, and no history of ideas can grant it stability. An agnostic at heart, Hjorth is a Christian moralist at best, and his dissociation from Pastor Lindekær's rhetorical outpourings, from backward politicians, and from Kristine's plump sensuality, is unavoidable. As shadows of the past, these liabilities are on a par with Professor Petersen and his camp followers whose sophistic discussion of the Eucharist and senseless assault on pantheism and panlogism in Hjorth's opinion consign the discussants to oblivion. Hjorth's reading of Strauss' polemics is chiefly an act of cleansing himself of theological squabble between an unstable natural world and a monotonous human reality.

Still, his separation from the past is most visibly enacted when Professor Petersen and Pastor Lindekær agree to put ideology before scholarship and fail Mr. Hjorth at his final university exam on account of his skeptical attitude toward Christian doctrine. Only one elected affinity can he count among his former establishment supporters, namely, Mrs. Lindekær, whose bracelet sports a serpent to his liking. The fact that it is not the seductive creep from the Garden of Eden, but the healing pagan symbol of medicine, coiling itself around the staff of Aesculapius, that he spots on Mrs. Lindekær's wrist, confirms that she too was a closeted free-thinker. Hjorth bids her farewell as the human exception to the inhuman rule he is rejecting. GL has reached its turning point.

III

At this point Gjellerup, in deferred accordance with the pattern of the *Bildungsroman*, returns the wounded but seasoned hero to his point of departure, the northern Schleswig province of his boyhood home, in order to explore how this young man's hard-earned experiences away from home might enable him to reclaim his land of origin as a personal realization of his god-given potential. Hjorth's integration of conflictual influences and personal sentiments, dearly attained in the Zealand countryside and in Copenhagen's clerical and bourgeois circles—and barely settled at the time of his departure for northern Schleswig—is here again exposed to divisive impulses. At the core of the experience is a personal victory in face of an academic failure, and a similar combination of triumph and defeat awaits him where he is going. A Danish province under repressive German authority since 1864, the national heartland of southern Jutland/northern Schleswig has seen its poster Danishness relegated from societal institutions to uncontaminated nature in a manner that fully resonates with the return of its prodigal son.

The dubious encounter between Hjorth and his homeland thus evokes an atmosphere of man's ideal purification in old sentiments—and an air of memorable Danish beech trees and cemeteries disturbed only by an attractive woman with a German accent. As a nexus between the returnee and his old world, this is a disrupted harmony and one that presents a replay of past dichotomies, albeit closer to home and presumably to a durable resolution. The new site of Hjorth's persistently "provisional and unstable position of rest" (Gjellerup 245)[4] is defined by his dual attraction to the German lady whose free-thinking spirit resembles his own, and to the southern Danish nationalists without a country who surround his family as a circle of neighbors and friends.

Here he is, then, with no exam and no home, yet in the process of mental homesteading in a climate of relativism and ecumenical tolerance and a mixed community of Danish peasants and well-to-do people indifferent to the Danish cause. To top it off, political party divisions in Denmark proper are viewed with particular skepsis by the estranged nationals south of the 1864 state border, to say nothing of the added skepticism expressed by Niels Hjorth's brother, a sailor with knowledge of American politics.

The stage is set for condensation of harmonious and disharmonious interactions between the protagonist and the German-speaking Ms. Johanna who ends up as the woman of the former's choice. A foster daughter of the local German vicar and nationalist, her familial and social setting invites both discord and confrontation; indeed, her presence elicits a host of Danish/Schleswig-Holstein/German sentiments, divided nationally in all directions and interlaced with a plentitude of personal and cross-cultural sympathies and antipathies, mutual affections and suspicions, and acts of tacit accord and open defiance. In a conciliatory tone Johanna wonders: how come the first Dane with whom she has a real conversation is—what is it called?—"so ein Jünger der Germanen," (a Teutons' apprentice) to which Hjorth responds with the rhetorical question: "[. . .] is not all of Denmark the Teutons' apprentice?" (335–36).

The implicit answer—embedded in the novel's title—is obviously to suggest a link between his personal and his country's national prospects and predicaments. The embodiment of pure soul and flawless moral inspiration, Johanna is brought up on German idealism that epitomizes individual humility and solitary harmony with nature. Her mentality is so refined as to border on emotional pessimism and melancholic shyness, on a general nervousness and a specific fear of death, but also on Danish culture at large with an empathy and understanding that matches her fiancé's pro-German Danishness. Conflictual residues remain and occasionally flare up in the course of the couple's spiritual intercourse, but disputes of religious import are considered seriously while linguistic confusions on Johanna's part are treated as terms of endearment to be welcomed into standard Danish (366).

At the same time the amalgamation and cross-acculturation of their respective attitudes come to symbolic fruition in the philosophizing—or rather theosophizing/anthroposophizing—gestures of a small ape enjoying their company. The arrangement betokens a tentative prefiguration of spiritual perspectives beyond the horizon of Nordic and German Christianity—and perhaps of Gjellerup's budding Indian propensities. Concurrently, Johanna gives Hjorth an opportunity to elaborate and disseminate the philosophical tenets he had contemplated in solitude earlier. At the center of his vision is a dualism situated right on the border between two ages: a nineteenth-century poetic perception of nature's elusiveness, changeability, and corruption, as opposed to Lessing's and his *Nathan*'s much more stable rational and moral discourse on comparable matters (367).

Hjorth's tale about an imagined visitor from Sirius and the latter's view of sublunary conditions is sanctioned evenly by narrative authority and the accompaniment of earthly nature, and so the tale serves as an object lesson of natural and spiritual, modern and historical, conciliation (370–71). In human perception, nature appears divided and the division is healed within nature by nature itself (367, 373, 379). And the implicit and explicit subjection of open-ended narrative realism to comforting poetic closure is not restricted to the spiritual realm of rational idealism; it also pertains to the political arena where Hjorth is now prepared to take on Professor Petersen in the election campaign.

As this 1877 campaign progresses, the democratic position is shown in a caricature meant—by the narrative—to discredit its reactionary promulgators and their dissimulation. When Hjorth is elected on the very ticket he opposed five years earlier, his personal development has become harmoniously integrated in the paradigmatic and *epochaltypisch* scheme of the novel, and his individual story has brought closure to society's schisms as well as to his own. His election to political office is portrayed in concert with his choice of a human soulmate (Johanna) and a nonhuman companion (the ape Sam). Yet the stylistic culmination of GL precedes this chronological and thematic finale with a more dramatic and problematic finitude.

IV

The site where GL's diversity of intellectual and attitudinal currents meet for final negotiation, and where its "provisional and unstable position of rest" is subject to the ultimate test, is the novel's chapter XCIV (379–85). It begins in typical fashion with an evocative image of the northern Schleswig countryside bathed in moonlight, literally a bright Nordic night around midsummer, when the memory of daylight is never completely absent and the moonbeams merge with the afterglow of sunset on whitewashed farm buildings. As day and night refuse to part ways, shadows lose their sharpness, and spots of light remain in the midst of darkness as evidence that nature is undivided and that the bright side of life is irrepressible after all.

Rendered specifically in the vocabulary of human affairs, as Niels and Johanna demonstrate in a subsequent conversation about politics and *Lebensanschauung* (world view), the supremacy and inclusiveness of modern perceptions of nature indicate a state of empty transcendence. Returning from discourse to nature, our couple now takes a walk down a path leading through a natural setting in which light and darkness blend on various levels of sensation: flashes of light and shades of dark intersect incessantly; corporeal beings clad in lightness protrude before receding into shadows; and counterfigures cloaked in black exit into dawning glades. There is an interplay between the path itself and the natural and anthropomorphous forms surrounding it, and the exchange amplifies the glances cast between the human strollers Niels and Johanna.

Eventually this cosmic dimension—with nature encompassing human subjects under a full summer moon—is (re)viewed for its existential significance. As the familiar pattern of interchangeable lightness and darkness unfolds and is repeated, there emerges a composition of polarized interdependency. It (in)variably connotes a human condition enriched by wistful and melting natural beauty, yet menaced by civilizing forces. Quite uncomfortably placed at center stage, Hjorth and his spirited feeling for nature stand for GL's alternative to civilization's transgressions. Radiating light in the darkness as he faces his beloved Johanna, his countenance has a softness to its glow that intimates harmony between an eighteenth-century moral code and the nineteenth-century Gospel of nature of which he is the novel's key representative.

As for backing of the protagonist's position, the epic narrator sanctions modernity as liberation from the limits of orthodox or transcendental doctrines imposed on nature. But the same narrator invalidates with no less authority impositions on nature attributable to any civilizing agenda. Altogether, nature is perceived by the narrative as modern *immanens*—viewed by agnostic pantheists for whom its spiritual dimension remains intact. Theirs is a Gospel of the natural here and now, whereas salvation in a confessional sense falls by the wayside. Temporal longing subjects the experience of nature to a moral aesthetics whose telos is self-experience. As when the biblical word becomes flesh, eternity becomes a quality of the moment. The empty transcendence shapes a spiritual fullness within the human and the present.

While political and societal depictions get both the first and the last word in GL—the election campaigns frame the narrative both literally and symbolically—they are saturated throughout with satire and caricature, blatant directness and stilted understatements, and mechanical rhetoric and imprecise polemics. The novel's descriptions of nature are generally less sarcastic and tendentious, but especially devoid of such strenuous and strained artistic measures is the stylistic oratory devoted to Gjellerup's summits of high-strung Platonic idealism.

GL is a *Lebensanschauungsroman* and *Bildungsroman* whose stylistic unevenness and exaggerations stem from attempts to articulate a conflict-ridden philosophy of life—attempts whose obstinacy merely throws the underlying conflicts into relief. The Teutons' Apprentice is the Sorcerer's Apprentice, whose moral rationalism supports modernity's liberation from orthodoxy and conventional wisdom, but not modernity's own ideological narrow-mindedness and modern man's self-glorification. The novel's resistance to modernism issues from within, and its propellant force is an essentialist nineteenth-century humanism. A tug of war between modernism and humanism dominates GL, as it does much of Danish, Nordic, and European literature after the modern breakthrough. Repercussions of this dynamic can be felt in Western intellectual history in such works as Adorno's *The Dialectic of Enlightenment*—and in papers for the University of Minnesota conference on "Rethinking Modernism."

V

Gjellerup's impact extends beyond naturalistic and symbolistic versions of modernity. On the one hand, its neoromantic spirituality calls forth an intellectual legacy dating back to Lessing's rational moralism and Schiller's romantic idealism; aimed at aligning the naturalistic foundation of symbolist rebellion with classical strands of spirituality, it is a balancing act intended to subject the modern to humanistic reflection. On the other hand, the attempted syncretism of transcendental, essentialist thinking and modernist formalizations has a future perspective in that it bears equally on *Jugendstil* and *art nouveau* as potential revitalizations of earlier modernist endeavors.[5]

The British critic Tony Davies, in his book on humanism, has provided a useful vocabulary for critiquing agendas like Gjellerup's. Of "the Hellenic ideal" Davies notes that it "belonged, for Hegel and Humboldt as for Goethe and Schiller, not to the remote past and the postmortem formalities of an ancient language, but to the future" (11). Indeed, for all its different variations, humanism of this origin offered "an idea that could at once rationalize an explosive and unpredictable modernity (as the triumphant achievement of heroic human endeavor), and justify or palliate its all-too-visible brutalities and inequalities" (Davies 19).

But not only is humanism a link to modernity enabling the artist to have it both ways, as I suggested earlier about Gjellerup; it also connects the individual with the universal: "Each of us lives our human-ness as a uniquely individual experience; but that experience, we are asked to feel, is part of a larger, all-embracing humanity, a 'human condition,' [. . .] [a] 'central [. . .] truly human point of view' " (Davies 21–22).

The power of this "central [. . .] truly human point of view" is nothing short of religious. It was "what the later nineteenth century dubbed, in lieu of the Christianity in which it could no longer believe, the 'religion of humanity' " (Davies 26). Two themes emerge from this essentialist construction: freedom and understanding, and "the two themes converge and compete in complex ways throughout the nineteenth century and beyond, and between them set the boundaries of its various humanisms" (Davies 27).

Karl Gjellerup's GL has been discussed earlier as an exemplary battleground for these converging and competing themes (with positivist humanism à la Comte on the sidelines). Indeed, there is precedent for propelling the "conception of humanism towards an identification with atheism and secularism" (Davies 30), as Gjellerup was also inclined to doing.

To account for these apparent contradictions, both within the humanist project itself and in regard to specific instantiations within the novel, it helps to be mindful of some distinctions set forth by Tony Davies. As opposed to essentialist humanism, another brand conceives of "Man" "not as an essential starting-point but as a destination" and underscores "less a given set of intrinsic qualities than the goal of an epochal and never-to-be-completed process" (Davies 31). Of direct relevance to the analysis of Gjellerup's GL is this summation of the latter humanistic stance: "If there is a 'human condition,' it is the condition of being always unconsummated, oscillating ceaselessly between the desire for fulfillment and the consciousness of failure. This is the condition that the nineteenth century called tragic and identified with modernity" (Davies 31–32).

Indeed it is, and it was precisely the same condition, bordering on personal tragedy, that Niels Hjorth experienced and sought to address as he moved from the sensually tempting Kristine to the spiritually healing Johanna; from the alienness of metropolitan Denmark to the surrendered Schleswig of his childhood; and from his sheltered political glibness on the political right to his role as political candidate much further to the left. Moreover, it was the condition of light and darkness, of merging and conflicting novelistic currents that brought essentialist depth and civilizing clarity to their narrative conclusion.

At this juncture, where humanistic resolution seems to have gotten the better of Gjellerup, Davies reminds us of Nietzsche, who in turn reminds us, in *Human All Too Human* (1880), of the futility of seeking truth "as something that remains constant in the midst of all flux, as a sure measure of things [. . .] But everything has become: there are no eternal facts, just as there are no absolute truths" (33).

Gjellerup would hardly disagree other than with Nietzsche's categorical rejection of the essentialist and humanistic "religion of humanity" as a passable gateway to the modernity that had occasioned this myth or "religion" in the first place. Inadvertently or not, resistance to modernism implies as much recognition thereof as any direct embrace in the wake of Nietzsche's antihumanism could ever lay claim to. The critical question is merely whether humanistic resistance to modernism can also match the authenticity of modernism's own offspring within the antihumanist tradition (Davies 48–49).

VI

According to Adorno, the answer is no. One of his foremost denunciations of humanism, *The Dialectic of Enlightenment*, portrays it as "an ideological smokescreen for the oppressive mystifications of modern society and culture, the marginalization and oppression of the multitudes of human beings in whose name it pretends to speak" (Davies 5). But in his seminal treatment of "The Decline of Modernism," Peter Bürger both qualifies and disqualifies Adorno's position. The latter has the rigidity of a "magnificent onesidedness" and entails an "anti-avant-gardism" and anti-neo-classicism, for that matter, in favor of the autonomy of art as all but sacrosanct (Bürger, *Decline* 35).

It is when this "coercion to formalization" finally "leads to emptiness" that "the historical avant-garde movements [. . .] demand [. . .] a return of art to life, the abolition of the autonomy of art," and that "the aestheticizing primacy of form is [. . .] replaced by the primacy of expression. The artist-subject revolts against form, which now confronts him as something alien" (Bürger, *Decline* 45–46).

Karl Gjellerup's artistic intervention in the modern breakthrough in Nordic literature around 1880 reflects similar concerns. As artistic form increasingly borders on pure formalization, and as more avant-garde-minded artists propose new challenges to artistic form, Gjellerup responds with a movement back to tradition in order to circumvent, if not obviate, the obstacles presented by modernity. While his objective is to overcome modernity with a spiritual pincers movement, the move, predictably, only confirms the predicament it was meant to resolve, and the emptiness of form it wished to escape becomes the very mold into which its escape route tends to disappear. While life and expression in Gjellerup's works do indeed meet, it is typically in a bloodless harmony that proves equally devastating to both and that ironically presages the destiny of much bolder artistic endeavors.

Still, there may be a way out of this no-win situation, winding its way between real, objective life and pure, subjective form, between materiality and reception. To clarify its direction, I cite from Danish philosopher Ole Thyssen's book *The Eyes of the Peacock: After Postmodernism* (1987): "So when you see the peacock fan its tail, you can indulge in the metallic colors and the confusion of eyes that stare at you from everywhere. But the many eyes must not blind you to the fact that these are all eyes on feathers, and that the feathers are feathers on a bird, and that without a peacock there would be no eyes whatsoever to look into" (143).[6]

While the *postmodern exclamation*, when you consider these beautiful eyes, is: What a bird!?—the *modernist question* is: Where is the content underneath the form, and the form underneath the ideology (or vice versa)?!

Both reactions pertain to dilemmas within such narratives as Gjellerup's GL and to consequences of these dilemmas. Is Gjellerup's resistance to modernism an opening up: directly to tradition, or indirectly to modernistic advancement of syntheses of life and form against form and ideology as rigid singularities? Or is his expansive reclamation of a spiritual form for naturalistic *immanens* merely a fiction substituting intertextuality for outmoded transcendentalism? Having enabled the question, the author would later take his case out of Western court and bring it before the Buddha. And the answer keeps blowing in the wind.

Notes

1. Translation mine.
2. Houe, "Karl Gjellerup" 172–83; see also Houe, "Begyndelsen på enden" 144–51.
3. Professor Petersen epitomizes Kierkegaard's theological anathema.
4. Translation mine. Further page references to this volume are given in the main text.
5. Paul and, most recently, Nybo, have suggested as much.
6. Translation mine.

Knut Hamsun's "White Negro" from *Ringen sluttet* (1936)—Or the Politics of Race

Monika Žagar

The Negroes were playing, and people were dancing on an oblong polished surface in the middle of the room—it was the same here as all over the world.[1]

Knut Hamsun published *Ringen sluttet* (The Ring is Closed, *RC*) in 1936, at the age of 77. In the 1930s, Hamsun and his family, disillusioned over parliamentarism, and fearful of organized labor and international bolshevism, rallied around Vidkun Quisling and his *Nasjonal Samling* (National Unification, *NS*) party. The *NS*, still split between various factions in 1933, had, by the end of 1934, developed into a party with a clear profile based on race as one of its main ideological axes (Bruknapp). Jon Alfred Mjøen, the internationally acclaimed eugenicist and an acquaintance of Hamsun, was considered one of the spiritual fathers of the party.[2] The various *NS* publications—*Fronten, Ragnarok*, and *Nationalt tidsskrift* for instance—that Hamsun read and sometimes wrote for, idealized the Nordic race and used other races as emblems of archaic, primeval aliens, and/or modern degeneration. As influential as Mjøen and *NS* propaganda might have been, Hamsun's race attitude had appeared as early as the 1890s. It colored his portrayal of Others in a number of his texts, most visibly perhaps in his 1889 book *Fra det moderne Amerikas Aandsliv* (The Cultural Life of Modern America, *CLMA*) and his 1910 play *Livet Ivold* (In the Grip of Life, *GL*).[3] The utopian primitivism of his 1917 novel *Markens grøde* (Growth of the Soil, *GS*) is also tainted by the skewed portrayal of the Lapps. Race also manifests itself in many ways in *RC*, not only in the location and function of a black community in Kentucky, a central organizing trope of the novel, but also in the attitudes and biases of the protagonists as well as the novel's narrator. This section of the chapter looks at what we would call in today's parlance, Hamsun's racism, as a component of his conflicted feelings about both modernism and primitivism.

RC is an illustration of Hamsun's engagement in a reckoning with modernity that, on the one hand, made the primitive attractive as a counterideal but, on the other, was complicated by his racism. In the first part of *RC* the primitive carefree way of life is represented positively but it soon evolves into a pointless, hopeless randomness. Much of the tension in the novel derives from playing off the attractive elements of primitivism against those elements of modernity that Hamsun scorned—women's liberation, globalization of cultures, shallow material values, urbanization, and racial integration—developments that Hamsun abhorred, and first depicted as American in *CLMA*.

In this part I illustrate why I believe Hamsun was harking back to his earliest book—his largely autobiographical *CLMA*—when, upon publication of *RC* he wrote to the editor Harald Grieg that the title means, "[. . .] that the last link in the chain connects with the first."[4] *CLMA* portrays, as I write elsewhere, freed black Americans and American Indians as uncivilized, with disgusting personal habits and low morals (Žagar "Black Man"; Žagar "Imagining"). American white women are depicted as corrupted by education, and as sexually active free thinkers who try to avoid motherhood. Democracy and modern values are active agents in the way each of these groups is permitted to live in America. *RC* would have the reader believe that all of these modern American features have now, in the mid-1930s, migrated to Norway.

RC is a novel set in a typical small coastal town in Norway in the early decades of the twentieth century. The newly independent Norway was at the time both provincial and global, for Norway was at the geographic margins of Europe while its fleet sailed virtually around the globe. The novel depicts the life of Abel Brodersen from boyhood through adulthood and his gradual dissociation from any permanent commitments in life. The action takes place predominantly in his hometown, his world travels recounted primarily through reminiscences. The crucial childhood relationship between Abel and the local beauty Olga mutates several times over their lifetime, with the early estrangement leading Abel to seek his fortunes abroad when he is but fourteen. When he returns, as a young adventurous man, Olga is engaged to marry a promising clergyman.

Abel's crucial experience is his prolonged second visit to America, where he and his wife Angèle live in a black village in Kentucky like content savages, away from modern, civilizing pressures.[5] The novel eventually reveals that Abel, in a fit of jealousy, tried to shoot his best friend Lawrence but, instead, killed Angèle. While Abel returned to Norway, Lawrence is eventually executed for the murder.

Back in Norway, the life of poverty in Kentucky is idealized and remembered as simple, happy, and erotic. The local pub's band of black musicians both invokes a link to the primitive lifestyle in Kentucky and simultaneously globalizes, somewhat anachronistically, Abel's otherwise typical Norwegian coastal community. Abel succumbs to the pressures of the hometown culture to be responsible and takes a job, yet each foray into "being somebody" is followed by a period of shedding all his material possessions in order to resume a minimal life in a decaying shack. As a metaphor for a primitive way of life, Kentucky regularly supports Abel's lack of ambition in Norway. Abel invokes Kentucky as a viable alternative lifestyle and thus justifies his desire to remain idle.

My proposition that the circle referenced in the title connects Hamsun's last novel to his first book, namely the already mentioned *CLMA*, through its focus on America, goes against the contention of several established critics. Robert Ferguson in *Enigma* (318) and Harald Næss in *Knut Hamsun* (153) contend that the imagery of the circle in the title alludes to *Sult* (Hunger), Hamsun's breakthrough novel from 1890. Atle Kittang implies the same through the wording of his own title. In spite of some common points connecting the two novels, I would argue that the comparison between *Hunger*'s protagonist Tangen and Abel does not hold. Tangen is a driven artist who hungers for success, while Abel is neither an artist nor driven; just the opposite, ambition and success are in fact repellant to him. There is a stronger link between Hamsun's description of Abel's lifestyle in Kentucky and Hamsun's cultural criticism in *CLMA*, the writing and publication of which predates *Hunger*. Ståle Dingstad's book, however, also supports the American connection. What connects the two texts, in spite of their differences, is, first, Hamsun's passages about blacks in America, and second, Hamsun's depictions of modern, emancipated women. By contrast, neither race nor America is mentioned in *Hunger*. Moreover, Abel settles not in the predominantly white and industrialized east coast or in the rural Scandinavian midwest, but rather in the black culture of the American South. He refers to America as the place where he comes from; he identifies with the black musicians from Kentucky who now perform in the local Norwegian wine pub.[6] His Kentucky identity, brushed aside by the established criticism in favor of the unifying trope of the starving artist reappears as that of a white Negro at the margin of the Norwegian community.

The turn-of-the-century response to Western industrialization, modernization, and materialism was often to turn to primitivism for redemption and consolation. While Western science, medicine, and psychiatry in particular, sought to prove the inferiority of non-Western peoples, Western artists and the general public often elevated the primitive to a place where authentic experience was far superior to the rational modernity of the West.

Still, the primitivist dream ultimately reinforced the racial divisions and elevated the primacy of the white. In this process, real geographical specificities were erased and the primitives envisioned, in Marianna Torgovnick's words, as "an inexact expressive whole" (20). The ensuing narrative of primitivism often conceptualized non-Western peoples as pure and simple, uncivilized, sexually unrestrained, brutal, and/or childlike. Hamsun gave many of these attributes to Abel. Primitivism had most to do with the longings and fears of the Western world, and as such, was constitutive in theorizing Western modernity. There is truth to Fred R. Myers' claim that "[t]he contribution of the primitivism debates to theorizing modernity has been the recognition of the role of the Primitive (external or internal) to constituting the modern" (14). In Western conceptualization, Myers continues, the primitive is taken as proof of the existence of social organization that is integral, cohesive, and wholesome. This in turn allows the modern to be described as fragmented, and the contemporary mass culture as "spurious" and "inauthentic" (Myers 17).

Acknowledging a hierarchy among the various Others—the noble Indian, the sly Oriental, the gossiping Lapp, the repulsive black—Hamsun participates in the examination, construction, reproduction, and dissemination of established tropes and images of the primitives. Yet discussion around Knut Hamsun's attitude toward modernity has focused, during the last three decades of the twentieth century, predominantly on the modernist "void," the creative process of writing, the concept of time, the male hero, and so forth.[7] Approaching Hamsun's oeuvre, instead, through the tropes of various Others, illuminates his modernity and modernism in a new light.

In Scandinavia, increased contact with different peoples through travel, immigration, ethnographic studies, museum displays, and so forth, reinforced, and simultaneously challenged the identity of being white, Nordic, and superior to others.[8] If we take Myer's claim that primitivism is essential to modernism's conceptualization of self, then the images of others should reveal some of the cultural baggage present during Hamsun's time. The way I read the epigraph to this chapter, Hamsun uses the black musicians as a metaphor of encroaching modernity and globalization. The black music band is reduced to a sign of increasing cultural leveling with none of the initial promise of an exhilarating exchange between the primitive and the civilized.

Hamsun's black metaphors have to be read against an intense debate, in both popular and academic circles, that has centered on race and degeneration in Norway and Scandinavia (as well as in Europe in general) since roughly the mid-nineteenth century.[9] The fundamental concern in this debate was, paraphrasing Nancy Stepan, to define, for each race in the entire world's population the most appropriate location on the evolutionary scale (97–116). The discourse of race became a powerful tool for framing historical changes and contemporary events. Eugenics, understood narrowly as a public and family health improvement project, could, when conceptualized more broadly, also be employed in defense of the white race. Jon Alfred Mjøen (1860–1939), for instance, who in 1905 founded an international eugenics organization based in Oslo, *Vindern Biological Laboratorium*, used his research to rally against immigration and interracial marriage. That Norway became an independent state in 1905 correlates with and highlights the need felt to establish a new collective identity that would include a racial awareness.

Mjøen, an acquaintance of Knut Hamsun, spelled out in his many articles and in his book *Racehygiene* (Race Hygiene) (1914) the fears and prejudices of many Norwegians that can best be summarized as fear of miscegenation. Mjøen maintained respect internationally as an eugenics expert and had significant popular support at home, yet remained an outcast from the Norwegian scientific establishment (Roll-Hansen, "Eugenic Sterilization" present volume). Still, the Norwegian Parliament, citing degeneration of a healthy Norwegian stock, passed a sterilization law in 1934 with only one dissenting vote. Eugenics measures were clearly supported evenly across the political spectrum.[10]

In more popular venues, exotic locations and races informed travel journals, immigration pamphlets, ethnographic writing of various sorts, and of course novels, all of which helped imagine and create separate identities for whites and others. In Scandinavia, these accounts are prefigured by sagas and the narratives of exploration and colonization of the inhospitable North that include similarly divisive descriptions of encounters between ethnic Scandinavians and the darker others (Jochens). What complicated this rather typical primitivism toward the end of the nineteenth century was widespread insistence in the Nordic countries on a symbiotic and authentic relationship with nature. Part domestic discourse in defense of traditional values perceived as endangered in modernity, and part acceptance of the continental European projection that imagined in the rugged North the last European primitivist enclave, Nordic primitivism became a source of national pride and an integral element of the Nordic man.

In general Hamsun recreates foreign places in his texts in line with the mainstream European writing about colonial territories, partially as a historical backdrop and partially as a magical location for living out libidinal impulses. He came into contact with non-European peoples during his two visits to the States and travels in the Caucasus and the Orient in 1899. A self-taught writer, he was also a voracious reader of canonical novels by established writers as well as of popular dime novels, semipopular scientific texts, and travel books. The black village in Kentucky where Abel enjoys an unbridled sexual life is one of the imagined magical locations. Abel's colonial America is constructed as a contradictory paradise where life unfolds as during its primitive beginning, where language is not used, and sexuality is not reined in by civilized codes of conduct. Abel elaborates on his vision of the good life in a description that collapses facets of America with a narrative about the tropics, where the "natives" are proud and happy, sexually free, and free from societal pressures to compete and acquire material goods. His virility constituting an essential part of his masculinity, Abel impregnates three women in the course of the novel. His wife Angèle is pregnant when killed. His mistress Lili gives birth to two children by Abel and two by her husband Axel. The once unattainable, middle-class Olga, unable to conceive with either her first or second husband, finally seduces and becomes pregnant with Abel. Still, modern in his restlessness and rootlessness, Abel is best defined by an absence of qualities; he has no ambitions and no obvious talents. Unlike characters in Hamsun's previous novels, Abel is neither a charismatic storyteller nor a diligent farmer; he is an emblematic, uprooted, modern everyman, yet one who fights for his right to remain idle and uncivilized.

It is productive to see *RC* as an echo of a book written in 1917 by the Dane Konrad Simonsen, *Den moderne Menneksetype* (The Modern Human Type) that discusses many of the degeneration and race issues in a popular form.[11] Dr. Konrad Simonsen (1877–1945) was known in Scandinavia primarily for his vocal opposition to the influential critic Georg Brandes and support of the ideas of German intellectual and industrialist, Walter Rathenau.[12] Simonsen's book contains much the same racial imaginary that informs Hamsun's texts, an imaginary that attributes sexuality, promiscuity, and an absence of civilized restraint of drives to inferior primitives. Simonsen's "analysis" of Southern and Northern peoples, and of modern mobility, resembles in many points the eugenics research propagated by J.A. Mjøen. Hamsun who first praised Simonsen's book in his 1917 short story "Nabobyen" was not the book's sole admirer; *Den moderne Menneksetype* went through ten editions in its first year. While it is easy to dismiss this book as a racist and anti-Semitic propaganda, as Allan Simpson did, it can be read productively as an expression of the *Zeitgeist* of the time.

Den moderne Menneksetype contains the well-known lament on the part of numerous European writers about Western modernity's material gains and the subsequent loss of intuition and creativity. Simonsen's complaints about modern technological inventions, the institutions of democracy, and easily available art and education as the root causes of the degeneration of society have also been rehearsed previously. Hamsun, an extraordinarily complex man who yearned for simple answers, shared with Simonsen to a large degree such views toward modern development. Abel's lack of ambition allows Hamsun to investigate the consequences of a radical rejection of the prevalent contemporary societal goals.

Simonsen couples his conviction about spiritual poverty in modernity with rapid degermanization of Germanic peoples due to their interbreeding with the lower races. While realistic about the pervasive impact of globalization on even the remotest Scandinavian communities, he glorifies the heroic Vikings as role models, and urges a return to traditional spiritual values. The bleak and disillusioned *RC*, set squarely in Simonsen's ideal coastal community, represents an extraordinary artistic response to both Hamsun's own earlier work and Simonsen's call for a spiritual renewal.

Hamsun had, as early as 1890, in his literary manifesto "Fra det ubevidste Sjæleliv" (From the Unconscious Life of the Soul), emphasized the role of what has become conventionally known as the "whisper of the blood, the pleading of the bone" (Bull 42). He boldly posited a subjective, instinctual writing that would track the minute shifts in the landscape of the mind and body, although he, a political radical at the time, simultaneously contributed to the predominantly realistic Scandinavian fiction of the last few decades of the nineteenth century with novels like *Redaktør Lynge* and *Ny jord* (both written in 1893). The focus on internal processes soon made him indifferent, and later hostile, to modern industrial development, which he viewed as a disruption of authentic experience.

America, which Hamsun visited twice in the 1880s, was in his view the epitome of modernity. Hamsun's *CLMA*, established him as one of America's harshest critics, portraying it as modernity's aberration, a country of material greed and mass mediocrity, with the exception of the vitality of American journalism.[13] In his later novels, America was the place where Hamsun dispatched useless characters to and from which immigrants returned restless and uprooted, like Abel.

The stereotypes of the promiscuous erotic blacks that Hamsun uses in *CLMA, GL*, and eventually in *RC*, fit into a broader tradition of expelling Others in the Western world: a vast array of various "white Negroes," be they the poor, criminals, revolutionaries, political radicals, Slavs, Gypsies, or Jews. The alignment of these disparate groups under the convenient label of "race," testifies that the label was used in unstable and shifting ways, as many scholars have claimed (McClintock 52–56). It could be used as synonymous with culture or nation, define ethnicity or subgroups within majority population, or invent and pinpoint distinctions between what we would now call classes. In Scandinavia, the Nordic peoples were traditionally pitted against the Lapps and the Finns who may or may not have looked different.[14] The absence of a difference in skin color, which complicated an easy definition of outsiders in Scandinavia, spurred Scandinavian racism to invent other signs of degeneration, such as barbaric language, sloppy habits of cleanliness, general slothfulness, a host of attitudes that Anne McClintock pointedly calls, although in a non-Scandinavian setting, "domestic barbarism" (53). Frequently, allegations of sexual perversion were used to depict, intimidate, and police the undesirables and outsiders of all sorts whose skin color may or may not have been remarkable. The narrative of imperial expansion having mostly come to an end, the distinction between the Europeans and the others, between the majority group and its minorities, was now displaced onto cultural values like cleanliness, polite behavior, proper discourse, and so forth, invoking the benefits of domestication.

As an artist who cherished independence, and as a Norwegian critical of British imperialism and American consumerism, Hamsun writes against the cult of the domestication of the wild, launching Abel into an imagined authenticity of a black American hand-to-mouth existence, and creating a narrative of a series of displacements. In the final analysis, Hamsun's portrayal of Abel collapses the us/them antagonism that essentially punctures the primitivist narrative: Abel ends up an outsider, a "white Negro," on both sides of the Atlantic.

The novel suggests that the black musicians and Olga essentially belong in the same category. Attracted to their voices and music, their exotic and erotic appearance, Olga is an embodiment of Hamsun's misogynist views of women. Olga never departs from the socially accepted cliché about blacks: they have velvet skin, stink, are musical, erotic, and promiscuous. What prevents her from realizing her vague dreams of sexual and social liberation are her (middle-) class pretensions, which are so often ridiculed in Hamsun's novels. In Olga's eyes, Abel too is an outsider, attractive, a bit dirty, exotic, and available.

Hamsun's depiction of the relationship between Olga and Abel reveals how he genders modernity as a process that undercuts and ignores male virility and privileges women in control. Hamsun saw in modernity not the emancipatory possibilities for women, but a shallow and barren life. Olga, described by a rather typical metaphor of an electric light without warmth, and with her speech consisting of disjointed sentences and snatches of unfocused thoughts, is not unlike a number of Hamsun's other women protagonists. A woman alienated from the authentic, "natural" life of motherhood who would rather read novels, smoke and shop, she has Abel at her mercy and discards him as a human drone after she gets pregnant.

Abel's final departure for America is the consequence of his realization that he has become superfluous on both sides of the Atlantic. While the end vaguely proposes that Abel might face criminal charges in connection with Angèle's death, it is unclear whether he will end up in the Kentucky black community, in prison, or somewhere else entirely.

How do we ultimately position this novel within Hamsun's oeuvre and in relation to Hamsun's cultural politics? In his book, Harald Næss calls Abel "lazy and optimistic" (*Knut Hamsun* 148). In his 1985 article, Næss characterizes Abel as Hamsun's "most modern hero." ("In Defense" 320). Atle Kittang labels Abel a disillusioned artist (303) and Ståle Dingstad, most recently, describes him as a cynic. Far from being either optimistic or artistic, or even cynical, Abel stands out as somebody who represents, rejects, and is unable to cope with modernity. In the exploratory process, Hamsun gives Abel's lifestyle a certain logic and value, yet ultimately collapses it into modern degenerate life as obvious from the metaphors of the racial and gender discourse. The narrative voice also degenerates, as Frederik Stjernfelt has claimed, from an omniscient voice into a voice that is synonymous with small town gossip (549). Most of the judgmental opinions about Abel, attributable to other protagonists are, at the beginning of the novel, explained, countered, and corrected by the narrator as a higher authority. The narrator's voice gradually changes, however, and blends into a collective judgmental voice while maintaining its aura of authority. The comments about Abel become harsher, and he is described as having, for instance, a "mismanaged brain,"[15] or is depicted as a "loony, a human wreck from Kentucky's valley of lost souls,"[16] or "a nameless one in a shed, a nothing, a loony."[17]

In conclusion, while *RC* initially endorses Abel's unambitious way of life in an attempt to recreate in Norway a worry-free and nonmaterialistic life style, it ultimately concludes that such attempts at modernity are doomed to failure. In the process the illusion of a primitivist escape is exposed as hollow. Even children, Hamsun's most cherished symbol of hope and resilience, are denied any redeeming features. Hamsun often "allows" protagonists who are social misfits or economic failures to be good fathers, like Oliver the cripple in *Konerne ved vandposten* (Women at the Pump) or Axel the farmer in *Markens grøde*. Avoiding moralistic judgments, and appreciating vitality, Hamsun portrays children born out of promiscuous affairs no differently from other children. Women who have been spoiled by education or modern cities are still sometimes given a last chance at redemption by having a child. Even Olga gets a chance, though she is not redeemed. Abel forecloses his own family line as he shoots and kills his pregnant wife Angèle in Kentucky. He remains an anonymous sperm-donor to Olga's child and to Lili's children. A man without successors, his biological children dispersed, Abel ends up absorbed into the vast American continent. What he leaves behind is equally unpalatable: a Norway forever changed by encroaching modernization symbolized by the black musicians from Kentucky.

The impossibility of resolving the contradiction within the primitivist critique of Western modernity results in a profound sense of despair in *RC*.

It might well be that Hamsun, out of a resigned disillusionment, turned to Quisling's party and the Nazi occupants of his country for a more optimistic message of cultural renewal that would in turn restore racial and gender purity. Why Hamsun would become an active Nazi supporter while many of his countrymen who shared his racist attitudes did not, remains inconclusive.[18] But his primitivist tropes certainly reveal a consistency in his worldview that would find many common points with Nazi ideas on race and modernity.

Notes

1. "Negrene spilte og menneskene danset på et avlangt gulvbræt, det var det samme her som over hele verden." Hamsun, *RC* 44; translation mine.
2. Jon Alfred Mjøen was a tireless advocate for eugenics health policies. He suggested, among other measures, alcohol consumption taxation, various support policies for women, biological registration of foreigners, prohibition of immigration, and a campaign to increase the number of children born to the healthiest Norwegian farmers. From 1919 to 1932, Mjøen published a journal *Den Nordiske Race*. Under the auspices of the *Nordische Gesellschaft*, he was a frequent lecturer in Germany in the thirties.
3. In this play Hamsun uses, as a metaphor of degeneration, the same gendered configuration of black man and white woman that he deplored in *CLMA*.
4. "[. . .] at siste Led i Lænken føier sig til første Led." Næss, *Knut Hamsuns brev*, letter 2517, 152.
5. Hamsun's original text has the events in America taking place in Kentucky; the English translation opted for Texas.
6. "Vi gik i skjorte, bukse og revolver der jeg kommer fra." (Where I come from, we walked in a shirt, pants, and a revolver) (46). "Ja de er fra Kentucky, sa Abel. Mine landsmænd. Vi sat om kveldene og hørte negrene synge hist og her." (Yes, they are from Kentucky, said Abel. My compatriots. We would sit in the evenings and listen to Negroes sing here and there) (57).
7. See for instance Kittang. It is correct to claim, I believe, that Kittang's Lacanian analysis of a selection of Hamsun's novels has set the tone of Hamsun research in Norway for almost two decades.
8. Some resources on the topic with a special focus on Scandinavia include: Christensen and Ericksen; Kent, especially chapters entitled "Germans, Xenophobia, and the Growth of National Identities" and "A Peculiar Institution: Slavery, the Tropics, and Scandinavia"; Kyllingstad; and Hansen.
9. Jon Alfred Mjøen, Ragnar Vogt, Johan Scharffenberg, O.L. Mohr, and Kristine Bonnevie were among the many Norwegian scientists who debated facets of biology, heredity, intelligence, and race, as well as the role of the state and its public policies. See also Roll-Hansen's article "Norwegian Eugenics."
10. On the socialist left, for instance, Dr. Karl Evang was the most vocal and influential supporter of a mild form of eugenics in the service of a better welfare state. Mjøen himself belonged to the Liberal Party (Venstre).
11. *Den moderne Mennesketype* was taken off the market in the early 1930s due to a public debate about its inflammatory racially charged statements. Hamsun's

efforts to have it republished show that he held it in high esteem over an extended period of time. Hamsun urged Aschehoug's director to reprint it (Næss, *Knut Hamsuns brev,* letter 2261, 460). In the letter, Hamsun refers to his own "linjer" (lines) about Simonsen's book from 1917 "som jeg ennu står ved" (that I still support). He adds that the book is "nøiaktig like aktuel som før," (just as current as before). After several weeks, on October 31, 1932, he turned to Grieg in Gyldendal to ask him to sponsor Simonsen (letter 2268, 465–66.) See also letter to Grieg (letter 2270, 467), in which Hamsun expresses readiness for his own financial support to Simonsen.

12. Simonsen, Konrad, *Georg Brandes*. Simonsen's inspiration came to a large extent from Walther Rathenau's two works, *Zur Kritik der Zeit*(1912) and *Zur Mechanik des Geistes: Oder vom Reich der Seele* (1913). See also Herf's discussion of Rathenau's ideas.
13. To read more about the role America played in the Scandinavian imagination of the nineteenth and early twentieth centuries, see for instance, Rossel. For an overview of representation of native Americans in early Norwegian immigrant writing, see Bergland.
14. See for instance Hansen's *Norsk folkepsykologi* in which he applies the theory of the long-skulls versus the round-skulls to explain moral values and election results.
15. Hamsun, "forkvaklede hjerne [. . .]" (62).
16. Ibid., "denne tomsong, dette vrak fra Kentuckys jammersverden" (108).
17. Ibid., "En navnløs i et skur, en ingenting, en tomsing" (114).
18. There were other prominent writers in Scandinavia who shared Hamsun's opinion on race and modernity. Expressing a strong belief in European supremacy, the Danish writer Johannes V. Jensen, for instance, examined the idea of progress and race in *Den lange Rejse* (The Long Journey). In the thirties, however, when *NS* appropriated race hygiene into its doctrine, Jensen distanced himself immediately from the idea of Aryan supremacy.

Eugenic Sterilization and the Role of Science—The Scandinavian Case

Nils Roll-Hansen

The practical impact of biological science on human life is growing quickly. At the same time the status and authority of science appears to be slipping in academic as well as general culture. But if we neglect scientific insight as a guide, how are we to control this development? Eugenics has received much attention as an expression of the dark sides of twentieth-century modernism. In this section I take a critical look at the role of science, in particular the science of genetics, in the rise and demise of this movement. I use the terms "eugenics" primarily to refer to policies and practices that aim to improve the genetic heritage (gene pool) of a population.

The founding of classical genetics in the early twentieth century represented a great step forward in the understanding of biological heredity. This stimulated the idea that mankind should take control of its own biological evolution, deliberately changing its genetic basis to create a better and happier species. Eugenic ideas had broad acceptance up to World War II influencing social policies throughout the political spectrum. But opinions on the means—segregation, sterilization, family planning, sexual education, restrictions on marriage or immigration, and so on—differed according to ethical attitudes and political goals.

At the beginning of the twenty-first century eugenics is a word with strong negative connotations. Nevertheless, new biological knowledge and technology is forcing on us social and political choices with eugenic implications. References to historical experience play a key role in present debates. But historiography has been insufficiently discerning with respect to different programs of eugenics and their relation to other aspects of social policy. One example is the tendency to interpret all sterilization as eugenically motivated. In some contexts sterilization had a primarily social and not a biological, eugenic motivation. As a means of contraception it was, for instance, important in women's emancipation and family planning.

Eugenic arguments have been influential in several areas of social policy, for instance in relation to marriage, immigration, and abortion. But it is eugenic sterilization that has attracted most interest and had the most important consequences—if we do not take into consideration eugenic justifications of the Holocaust and other genocides. In the following passages I focus on sterilization, trying to sort out the role of eugenic and noneugenic justifications, as well as the impact of expert knowledge about human genetics. I use Germany as a contrast to show more precisely the character of Scandinavian eugenic thinking and sterilization practice.

The Introduction of Eugenics in Scandinavia

Eugenics came to Scandinavia as an intellectual movement during the first decade of the twentieth century. Inspiration came mostly from Germany. In Sweden a society for race hygiene was founded in 1909 as a branch of the German-based International Society for Race Hygiene (Broberg and Tydén *Oönskad*; Broberg and Tydén, "Eugenics in Sweden" 83). In Denmark the movement was led by the Anthropological Committee where most members were medical doctors (Koch, *Racehygiejne i Danmark* 134–37). In Norway the pharmacist Jon Alfred Mjøen became a leader of eugenics and an influential public propagandist (Roll-Hansen, "Norwegian Eugenics").

Mjøen formulated the so-called Norwegian Program for race hygiene that attracted broad international attention. This was an inclusive progressive program for social reform including taking measures like economic support for mothers, tax exemption for those who had a family to support, the fight against poisons like alcohol, nicotine, and lead from industry, institutional segregation of the mentally retarded, the insane, and alcoholics, as well as sterilization of sexual criminals. When Mjøen published his popular book *Racehygiene* [Race hygiene] in 1914, it was sharply criticized by biological and medical scientists for its faulty presentation of biological facts and misleading claims about the effects and feasibility of various practical eugenic measures. The leading critic was a young medical doctor, Otto Lous Mohr, who later became an internationally prominent expert in human genetics.

Mjøen was an active member of the Liberal Party with good contacts in the government. He had already established his own private biological institute doing alcohol studies for the government as well as self-initiated research into eugenics. His critics were worried that this laboratory should develop into a state institute for eugenic research. On their proposal the first Scandinavian institute for genetics was established at the University of Oslo in 1916. Relevance to social policy was a crucial part of the justification. The first head of the institute was the zoologist and geneticist Kristine Bonnevie, first female professor at the University of Oslo. Mjøen's opponents organized themselves into the Genetics Society while Mjøen had already created the Norwegian Consultative Committee for Race Hygiene that included a number of prominent citizens—humanists, politicians, and lawyers. In Norway there was a sharper split between the popular eugenic movement and the biological and medical expertise than in the other Scandinavian countries.

In Sweden a government-financed institute for race biology was established in 1921 with the medical doctor and eugenic enthusiast Herman Lundborg as head. In Denmark the internationally famous geneticist Wilhelm Johannsen worked to institutionalize human genetic research with a view to its medical and social applications, but warned against premature application. A Danish institute for human genetics and eugenics opened in 1938 with Tage Kemp as head (Koch, *Racehygiejne i Danmark*).

Scandinavian Sterilization Laws and Practice

Sterilization laws that lasted well into the 1960s and 1970s were introduced in Denmark in 1934 and 1935, in Norway in 1934, and in Finland in 1935. In Sweden a law of 1935 was revised in 1941 providing for a more radical and coercive sterilization practice. These laws were introduced with a high degree of political consensus and were considerably more moderate than eugenic enthusiasts like Mjøen or Lundborg wanted.

In principle sterilization was voluntary. But for socially marginal groups the element of coercion could be strong. For instance, for women with many children and a poor economy consent to abortion could be dependent on sterilization. In such circumstances it even happened that sterilization was carried out without the knowledge of the person sterilized. Institutionalized young boys and girls with asocial tendencies were often under strong pressure, sterilization being a condition for leaving the institution.

The Norwegian 1934 law is representative, though perhaps somewhat more insistent on voluntariness than the laws of the other countries. Sterilization was permitted for three categories. First, people above twenty-one with full legal rights and a "reason worthy of respect" (aktverdig grunn) could be sterilized on their own personal application (§3.1). Second, people under twenty-one, or those who were not legally competent for other reasons could apply on similar grounds with the written permission of their guardian (§3.2). Third, people who were not capable of applying due to mental illness or severe mental retardation could be sterilized on the application of a guardian or curator "when there is no hope for recovery or substantial improvement" (§4). The more or less compulsory sterilizations of mentally retarded or ill persons and social outcasts are found mainly in categories two and three. Sterilizations in these two categories peaked with approximately 100 per year around 1950 and then dropped. After 1950 the first category was prevalent. Such sterilizations rose exponentially from approximately 5 per year in the mid-1930s, reaching around 200 per year by 1950 and 5000 by 1977 (Haave 152–60).

The main change in the new Norwegian sterilization law of 1977, still in force, was to make sterilization in the first category (normal legally competent persons above twenty-one years) a private matter between client and doctor, not requiring any official permission. This represented the full liberalization of voluntary sterilization for normal persons. The formal legal basis for nonvoluntary sterilizations remained the same, however. This situation is different from Sweden where the new law of the 1970s permits only voluntary sterilization, with the consequence that persons legally incapable of giving such consent cannot be sterilized.

It appears that the support for eugenic sterilization in Scandinavia culminated at the end of the 1940s. During the late 1930s and the 1940s many medical doctors, and especially psychiatrists, supported sharper sterilization laws allowing more coercion and thus achieving a more effective sterilization of mentally retarded. In Norway there was no new law passed by ordinary legislation, but a Nazi law was introduced under the Quisling regime during the German occupation. The frequency of sterilizations was two–three times higher during the two and a half years of the Nazi law, 1943–45, than in the periods immediately before and after (Haave 155). In Sweden the new law of 1941 was accompanied by a sharp rise in the number of sterilizations. At first the majority was justified by the so-called eugenic indication. But at the end of the 1940s "medical indication" took over as the main justification (Broberg and Tydén, "Eugenics in Sweden" 109). In Denmark sterilization of mentally retarded under the 1934 law reached a level of about 250 per year by the late 1930s and declined quickly after 1950 (Koch, *Tvangssterilisation i Danmark,* figure 4).

Eugenic justification, aiming to improve the gene pool of the population, no doubt played a significant role in sterilization practice during the 1930s and 1940s. But even in this period it appears that social justifications, for instance, family planning, improving living conditions for mothers and children, avoiding situations where incompetent persons were responsible for the upbringing of children, were more important. Haave argues that in Norway the social reason was the dominant motive in the sterilization of mentally retarded in the 1930s (213). Koch classified registered sterilizations of the feebleminded into three categories according to the justification given in the applications: only genetic reasons, both genetic and social reasons, and only social reasons. She found that the first category was insignificant throughout the period from 1934 to 1968. There was a dominance of the purely social over the mixed cases up to the early 1940s, parity between these two categories from then till the early 1960s, and from then on once more dominance of the purely social category. Koch's statistical results indicate that in Denmark eugenic reasons, in the biological sense, were mostly insufficient to justify sterilization of mentally retarded (Koch, *Tvangsterilisation i Danmark*, figure 11).

Eugenics after 1945

Eugenic sterilization did not immediately disappear with the experiences of Nazism during World War II. Until 1976 official Swedish statistics listed the same three categories of sterilizations: eugenic indication, social indication, and medical indication. But the number of Swedish sterilizations on eugenic indication declined sharply from more than one thousand per year to less than one hundred during the 1950s. By then eugenic ideology had lost public favor. However, it is telling that as late as 1955 the Norwegian director of health, Karl Evang, argued that the sterilization of the feebleminded ought to be intensified for eugenic reasons. This does not necessarily mean that Evang saw eugenics as the main reason for sterilization of the feebleminded. But it does show that eugenic thinking was still acceptable and influential.

Evang, a left-wing social democrat, was a powerful head of the Norwegian health service from 1939 to 1972, with a five-year break during the German occupation from 1940 to 1945. He was trained as a medical doctor and was, for a short period in the mid-1930s, research assistant for Otto Lous Mohr. In 1934 Evang published a pamphlet, *Rasepolitik og reaksjon* [Race politics and reaction], where he condemned the racist eugenics and population policies of Nazi Germany. He also warned strongly against radical eugenic measures based on social and sexual prejudice. But he accepted a moderate eugenic policy, including eugenic sterilization, as long as it was based on what he considered sound democratic and scientific principles.

What motivated Evang and his likes to promote a limited but still explicit eugenic sterilization practice even after 1945? The standard story depicts eugenics as based on a lack of genetic knowledge, prejudices against lower classes, women and marginalized social groups, authoritarian disrespect for individual rights, and a utopian modernism. Evang and other Scandinavian social democratic leaders no doubt had a paternalistic attitude and great faith in social planning. But they also championed the equality and the rights of lower classes, women, and social outcastes. Politically social democracy was starkly opposed to Nazism.

It is often claimed that eugenicists did not clearly understand that for recessive traits sterilization, or other means of preventing procreation, would have a very small effect. However, the so-called reform eugenicists took care to consider the most advanced genetic knowledge and were well aware of such problems. For very rare recessive traits the effect would be small indeed. But for conditions that appeared in the population with frequencies of the order of 1 percent, substantial reductions in the course of a few generations appeared as possible according to the contemporary state of genetic knowledge, until around 1960.

In his 1955 report on sterilization in Norway, Evang deplored the diminishing rate of eugenic sterilizations and recommended "measures aiming at more frequent sterilization according to the law in cases of clearly hereditary disease of a more serious nature" (*Sterilisering* 48). He suggested "a substantial increase in the use of sterilization of feeblemindedness." Though many countries had been too optimistic with respect to reducing the frequency of hereditary disease through sterilization, Norway had been too pessimistic, argued Evang. The average annual number of sterilizations of the mentally retarded and ill in Norway in the period 1945–1954 was only eighty-seven. In Sweden the frequency was several times higher. However, even there the number had dropped rapidly, from 937 in 1945 to 277 in 1952 (Evang, *Sterilisering* 34–41). As expert authority, Evang relied on Nils von Hofsten.

Justifying Eugenic Sterilization of the "Feebleminded"

Nils von Hofsten was the main advisor to the Swedish government on eugenic sterilization from the 1930s till the 1950s. He was a well-known political liberal and professor of zoology and published the first serious Swedish textbook of genetics in 1919. In a 1944 paper on "[t]he hereditary effects of sterilization" von Hofsten discussed the possible eugenic effects of Swedish sterilization practice. The hope that the new law of 1941 would increase the frequency of sterilization of the mentally retarded, in particular the group of "feebleminded," had been more than fulfilled, he claimed. Already in 1943 there were close to thousand such sterilizations, similar to the number that each year reached fertile age.

In von Hofsten's calculations of the possible eugenic effect, one assumption was that 75 percent of all feeblemindedness is hereditary and can be accounted for in terms of classical Mendelian inheritance. This high degree of heritability was assumed by many experts on psychiatric genetics at the time. Von Hofsten recognized that hereditary feeblemindedness was "not a biological unity." He assumed that it depended on "at least two, most likely at least three genetic factors" (Von Hofsten 179). But he argued that a complex mechanism including both recessive and dominant factors could well be equivalent to a model depending on a single recessive gene. It was well known from genetic literature that such a model, with random mating and 100 percent negative selection, would give a reduction from 1 percent to 0.7 percent in frequency in two generations. For Sweden this meant 19,000 feebleminded, by no means an insignificant eugenic effect, held von Hofsten ("De arvsbiologiska verkningarna" 179).

Gunnar Dahlberg criticized this argument. He had taken over as professor and head of the State Institute for Race Biology in 1936 with backing from his social democrat friend Gunnar Myrdal. His criticism of von Hofsten's eugenics was both sociopolitical and scientific. Such policies would discriminate against women and other oppressed groups and produce much suffering. Dahlberg also judged von Hofsten's assumptions about the genetic mechanisms to be too optimistic (235–36). Von Hofsten accepted Dahlberg's view for the relatively rare hereditary diseases and also for schizophrenia and manic-depressive insanity. It was only for feeblemindedness that he found eugenic sterilization to be justified. As late as 1963 he published a survey of *Sterilization in Sweden 1941–1953*, which supported eugenic sterilization of the feebleminded.

Tage Kemp's view was similar to von Hofsten's. Kemp was head of the Institute for Human Genetics at the University of Copenhagen and organized the first international congress of human genetics in Copenhagen in 1956. In 1957 he gave the Galton lecture in London, later published in *The Eugenics Review*. "Genetic hygiene" was Kemp's terms for a eugenics emphasizing voluntary cooperation. He estimated that selection against feeblemindedness would reach a level of 50 percent for the period 1951–70 if sterilization kept the same rate. But he cautioned that "[t]he effect of this negative selection will depend on the way mental defectiveness is inherited." Kemp still relied on high heritability of mental deficiency, called "empirical genetic prognosis": With two mentally defect parents, 60–90 percent of the children would be mentally defect, with one such parent, 30 percent (Kemp 17).

Psychiatrists' Support for Eugenics

Strong hereditarian attitudes were common among Scandinavian psychiatrists in the early post–World War II period. Ørnulf Ødegård was director of the national Norwegian Psychiatric Hospital and much used as advisor for the Norwegian government. According to a 1941 textbook that he coauthored there is a 50–60 percent risk of feeblemindedness if one parent is feebleminded and 85–90 percent if both are (Ødegård et al. 26). Apparently Scandinavian and German psychiatry was more hereditarian than was Anglo-Saxon psychiatry at this time. An official British report on mental retardation reported similar figures from German studies (Brock Committee 131–34), but its own conclusions were considerably more cautious both with respect to percentages and the role of biological heredity (Brock Committee 21). Similar conclusions were reached by an American report from the same time (Kevles 167).

In the late 1950s Ødegård served as genetic expert on a committee to review marriage regulations on medical grounds (Giæver, "Marriage and Madness" 9–13). According to the marriage act of 1918 "he, who is insane" is not allowed to marry. The "insane" at this time included the severely feebleminded (*åndssvake av høyere grad*). The committee report of 1959 proposed a revision according to which the insane, the feebleminded, and drug addicts would not be allowed to marry without special permission from the government. This permission could be made dependent upon sterilization. An appendix written by Ødegård claimed that poor results from therapy in the early twentieth century had motivated an exaggerated hereditarianism, but at present there was a "tendency to underestimate what can be achieved by eugenic measures." This claim was substantiated by referring to the results of von Hofsten. The marriage act finally passed in 1969 simply retained the prohibition for the insane and feebleminded without adding the eugenically motivated clause that permission might be given on the condition of sterilization.

Already in the 1970s a new round of revision was initiated. The Ministry of Justice now turned to other psychiatric experts. Referring to recent scientific results two experts claimed that the heritability of mental retardation had earlier been much overestimated and recommended that prohibitions on marriage for the insane and mentally retarded be removed. The new law of 1991 contained no such clause (Giæver, "Marriage and Madness" 16–17).

The strong hereditarian attitude of psychiatrists was supported by twin studies of schizophrenia. Two large studies by Franz Kallmann, a German psychiatrist who had to flee to the United States due to his Jewish ancestry, showed a large difference in concordance numbers,[1] 86 percent for monozygotic twins and 15 percent for dizygotic.[2] Even if other researchers obtained a somewhat smaller difference, Kallmann's results were widely accepted until the 1960s.

It was a surprise to psychiatrists when a Finnish study showed discordance for all of sixteen monozygotic pairs of twins (Tienari). Soon a Norwegian study confirmed that concordance was lower than had been previously assumed both in monozygotic and dizygotic twins (Kringlen 1964). A methodologically careful further study of altogether 342 pairs of twins, based on a register containing all admissions to Norwegian psychiatric hospitals after 1916 gave a concordance of 5–14 percent for dizygotes and 28–38 percent for monozygotes.[3] These remain authoritative figures until the present.

Comparing Sterilization in Scandinavia and Nazi Germany

For a brief period in August and September 1997 the story about sterilization in Scandinavia attracted the attention of the world's mass media: 60,000 people had been sterilized in Sweden and 40,000 in Norway. Considering the size of the population in these countries these Swedish and Norwegian numbers appeared comparable to the 3 to 400,000 sterilizations under the Nazi regime in Germany. This was interpreted to demonstrate that social democratic regimes in some respects had been as brutally oppressive of individual liberty as the regimes of Hitler and Stalin (Broberg and Tyden "När svensk historia").[4]

This sinister interpretation of Scandinavian sterilization practices, emphasizing the similarities to the German case, has also made its way into the scholarly literature. One example is the comparison of Sweden and Germany in the 1999 paper, "Science and Political Culture: Eugenics in a Comparative Perspective," by the German sociologist of science Peter Weingart. Other authors have published similar interpretations and claims.[5]

A problem with Weingart's analysis is that it blurs the difference between science and politics, that is between activities that primarily aim to understand the world and activities that aim to change it. A traditional "rationalist" view is that while science aims to produce and propagate knowledge, politics makes use of knowledge for social and other practical aims. This is meant as an analytical distinction and does not imply that activities can be separated into purely scientific on the one hand and purely political on the other. Policy can never be derived from scientific knowledge alone; it also depends crucially on social aims or values. To understand, criticize, and control political programs like eugenics, society needs institutions that support a science that is not bound to specific political objectives but is oriented toward knowledge—theories and facts—of common and general interest. A "pure science" where politics has no role does not exist in the real world. But a relatively autonomous and sufficiently vigorous and authoritative basic science can be an important basis for political and moral criticism. Such a view does not imply that good science is necessarily morally good. On the contrary, the consequence is that the best of science can well be combined with the worst moral or political values and support definitively bad policies.

In his introduction Weingart recognizes eugenics as a political program rather than a science: "[. . .] one can perceive the development of eugenics as a science-based social technology which is implemented in varying political cultures in different ways" (163). But in the rest of the paper eugenics is simply referred to as "science." His claim that "the development of science is *relatively independent* from cultural and political events" (163) thus appears to cover policy (eugenics) as well as science (genetics). In the following I show how Weingart's argument that eugenics was much the same in Germany and Sweden, independent of the political context, trades on this ambiguity.

I agree with Weingart that there are no good reasons for "bracketing" the science of Nazi Germany as extraordinary and fundamentally different from science in liberal democratic countries (164). No doubt some excellent genetic science was done in Germany, even during the Nazi period. But this did not preclude invalid appeals to science in legitimating Nazi policy. It could be appeals to bad science (quackery) as well as to good science in combination with bad values. Geneticists with liberal and socialist inclinations criticized Nazi eugenics on both accounts. On the one hand it was in part "unscientific," for instance, when it assumed that there existed reliable scientific evidence that conditions like epilepsy, feeblemindedness, alcoholism, homosexuality, and so on were to a high degree genetically determined. Solid evidence for such claims did not exist, argued Scandinavian, British, and American geneticists like Gunnar Dahlberg, Otto Lous Mohr, J.B.S. Haldane, Lionel Penrose, and Herman J. Muller. On the other hand these critics were acutely aware that eugenic policy depended on values no less than factual beliefs. A mainspring of their criticism was revulsion against political aims and social values contrary to those of the liberal democratic society that they believed in.

Weingart recognizes that a fascist government "was responsible for the crucial transition from voluntary to compulsory sterilisation" in Germany after 1933. But he also claims that a similar development took place in Sweden. The rights of the individual became subordinated to those of society in similar ways: the "autocratic philosophy" underlying eugenics and sterilization "may explain, amongst other things, how thin the dividing line between Social Democratic and National Socialist sentiments actually was with respect to the role of the state and eugenic practice" (Weingart 167).

Weingart disregards the fact that Swedish law and practice, in contrast to the situation in Nazi Germany, continued to emphasize voluntary sterilization as the basic norm. Scandinavian countries had nothing similar to the German *Erbgesundheitsgeriche*, a legal institution to secure the enforcement of compulsory sterilization. Furthermore the German law prohibited sterilization for social reasons. In Scandinavia such indications were legal and probably more important already from the 1930s than genetic indications.[6] This reflected the opinion of critical experts like Mohr in Norway and

Dahlberg in Sweden. They claimed that knowledge about human heredity was too uncertain to justify programs of eugenic sterilization, but they accepted social justifications.

After the Nazi takeover in 1933 public debate and criticism in Germany was heavily suppressed. Ideological "Gleichschaltung" paved the way for a radicalization of eugenic policies in accordance with Nazi ideology. The uncertain nature of knowledge in human genetics was set aside, and women's obligation to bear children for the country overruled the goal of social equality for the sexes. Even the majority of geneticists served the regime with little protest.

In his historical comparison of sterilization in Sweden and Germany Weingart makes misleading use of statistics. Most of the estimated 350,000 sterilizations under the Nazi law of 1933 were carried out in the course of a few years, before 1940. This points to the rushed, arbitrary, and violent nature of the German program. In Sweden the 63,000 officially recorded sterilizations took 40 years. The majority, about five-sixths, were carried out after 1945. For this period Weingart provides no statistics of sterilizations in Germany. Furthermore, Swedish statistics differentiate between "eugenic," "social," and "medical" indications. About two-thirds of the 63,000 Swedish sterilizations were classified as medical and the great majority of these were carried out after 1945 (Broberg and Tydén, "Eugenics in Sweden" 109–10). Most medical sterilizations in Sweden were probably wanted by the persons in question, mainly women, and cannot be classified as compulsory.

In concluding that "the development of science (here eugenics) is hardly directly affected by political circumstances," Weingart (175) conflates science and politics. He apparently holds that eugenics as a social policy and practice is also relatively independent of political context: There was "a virtual identity of the eugenic and race-hygiene discourse in Sweden and Germany as well as a striking similarity in the sterilization practice" (Weingart 173). It is hard to see how this claim can be substantiated, either for the period between 1933 and 1945 or the period from 1945 to the 1970s.[7]

Concluding Remarks on the Relation of Science to Politics

Comparative analysis of eugenics in Scandinavia and Germany is useful for developing our understanding of the political role as well as the political dependence of science in modern societies. The misleading aspects of Weingart's analysis brings out the importance of a clear conceptual distinction between science and politics, that is, between the production of generally valid knowledge and practices that applies such knowledge for particular social and political purposes. There is, of course, no sharp separation of scientific from political activities. That scientists participate in politics and politicians in the regulation of science is as it should be. The point is, I argue, that the production of general knowledge about human heredity and the promotion of social policies with the help of such knowledge are different functions in a liberal democratic society. In addition to their primary responsibility as citizens and participants in the cultural and political discourse, scientists have an extra social responsibility due to their special knowledge. By suppressing liberal cultural and political discourse, totalitarian regimes also suppress this special responsibility of scientists. In Scandinavia, as well as in Britain and in the United States, science retained a good measure of autonomy from the political system. There was room for sharp public criticism of eugenics, and the excesses of Nazi Germany were avoided.

The comparison of eugenics, and sterilization policies in Scandinavia and Nazi Germany shows how genetic scientists under liberal democratic regimes with freedom of speech were able to restrain eugenic utopianism both in theory and practice. Lacking respect for sound scientific evidence and argument appears to have been important where the most objectionable eugenic policies gained ground. In this sense at least there was a significant link between good science and good policies.

Notes

1. The concordance number is the percentage of the pairs that share a certain property, for instance schizophrenic insanity.
2. See Kallmann, "The Genetic Theory" and *Heredity in Health*.
3. See Kringlen, "Schizophrenia in Twins."
4. *The European*, 11–17 September, 1997, 5, 14–15.
5. See for example Zylberman; Weinstein and Stehr; Etzemüller; Spektorowski.
6. See Runcis; Koch, *Tvangsterilisation i Danmark*; Haave; and Tydén).
7. For an overview linking history to present issues concerning sterilization of mentally retarded, see Haavie.

Section III

Science, Technology, and German Modernism

Reactionary Engineers? Technocracy and the *Kulturfaktor Technik* in Weimar Germany

Andreas Michel

My interest in the notion of technocracy was sparked when I began teaching at an Institute of Technology. In the humanities and social sciences, particularly in the more theoretical pursuits of critical theory and cultural studies, the rise and influence of technology in modern society is generally depicted in an unfavorable light. So much so that in many accounts of the social impact of technology, the notion of technology slides all too easily into technocracy. In this usage, technocracy, far from representing the utopian promise of a just management of social resources, serves as a catchall term for an increasingly technologically administered society, where politics itself has come to an end.

The slippage from technology to technocracy is surprising since there seems to be general agreement among historians as to the periods in modern German history when it is warranted to speak of a desire for political rule by engineers. Stefan Willeke has in 1996 provided an interesting account of technocratic movements between the World Wars (Willeke in Dietz). It appears that the first truly technocratic desires emerged in the United States in the wake of Thorstein Veblen's utopian ideas for a "Soviet of Technicians," which was to administer social justice on the basis of the factual knowledge of its members. German engineers began to pick up on these American ideas, but not without transforming them to a German context. This context is the *Kulturfaktor Technik*, that is, the discursive attempt by German engineers to prove that technology is part of *Kultur* (discussed in detail shortly). The first truly technocratic ideas surfaced in the pre-Fordist visions of *Gemeinwirtschaft* developed by Walther Rathenau and Wichard von Moellendorff during World War I; a second wave occurred with the founding of explicitly technocratic societies at the end of 1932. These societies, which came into being shortly before the Nazi takeover, were dissolved in 1937. Thus, both properly technocratic endeavors were relatively short-lived. These facts notwithstanding, literary and philosophical texts continue to demonstrate slippage between the notions of technology and technocracy.

In his book *Neue Sachlichkeit 1924–1932*, for example, Helmut Lethen dedicates a whole chapter to technology in Weimar. He studies the cult of technology in literary and cultural productions (Brecht/Bronnen) as well as in popular writings such as *Technikerromane*. It is fair to say that he does not depict Weimar infatuation with and fear of technology in a favorable light. Not only is technology exclusively portrayed in terms of *Rationalisierung* and *Amerikanisierung*, but it is the very example of a mentality that conceives of human beings in terms of efficiency (*Rentabilität*) only. In Lethen's account, technology prefigures the fascist politics of the Nazi state (*Neue Sachlichkeit* 59–82).

In the course of this description Lethen's language constantly slides from *Technik* to *Technokratie*. Of course this is hardly surprising, since his ideological parameters are strongly influenced by Horkheimer's and Adorno's writings for whom the true essence of technology surfaced in the Holocaust (*Dialectic of Enlightenment*). In their work, technology is merely another word for instrumental reason that, because of the seamless grasp it holds on every aspect of society, is easily likened to technocratic rule. Similar examples can be taken from the writings of Herbert Marcuse, and it can also be shown that Martin Heidegger's very different understanding of technology as *Seinsgeschick* nevertheless concurs with this assessment when it comes to modern technology (Heidegger; Zimmermann, *Heidegger's Confrontation*).

I am fascinated by this seemingly pervasive tendency in humanistic criticism, and by the negative evaluation of technology and efficiency in general all the way up to Lyotard and Baudrillard. My current research is guided by the question of to what extent the instrumental reason paradigm may still show us humanists in the grip of the German mandarin tradition (Fritz Ringer), one that devalues the accomplishments of what German ideologues in the early twentieth century called *Zivilisation* as against those of *Kultur*.

In the following passages, I address a small aspect of this larger question by looking at a sample of writings by German engineers between the World Wars. One of the few critics to have dealt with these texts is Jeffrey Herf in his book entitled *Reactionary Modernism* (1984). Here the same pattern of the devaluing of technology occurs, despite the fact that Herf explicitly distances himself from the dialectical view of the Enlightenment made famous by his intellectual mentors Horkheimer and Adorno. By challenging some of Herf's conclusions regarding the writings of the cultural politicians among German engineers, I hope to contribute to a reappraisal of Weimar modernism.

I

Herf's own master narrative attempts to capture the ideological standpoint of the conservative Weimar intellectuals whom he calls reactionary modernists: Spengler, Jünger, Heidegger, Schmitt, Freyer, and Sombart. Their intellectual position, according to Herf, is marked by a central paradox: "It is paradoxical to reject the enlightenment and embrace technology at the same time, as did the reactionary modernists. Their claim was that Germany could be both technologically advanced *and* true to its soul" (3). For Herf, this position is paradoxical because the term "soul" denotes "antimodernist, romantic, and irrationalist ideas present in German nationalism"—a conception that must be seen at odds "with the most obvious manifestation of means-ends rationality, that is, modern technology" (1).

Herf identifies this tradition as *reactionary* in order "to emphasize that it was a tradition of the political right [. . .]. The conservative revolutionaries sought a cultural-political revolution that would revitalize the nation. They were reactionaries in that they opposed the principles of 1789" (Herf 11–12). They were *modernists* because "they were technological modernizers: that is, they wanted Germany to be more rather than less industrialized. [. . .] They articulated themes associated with the modernist vanguard [whose] central legend was of the free creative spirit at war with the bourgeoisie" (Herf 12).

Synthesizing the main characteristics of Herf's master narrative, one might say the following: reactionary modernism integrates modern technology into (German) *Kultur*. However, it rejects all other aspects of Western modernity, in fact it remains antimodern in all respects except the will to power represented by technology. Germany's reactionary modernists thus effect a selective appropriation of Western modernity, rejecting Enlightenment rationalism, as well as political and economic liberalism.

It is worth noting here that Herf's interpretation of modernity differs markedly from the one espoused by Horkheimer and Adorno in *Dialectic of Enlightenment*. For Herf, the essence of modernity is not instrumental reason as such, as it is for them. It is not Reason that is to be blamed for the Holocaust, but rather the illiberal tradition of a German *Sonderweg*, unable to fully assimilate the values of Western modernity. What Horkheimer and Adorno attributed to an excess of Reason is for Herf really a *lack* of Reason.[1]

According to Herf, Weimar engineers formed an integral part of this cultural appropriation of technology. In a chapter entitled "Engineers and Ideologues," he argues that "the cultural politicians of German engineering began to reconcile technology and culture in a nationalist synthesis long before World War I" (Herf 153). As I show shortly, it is true that throughout the first three decades of the twentieth century German engineers did indeed attempt to justify their profession as well as technology in general in terms of the values of German *Kultur*. But Herf's claims go farther: they include engineers in the seamless web of antimodern values connected with the reactionary modernist tradition, among which are romanticism, irrationalism, anti-intellectualism, and antiparliamentarism. All these tendencies end up supporting a German nationalism that by 1932 leads, almost naturally, into a technocratic allegiance with National Socialism.

I test Herf's conclusions by looking at a keynote speech given at an engineering congress in 1924. The text can be found in *Technik und Kultur*, probably the most prominent engineering journal, published by the *Verband Deutscher Diplom Ingenieure* (Association of German Academic Engineers).[2] I am interested in whether or not this keynote address supports Herf's claim concerning the irrationalism, anti-intellectualism, antiparliamentarism, and right-wing nationalism of the German engineering profession between the wars.

II

The principal issue for the cultural politicians among German engineers in the late nineteenth and early twentieth century was the attempt to gain recognition for the undeniable contributions of their work to human progress. This was no easy task in a culture whose elites were exclusively recruited from the aristocracy, military, the *Beamtentum*, and the bourgeoisie. In their search for recognition German engineers came up against at least two obstacles. The first is the late-eighteenth-century tradition championing the romantic-humanist ideal of *Bildung*. *Bildung*, best understood as a state of refined cultivation, focused on the inner growth of the individual as fostered by the study of the classical texts of antiquity. From the point of view of *Bildung*, the achievements of technology contributed merely to the perfection of the outer surface of life. The second obstacle fueling the rift between technology and the humanists was the perception that technology was in collusion with capitalist exploitation and the world of commerce. Both these obstacles contributed to a climate in which technology and its advocates were perceived by the reigning intellectual elites as corrosive elements, liable to destroy or diminish German culture.

During the late nineteenth and early twentieth century, the engineers' struggle for recognition occurred in a national context that had become crystallized around the binary opposition of (German) *Kultur* versus (Western, primarily Anglo-American) *Zivilisation*. Whereas *Kultur* was held to develop the inner core of human nature organically, with an emphasis on personal perfection (thereby contributing to the growth of a social "soul"), the concept of *Zivilisation* represented little more than the surface allure of material gains made possible by commercial and technological innovations. Being squarely identified as representatives of mere *Zivilisation*, the cultural politicians among German engineers decided upon the strategy of emphasizing the *Kulturfaktor Technik*: they argued that technology is not merely about material gain and comfort, but is instead an inherent aspect of the organic growth of *Kultur*.[3]

Technik und Kultur, the above-mentioned journal of the Association of German Academic Engineers, captures this strategy in its title. With their journal, engineers intended to lobby for the cause of technology in the register of the German philosophical tradition. One prominent contributor to *Technik und Kultur* was Carl Weihe (1875–1954), a patent lawyer and salaried professor at the University of Darmstadt, where he lectured on the history and culture of technology. Weihe also served as editor for *Technik und Kultur* from 1921 to 1928.

On June 22, 1924, in Frankfurt am Main, Weihe delivered a keynote address to the National Congress of Academic Engineers. His title, "The Cultural Tasks of the Engineer," captures the programmatic character of the speech. On the one hand, his speech is an affirmation of the role of technology in modern industrial society; on the other, it is a plea to see technology not as representative of Western *Zivilisation* but rather of German *Kultur*. Despite my ascription of "German" to *Kultur*, Weihe's speech is anything but nationalistic. Although he mentions in passing the harsh conditions of the Versailles Treaty, his address is not couched in the aggressive, antidemocratic rhetoric of political radicalisms prevalent at the time; instead, it is closest in temper to an enlightened disquisition on the role of technology in society. As such, Weihe's speech offers an interesting articulation of values associated with *Zivilisation* presented in the register of *Kultur*.

As is hardly surprising for a keynote address given at the most prestigious academic engineering congress, Weihe's speech revolves around the world of work and of possible strife between management and labor. The engineer's tasks of Weihe's title are elaborated between this world of labor and the ideals of German *Kultur*. True culture—*Kultur*—for Weihe consists of the harmonious coexistence and mutual interdependence of three aspects of human labor: the labor of the mind (in philosophy, science, government), of the soul (in ethics, religion, and art), and of technology (in manufacture, industry, trade, and agriculture). In Weihe's view, these three areas of human labor cannot thrive without each other; for instance, there can be no government without a conception of ethics and no scientific research without technical instruments. Only if these areas harmoniously coexist can one speak, claims Weihe, of a "true culture that is neither a supraculture (*Überkultur*)—tilting to one side, toward the aesthetic, for example—nor a senile subculture (*Unterkultur*) that has become petrified as *Zivilisation*, to employ Spengler's terminology" (46).

What, then, are the tasks of the engineer with respect to the maintenance of *Kultur*? According to Weihe, the first task of the engineer is, not surprisingly, to exhibit particular care in the cause of technology. Although Weihe, as a matter of course, regards technology as the foundation of all *Kultur*, he admits that the pursuit of technology has also had its problems. He concedes, for instance, that

> technology, whether in the guise of slave technology in antiquity or, on occasion, as industrial technology in modern times, has proven hostile to *Kultur*, has even at times altogether denied it. Where this occurred, man's humanity as well as his rights were violated for the benefit of the few who knew how to extract excessive profit from the work of others. (Weihe 46)

Yet on balance Weihe holds that the benefits of technology far outweigh its darker aspects. The age of industrialization and the rise of technology have brought advances in all fields of human life, particularly in the areas of nutrition, health, and human comfort. It is the engineers' task to keep their focus on inventions and to develop further applications for the well-being of society. Engineers, in Weihe's view, are thus the (unacknowledged) true leaders of modern society, and they ought to take pride in this fact.

But this constitutes only part of the engineers' task; here they are in their own realm so to speak. What, then, is the engineers' role in *Kultur* at large? Weihe offers three suggestions. First, engineers have to play the role of enlightened mediators (*Aufklärer*) in labor disputes; secondly, they need to take responsibility for the education of the workers; and, thirdly, they have to be responsive to the spiritual element of technology, the *Geistige in der Technik* (Weihe 48). In this context Weihe develops the notion of *technological idealism*, an oxymoron in terms of the German intellectual tradition he is courting. This conceptual dissonance is of course intended. The notion of technological idealism as well as the three suggestions mentioned betray Weihe's desire to employ the framework of *Kultur* to win the support of the *Bildungsbürgertum*, the cultivated bourgeoisie, for the efforts of the engineers.

Weihe's first suggestion enjoins engineers to function as enlightened mediators in the workplace because they are the ones most familiar with the work of the laborer; because of this they find themselves in a good position to arbitrate disputes concerning workers' rights and duties. As mediators, engineers are able to stand above the fray, so to speak, and to judge labor situations on the basis of their own deeper knowledge. This knowledge must be gained, surprisingly, through reflection on what makes mankind human:

> The engineer, in particular the academically trained engineer, has the duty to reflect deeply on the nature of mankind, to study the worker and his thinking, and to hold technical management and the process of production up to the measure of mankind. He has to gain an understanding of how work and the mode of production impact upon the human body and soul. (Weihe 47)

While I have no desire to ridicule such laudable moral activity on the part of anyone in society, it nevertheless strikes me as odd to *expect* this kind of moral introspection on the part of engineers—not because they ought not to reflect deeply or because they are unable to, but because they have to fulfill different tasks in modern society, tasks that have to do with efficiency and scientific measurement rather than with the care of the soul. Such tasks can be defended in their own right rather than in terms of a call for moral introspection. Weihe's rhetoric is designed to convince the educated classes of how close German engineers really are to the hallmarks of *Kultur*.

Closely related to this first aspect is Weihe's second suggestion, according to which the engineer is to take on the task of educating the worker. The fundamental objective of this education imperative is to make the worker realize that his work is not alienated:

> Only when the worker understands what he does, when he knows the place of his own work in the order of individual and communal production, when he knows where exactly he fits in as a necessary link in the mechanism (*Räderwerk*) of the economy, only then will he experience inner satisfaction in his work, only then will he feel the sanctity of work. This [knowledge] will raise not only the quality of the product but elevate the human being itself. (Weihe 47)

The last sentence in this passage, the twofold liberation (of product and human being) attained through the worker's reconnection with his inner self, recalls the moral idealism of the German intellectual tradition. Through a nonalienated relationship to his work, the object (the product) and the subject (the laborer himself) find themselves *perfected*. Striving toward moral perfection is, of course, one of the central tenets of German

Bildung. In more general terms, alienation (i.e., that which keeps human beings from perfecting themselves), has—from Rousseau to Schiller, from Hegel and Marx to Weber—accompanied the rise of industrialism as a staple of critique. Indeed, during the mid-1920s, the time of Weihe's address, the principal German attacks on Taylorism—the scientific study of labor based on the stopwatch—are partially couched in the terminology of alienation. Weihe here coopts the notion of work as self-realization, prevalent in the German notion of *Kultur*, and applies it to technology. And he continues:

> If we thus succeed to reconnect the worker with the inner experience of his labors—as was the case with small tool artisans during the Middle Ages and the Renaissance—then the creative drive will stir in him. (Weihe 47)

The creative drive, the *Schöpferdrang*, represents the pinnacle of the German nomenclature of *Kultur*. Indeed, the entire field of connotations around *Kultur*—such as inner experience, personal growth, and organic work—is animated by the creative drive. As such it is the very antithesis of technology, of all machine-like and mechanical modes of being. The creative drive is mankind's connection to the unconditioned, the spiritual, and the divine. If this is so, there seems to be, at least at first sight, a fundamental incongruence here between technology as the essence of the mechanical and the dynamics of the creative drive. However, by suggesting, as Heidegger will do in the early 1930s, that *art*—the primary instantiation of the creative drive—and *technology* are manifestations of the same creative human impulse, of *techne*, Weihe closes the gap between creativity and technology. If the worker, invoked in the passage, becomes again, through the offices of the engineer, like the artisans during the Middle Ages, he will be able to rekindle

> the creative drive, from which stems all technology, and which can be observed in the work of the least laborer once it is kindled [. . .]. The creative dimension is the highest power in man. It elevates man above nature. He builds into the existing world a second nature, born of his mind, made by his hands, and suffused with his soul. That is technology, our technology. (Weihe 47)

The creative drive turns the worker into an artist and conceives of both worker and artist as analogous to God the creator. The phrase "our technology" is a clear reference to the merger that Weihe is attempting between the German discourse of the soul and that which such discourse would consider to be the alienating consequence of technology. The personal pronoun *our* says that this, the creative drive, which impels the making of the artwork and is one of God's primary attributes, is also the essence of technology. It seems safe to say that both Weihe's description of the factory worker's labor conditions and his views of technology are designed not for the engineer, who probably knows better, but rather for the German educated class, the *Bildungsbürger*.

The third and most important cultural task of the engineer takes off from this *rapprochement* between technology and art. This is the point where the spiritual dimension of technology, the *Geistige in der Technik*, comes into play. Having first established that art and technology originate "from the same root" (48), Weihe now proceeds to differentiate the two according to the manner in which they fashion their objects. And it is this distinction that will allow him to claim for the engineer a social status equal if not superior to that of the traditional humanistic elites.

Weihe's argument runs as follows. In both art and technology, the final product derives from the *idea*, the invention that forms spontaneously in the inner realm of the individual. In art, this happens subconsciously, and "the beauty of the finished work surprises even its creator" (Weihe 48). Here, the creative drive that brings the idea to fruition is spent exclusively on the act of achieving the beautiful form (*Schönheitsform*) of the product, without concern for any purpose. In the case of technology, on the other hand, turning idea into product "requires a keen process of reflection that must always be mindful of its purpose" (Weihe 48). Here the creative drive is determined by the object's purposive form (*Zweckform*). According to Weihe, the *spiritual dimension in technology* emerges when, during the creation of a product, beautiful form and purposive form grow organically from the product's essential possibilities. And when it comes to technical products, only the engineer—the person who really understands purposive form—is able to realize and recognize *beautiful* form in the product. Thus, once they have schooled themselves in the traditions of beautiful form, it is the principle task of engineers to enrich society, as only they can, with new technological objects. Thus, at the close of Weihe's address, the ideas of German *Bildung* triumph, and it is the engineer, not the poet or the philosopher, who is in charge.

In his address to the National Engineering Congress, Weihe makes a plea to the established German elites to accept the engineer as one of their own. The engineer's distinction is that he, like no one else in society, understands the inner nature of technology and can translate it into social reality. Weihe's delineation of this ability, as well as the vocabulary he uses, fits neatly into the reigning idealist framework of *Kultur*. In Weihe's utopian vision, the engineer, once trained to recognize the beautiful content of technology, will "help usher in a new idealism, a technological idealism" (49). With Weihe's concluding remarks, the ideological merger between *Kultur* and technology is articulated and envisioned.

The last term, "technological idealism," should make clear how idealistic the German interpretation of technology had become during the Weimar Republic. From a contemporary perspective of even the most circumspect acceptance of technology *as instrument and tool* rather than as spiritual manifestation, one can only marvel at the lengths to which the cultural politicians among German engineers went in order to make technology acceptable to the ruling elites. Thus, my analysis corroborates Herf's basic thesis, according to which German engineers' felt constrained to champion *Zivilisation* in terms of *Kultur*.[4]

III

There is, however, a second thesis in Herf's book when it comes to German engineers—a thesis that I believe is overhasty and in need of differentiation. I am referring to the claim according to which "a reactionary modernist tradition [. . .] developed inside the German engineering profession" (Herf 152). Herf maintains that, like the literati, the engineers held irrational, anti-Enlightenment views; they were convinced that their support of "technology would have to be legitimated without succumbing to Enlightenment rationality" (155). This statement expresses the general tenor of his chapter "Engineers as Ideologues." In light of these claims, it is worth taking a second look at the results of the analysis.

Herf suggests without qualification that "[the engineers] excoriated the Weimar Republic as a swamp of political chaos and cultural despair" (163). However, in 1924, Weihe's keynote address is anything but an excoriation. Rather, it is a reasoned attempt at including engineers in the leading administrative circles of a society *based on the values and ideas* of *Kultur*. One might disagree with these particular values and ideas, but such disagreement does not make them irrational. In his speech Weihe sets forth his version of the dialectics of beautiful and purposive form. In doing so, he calls for the social acceptance of technology and its benefits on rational, not irrational, grounds. Contrary to Herf, I am therefore suggesting that Weihe's address, and in my view the bulk of his contributions to the journal *Technik und Kultur*, do not belong in Herf's column of reactionary modernists. Weihe and most of the German engineers publishing in *Technik und Kultur* are far from rejecting reason as a means in the pursuit of technology.

This is not to deny that they were quite eager, on political grounds, to make compromises with the ideals of German *Kultur*, as we have seen. From today's point of view these compromises may seem quaint and unconvincing. But to call them quaint is not the same as ranging their proponents under the rubric of reactionary modernists. The question is whether their pronouncements entail the rejection of democratic and

Enlightenment values or, alternatively, if their articulation of the *Kulturfaktor Technik* was compatible with such values. In the case of Weihe, I believe this question must certainly be answered in the affirmative.

If my analysis is correct, that is, if Herf overstates his case at least with respect to Carl Weihe, the question arises as to why he would do so. In conclusion, I speculate as to what might have induced Herf to include German engineers in the company of reactionary modernists.

Herf's interpretation of German history, like most accounts of it after 1945, begins with Hitler—that is to say, all events in German history are interpreted from the perspective of the inhumanity of World War II and, especially, the Holocaust (Fulbrook). The danger of such an approach is that the smallest hint of any divergence from our post-Holocaust point of view is viewed as potentially preparing, contributing to, or supporting the horror. Statements such as "What began as an indigenous tradition of German engineers and right-wing literati ended in slogans administered by the Nazis" (Herf 16) and "The predominant tradition of German engineers was heavily ideological and merged with Nazism in important ways" (154) at least potentially betray a logic that will see the emergence of Nazism in any deviance from the Western path of political development.

It seems that, in the case of German engineers, Herf's analysis has succumbed to this danger. Framed by the paradigm of the "politics of cultural despair" developed by George Mosse and Fritz Stern, Herf holds most questionings of Enlightenment reason and economic liberalism to be irrational and unreasonable expressions of a revolt against modernity. Thus, when engineers like Weihe appeal to idealist concepts of soul and *Geist* in order to advance the cause of technology, Herf automatically sees them within the reactionary modernist tradition. He overstates his case because he disregards the specific difference between the cultural engineers and the literati. To suggest that the engineers, like the reactionary modernists, were "irrationalists who despised reason and denigrated its role in political and social affairs" (13), or better yet "cultural revolutionaries seeking to restore instinct and to reverse degeneration due to an excess of civilization" (12), seems, based on the evidence above, to be a misreading.

During the Weimar Republic at least, such a rejection of reason, intellect, and internationalism in favor of *Volk*, instinct, and race does not apply to the engineering discourse. The mere desire to integrate technology into an admittedly idealist version of *Kultur* does not suffice—contrary to what the "cultural despair paradigm" might suggest—to include the engineers among the reactionary modernists. Carl Weihe's understanding of *Kultur*, despite his borrowings from German idealism, is not parochial, or nationalistic, but rather supra- or international. *Kultur*, in his view, represents human culture, including technology, as the unidirectional process of human progress. In some sense, then, Weihe is a representative of an earlier, late-eighteenth-century German discourse on culture—prior to the *Sonderweg* of German *Bildung*—one that saw *Kultur* and *Zivilisation* as perfectly compatible.[5]

A closer reading of the writings by the cultural politicians among German engineers, such as I have performed here, can help us articulate the conceptual and ideological differences within Weimar modernism, where universalism and nationalism, modernism and antimodernism, coexist in uneven measure.

Notes

1. Thus Herf's critique of Horkheimer and Adorno: "What proved so disastrous for Germany was the separation of the Enlightenment from German nationalism. German society remained partially—never 'fully'—enlightened. Horkheimer and Adorno's analysis overlooked this national context and generalized Germany's miseries into dilemmas of modernity per se. Consequently they blamed the Enlightenment for what was really the result of its weakness" (10).
2. *Technik und Kultur* appeared from 1909 to 1934, when it was discontinued by the Nazis. For the history of the journal, see Dietz, 105–30.
3. See contributions in Dietz and Hard.
4. An earlier version of section II appeared as "Culture and the Engineer: German Discourse on Technology in the Weimar Republic," *Humanities & Technology Review* 20 (2001): 1–21.
5. See Bollenbeck. He distinguishes a broad, late-Enlightenment (ca. 1775) from a narrow, neohumanist (ca. 1800) concept of culture. While the former concept includes the totality of human activities, the latter inaugurates the process that will eventually lead to the late-nineteenth-century distinction between inner (*Kultur*) and outer (*Zivilisation*) forms of cultivation. See particularly 93–160.

Science, Art, and the Question of the Visible: Rudolf Virchow, Hannah Höch, and "Immediate Visual Perception"

Thomas O. Haakenson

> *We [. . .] learn definitively, that the operation of light takes place in the interior of the human body, and that it is a mere superficial [peripherisches] organ of the human body—not in fact the brain, but the eye itself—which experiences this operation. We learn that this photography is, in fact, not a mental operation, but a chemical procedure, which is perfected by the co-operation of certain vital processes, and that, in reality, we do not see external objects, but the pictures of our eye. (11)*
>
> —Rudolf Virchow
>
> *The Freedom of Science and Teaching in the Modern State*

In the 1926 photomontage *Denkmal II: Eitelkeit* ("Monument II: Vanity"), the artist Anne (Hannah) Therese Johannah Höch combines the allure of traditional portrait nudes and the artifacts of an apparently primitive Otherness.[1] Part of a series of such images titled *Aus einem ethnographischen Museum* (From an Ethnographic Museum), Höch's concatenation of European tradition and anthropological abjection does more than display (Makholm 198–99).[2] Much like a Germany trying to reconcile the incommensurabilities of modernity, of political and economic fluxuations, and of scientific innovation and modernist fetishization of the "primitive other," Höch's photomontage seeks to reorient the spectator's perceptual relation to the new and the old, the familiar and the unfamiliar.

Such a perceptual reorientation suggests an innovative engagement: in the photomontage *Denkmal II: Eitelkeit*, display becomes a vehicle through which to offer alternative if implicit visual interpretations of some of science's evidentiary objects. Prior to and during the early years of the development of anthropology as a formal discipline in Germany in the late nineteenth and early twentieth century, scientists grappled extensively with the implications of supposed racial, evolutionary, and biological differences among Europeans and non-Europeans. By juxtaposing signifiers of racial identity (i.e., the white female body) with those of anthropological otherness (i.e., non-European sculpture), Höch does more than continue a fascination with the primitive, popular within German art circles at the time. David Pan suggests that primitivism might be thought of, in part, as a critique of science that "emphasizes that technological progress does not change the existential situation of the modern compared to the primitive" (6). Kristin Makholm extends this line of thought in examining Carl Einstein, a key proponent of primitivism, and his concerns with museums that separated their *Schausammlungen* (display collections) from their *Forschungsinstituten* (research institutes), indicating that scientists and museum directors simply had exoticized anthropological others rather than understood primitivism as, in part, a criticism of European epistemology (242 fn. 529). By focusing on the use of display, artists such as Höch, I would like to suggest, provide a way for us to rethink developments in the life sciences and the impact that these developments had on German modernisms. Specifically, and in comparison to the issues associated with Peter Bürger's "historical avant-garde," the critical energies of artists like Höch might be viewed as directed at modern science's optical certitude rather than at the separation of art from the quotidian.

In this part, the "life sciences" refers to a broad array of fields, many of which have some relation to biology (Magner). Scholars such as Timothy Lenoir and Lynn K. Nyhart locate the emergence of modern biology in the early nineteenth century, and detail its unique conceptual, institutional, and disciplinary development in Germany. Recent work done in the history of anthropology by scholars such as Benoit Massin, H. Glenn Penny, Robert Proctor, and Andrew Zimmerman shows the extensive relationship between biology and *Anthropologie* (anthropology, but often used as synonymous with physical anthropology). Taking these various concerns into account, the goal of this section is to examine the way in which an artist such as Hannah Höch, aware of developments in the life sciences and the impact of these developments on public perception, challenged science's supposed visual objectivity.[3]

The Problem of Perception

Notable among recent projects assessing the relationships between art and science is the work of Jonathan Crary, who provides a challenge to traditional art historical studies of representation and to technologically determinist accounts of the development of photography and cinema. Crary examines "a new valuation of visual experience" that has its origins in the early nineteenth century, describing vision as embodied neither in the human subject nor in particular styles of artistic representation. Rather, he suggests that visual truth was—and, to a great extent continues to be—based on "an unprecedented mobility and exchangeability, abstracted from any founding site or referent" (Crary 14). The origins of this visual abstraction are found, according to Crary, in the increasing interest in retinal processes in the nineteenth century, an interest associated with the field of physiological optics.

Education reformers and popular scientific venues in the nineteenth century sought to employ increasingly visual devices such as the Straight-Rest and the "spectatorium" to standardize the experience of supposed optical truths, such as the correct posture to prevent degeneration of the eyes or the implications of electricity on the organs of humans and animals. Aware of these cultural changes, promoters of the observational and experimental approach to the life sciences were confronted with the fact that an a priori knowledge no longer guaranteed the universality of visible facts. The realization meant not only the need to standardize observational and experimental methods to account for the new insights about retinal processes, but also led to the disconcerting discovery that vision itself might be susceptible to degenerations caused by incorrect instructional methods or improper displays. The increasing credibility of the methods associated with instruction through visual aids, or *Anschauungsunterricht*, as well as the explosive growth in the number of German museums in the late nineteenth century suggest that those interested in popularizing and promoting new approaches in the life sciences were nevertheless able to devise foundations for establishing the supposed truth of visual information.

Along with the mechanical and technical means by which the insights of physiological optics were disseminated, popularizers and promoters often utilized semifamiliar concepts in their attempts to establish new normative criteria of visual truth. In Germany, one such concept was that of an *unmittelbare Anschauung*—of an "immediate visual perception."[4] Individuals in a number of the life sciences used the concept in their attempts to popularize scientific knowledge and to incorporate the insights of physiological optics as to how the eye actually processes information. The idea was incorporated into a number of museological initiatives in Germany in the late nineteenth and the early twentieth centuries.[5]

The concept of *unmittelbare Anschauung* referred to the ideal—and what many scientists believed were the only correct—conditions for optical assessment. For scientists such as Rudolf Virchow, "immediate visual perception" meant that optical information left impressions on the retina, impressions that were communicated directly to the brain. The eye, and not the brain, served as the initial site for the processing of optical information, an insight that Virchow felt demanded "a new starting-point of analysis for the understanding of our relations to the external world, and for discriminating more precisely the merely mental [geistigen] part of vision from the part of it that is purely physical [körperlichen]" (*Freedom* 11–12). Virchow and others became convinced that the best way to ensure correct mental comprehension of a visual representation was to create conditions that allowed the eye to "measure" the object accurately rather than to depend upon a priori cognitive abilities.

Virchow's scientific work transcended a number of fields, from physical anthropology to cellular pathology. His emphasis on "immediate visual perception," fostered by his relationship to his advisor Johannes Müller and his affiliations with colleagues Herman von Helmholtz and Emil Du Bois-Reymond, influenced the display strategies of his protégés greatly, including the sexologist Magnus Hirschfeld and the U.S. immigrant Franz Boas. Whereas Müller's ideas about specific nerve energies and the relationship of these energies to sense perception were key for Virchow's early work, especially his dissertation, the further research of Du Bois-Reymond and von Helmholtz into the empirical conditions of perception—that is, the "world out there" and not simply the sensations internal to the human body—became an increasing concern for Virchow. His attempt to emphasize the empirical conditions of perception in his public and professional scientific practice—most notably in his Institute of Pathology—influenced later display techniques, including those of Hirschfeld's Institute for Sexology and of Boas and his contextual displays of anthropological artifacts.

That someone like Virchow was a strong and vocal proponent of an "immediate visual perception" in public venues as well as in professional scientific practice was no minor endorsement. While Virchow was a respected scientist and researcher, he was also an extremely well-known politician and public figure. He wrote a number of works that located the root of medical problems in public policy, beginning with a text in 1844 titled "Zur Geschichte des Carthauses in Schivelbein" (On the History of the Carthauses in Schivelbein). As a result of this early essay, he was appointed in 1848 to investigate an outbreak of typhus fever in Upper Silesia. His report criticized primarily the government and its misdirected approaches toward treating the effects and not the sources of typhus—that is, the disease and not its origins in improper sewage and waste removal. Such an approach to medical issues, what some undoubtedly labeled proto-socialist, was radical for the period.

It was only upon his return to Berlin in 1856, however, that Virchow became involved actively with a number of explicitly political affairs.

Importantly, he sought increasingly to combine his public and political concerns with his scientific research and activities. He was elected to the Berlin City Council in 1859, to the Prussian Diet in 1861, to the German Reichstag from 1880 to 1893, and founded the *Fortschrittspartei* (Progressive Party). Virchow held his post on the City Council for over forty years, until his death on September 2, 1902. The results of this combination of public and professional activities included his various attempts to change the way in which people engaged science. Indeed, his insights into optical processes had direct implications not only for his research practices but also for the public display of his evidentiary objects, issues that were key in the construction of his Institute of Pathology.

In 1896, Virchow announced to an assembled crowd of dignitaries and invited guests at the Charité Hospital's Institute of Pathology in Berlin the construction of what he believed to be an important facility for training the lay public in the most appropriate techniques of optical assessment.[6] The facility, the Museum of Pathology of the Royal Friederich Wilhelm's University, would house an unusual collection taken from over 23,600 cellular and anatomical-pathological specimens that Virchow and his colleagues had amassed for much of the nineteenth century. Virchow's hope was that the new Museum of Pathology would demonstrate to the public the most appropriate optical assessment of the specimens on display through an emphasis on "immediate visual perception."[7]

On June 27, 1899, Virchow gave the keynote address that opened the Museum of Pathology, the first of three buildings to comprise the new home of the Institute of Pathology. In the opening address, Virchow spoke of the potential significance of the museum with respect to the public reception of scientific research and in contrast to the type of engagement enabled by the popular press:

> [. . .] For the first time on this occasion a plan's potential is realized and that on behalf of the High Ministry which conceived of this plan: Namely the possibility for entrance into the Institute for the general public. Today, where through the universal distribution of the press and the circulation of literary publications, the public is made aware in a certain way on a daily basis of the progress of [medical science]—and naturally also the set backs that also occur—one can hardly meet in lay gatherings where one would like to say something completely new such that it would not have already been shared in some worldly form or another. The difference between us and them, [in] what the general press offers, is based only in the assurance [of the accuracy of] the evidence, with which we offer here absolute familiarity and the greater ability to represent it in an understandable way. What was missing and what has always been close to my heart was the immediate visual perception [of the evidence itself]. (Virchow qtd. in Krietsch and Dietel 2–3; my translation)

Explicitly contrasting the potential of the new facility with the public understanding of and interest in the sciences as evidenced in the popular press, Virchow indicated that the Museum of Pathology would provide a physical venue for him and his colleagues to showcase the advancements in their research.

For many, the initial trepidation about the public's ability to understand complex scientific problems had transformed by the end of the nineteenth century through an emphasis on the new means for the display of scientific knowledge. Constantin Goschler notes that Virchow juxtaposed the concept of *schauen* ("to look") with *sehen* ("to see") and valorized the latter term as a trained ability to view scientific evidence correctly, to learn the culture of correct optical assessment (206). Virchow felt that the distinction between *schauen* and *sehen* could also be taught to the lay public. He emphasized his and others' belief in "immediate visual perception" as a necessary precondition in the public presentations of scientific knowledge about the body.

More than just another official event then, the opening of the Museum of Pathology was an indication for Virchow that years of campaigning and innumerable appearances had already begun to produce their just results. The exhibition space would allow the public to gain access to objects and evidence to which he, his colleagues, and his pupils already had access, in some cases for decades. Indeed, Virchow emphasized during a public address at the University on August 3, 1893, the need for such direct sensory engagement:

> On all sides the conviction was evidently taking root that the natural sciences can be understood only by the observation of nature herself, and that the effective combination of science and tangible objects requires provisions on a large scale, such as can be afforded by museums, collections, laboratories, and institutes. This conviction became particularly strong when it was realized that experimentation is the most important means of forcing nature to reveal the essence, causes, and development of a phenomena. ("Founding" 692)

For Virchow, public and professional access to "tangible objects" would be the best means by which to "observe nature herself" and, via experimentation, to force nature to reveal the laws of "her" development.

Similar to other scientific venues and displays popular at the time, Virchow's museum sought to make the life sciences understandable for and acceptable to the lay public via visual display. In an exhibit titled *Volkskrankheiten und ihre Bekämpfung* (The Fight against Public Diseases) that appeared in Dresden, Munich, Kiel, and Frankfurt in the early twentieth century, the exhibit organizer, Karl August Lingner, sought to introduce the public to the complex scientific ideas of Robert Koch in a way that was visually accessible: "[Lingner] inscribed himself into the tradition of eighteenth-century Enlightenment to propagate the idea that 'visual instruction' was the most appropriate form of 'mass instruction' for transmitting established knowledge in a way intelligible to all" (Brecht and Nikolow 517). Much like in Virchow's displays, in the *Volkskrankheiten* exhibit the "connections between the dissemination of diseases and the strategies to combat them were to be visible at first glance" (Ibid. 522). Whereas the curator Lingner was concerned in the *Volkskrankheiten* exhibit with the way in which diseases were spread and could be prevented, Virchow was focused in his museum primarily on pathological developments and their impact on the human form. Both Lingner and Virchow, however, sought to present this specialized scientific information in a way as easily—and as visually—accessible to the lay public as possible.

Virchow's emphasis on display and his desire to educate the public as to developments in the life sciences perhaps provide unique German perspectives on the issue of pathology, although Virchow's work undoubtedly had a significant effect on scientific research beyond national borders. The French medical historian Georges Canguilhem describes Virchow's concept of pathology as "physiology with obstacles" (207), suggesting that for Virchow pathology was a deviation from supposed normal physiological processes and biological developments, and that for some reason—environmental, cellular, anatomical, or otherwise—these processes and developments had deviated from what was understood to be their most common paths. Thus, for Virchow, pathology was not an abnormality, in the pejorative sense, but rather simply a physiological and developmental phenomenon that was not as common as supposed normal phenomenon. The body that exhibited pathological development, in other words, was by no means "unnatural." Despite the clarification of Virchow's pathology as "physiology with obstacles," Canguilhem pays relatively little attention to the German scientist, perhaps one of the most influential scientific figures in pathology in the late nineteenth and early twentieth centuries. One of Canguilhem's most well-known protégés, Michel Foucault, also fails in his influential *The Birth of Clinic* to devote any attention to Virchow's work, despite the fact that the book purports to provide an "archaeology" of medical vision.[8] As a result of these avoidances and absences, both Canguilhem and Foucault fail to help explain the way in which someone like Virchow could seek actively a public-pedagogical engagement as part of his scientific activities. Virchow's science did not distinguish between private research center and public clinic, as does Foucault in his study. Rather, Virchow's emphasis was on professional scientists' as well as the public's ability to *sehen lernen* (learn to see).

It was in the display objects in the Museum of Pathology that Virchow sought to demonstrate the insightfulness of his approach and to standardize the optical dimensions of his science through an emphasis on "immediate visual perception." Displays of unusual developmental and anatomical bodies included fetuses exhibiting holoprosencephaly, a condition resulting from the failure of the anterior portion of the embryonic brain to undergo proper segmentation, as well as examples of cranial malformations, such as hydrocephaly and microcephaly. While such displays had existed in mostly private collections for centuries, Virchow had been able to secure state support for the public display of such objects, in effect generating further official, political support for his public and professional scientific ideas. One of the most popular groups of specimens included the so-called Janus Head, a condition resulting when a fertilized egg does not completely split in half. In comparison to such venues as Castan's Panopticum, in which microcephalic specimens—including live human subjects—had become commonplace, Virchow sought in his museum to explain the biological and developmental conditions that led to such conditions. While anatomical-pathological specimens had been—and continued to be—displayed in special theaters and in local venues, the opening of Virchow's Museum of Pathology marks an increasing belief that lay persons could be trained to assess objects scientifically if given the correct conditions for an "immediate visual perception."

Mediated Visions

One of the fields in which Virchow's emphasis on *unmittelbare Anschauung* had immediate and lasting implications was anthropology. His emphasis on physical anthropological measurements in contrast to speculative approaches to evolution is well known, and emphasized the detailed testing of scientific hypotheses before such hypotheses were endorsed in public forums.[9] The Museum of Pathology allowed him to connect further a number of pathological and anthropological issues.[10] In contrast to the emphasis on "immediate visual perception" that would inform Virchow's and his colleagues' displays of scientific evidence, artists such as Hannah Höch would suggest a more critical approach. Her work neither accepted Virchow's emphasis on "immediate visual perception" nor the ideas of his protégé, such as Franz Boas, who emphasized holistic or contextual displays of artifacts rather than the display of individual specimens (J. Berman 215–16). Höch's photomontage series *Aus einem ethnographischen Museum* suggests the limitations of strictly "physicalist" (i.e., physical anthropology) as well as "cosmological" (i.e., Boas's more explicitly contextual) approaches to anthropology. Through their incorporation of anthropological objects as well as signifiers of everyday European life, Höch's photomontages show that both physicalists and cosmologists depended upon a biased "immediate visual perception" to underpin their knowledge claims.

Unlike Boas and his emphasis on context in his anthropological displays, Höch's use of photomontage demonstrates a concern that the culture not only of "exotic others" but also of indigenous Germans should be subject to critical examination. Höch was an avid reader of scientific periodicals and a collector of illustrated and photographic images; she also frequented many of Berlin's institutes and museums. She utilized a number of images of objects and artifacts that Boas had collected and were on display in Berlin, especially objects and artifacts from what he described as the Kwakiutl Indians of the North American Northwestern coastal region.[11] Höch suggests through her juxtaposition of supposedly primitive others and modern subjects in her photomontages that no amount of context can reveal that the anthropologist's own culture is subject to change, that "immediate visual perception" does not mean eternal knowledge. Thus, while projecting ideas of "vanishing peoples" onto anthropological others was a strategy through which Europeans could ease their own sense of instability associated with the massive social, political, economic, and cultural changes of the period, Höch refused to provide a visual archive of "vanishing peoples" in her creations, thereby suggesting a need to confront the problems of modernity as European ones—not as projections of loss and primitiveness alleviated through elimination or fetishization of the "anthropological other."

Rather than situate Höch's photomontages in this complex anthropological and visual tradition, scholars have often dismissed her photomontages as simply disturbing private fantasies or as irrelevant. As a result, she often is not included among the radical and innovative avant-garde artists of the day. However, her work demonstrates an important example of the untenable assumptions of avant-garde inclusion and radicalism during the 1920s. Art historians such as Peter Boswell and Maria Makela have, for example, charted the way in which Höch was excluded from Berlin Dada events because she was perceived to be too concerned with formal artistic standards and hence not radical enough to be an avant-garde artist (2). A reassessment of her work is particularly relevant given Peter Bürger's description of Dada as "the most radical movement of the European avant-garde," a qualifier bestowed because, rather than simply altering styles and representations of previous art movements, Dada attacked art as a social institution (*Theorie* 28–29).

Such a description of Dada does not apply to Höch, who was actively involved in the activities of the Berlin Dada group because of her interest in art as a means to achieve social change. Her work, however, consisted primarily—but not exclusively—of paintings and photomontages, not the political protests or public spectacles so often associated with Dada. Höch's work was innovative epistemologically. That is, her use of photomontage, an art form associated with the word "montieren" (to assemble or mount), refers to what Boswell and Makela describe as the "piecing together of photographic and typographic sources, usually cut from the printed mass media" (2). Often, other Dadaists depended upon the new unity produced by rephotographing their photomontages to create a smooth and seamless surface representation. Höch never rephotographed her work or manipulated negatives in the darkroom. She refused to assume that visual representations conveyed truths. Refusing to engage in such "photographic artifice," she preferred instead "to accept the evidence of hand cutting over the creation of a seamless image or the mass-production of images" (Boswell and Makela 2). In leaving these evidentiary traces, Höch reminded the viewer that her images had been manipulated and, implicitly, of the material limitations of the medium of photography. Höch made explicit photomontage's incorporation of different source materials into an arbitrarily constructed new unity. Consciously defying photographic convention, she refused simply to try to *represent* objects but sought rather to invoke an optical strategy made possible by the photomontage technique that *criticized* the reductive nature of visual representation itself.

In *Die Süße* (The Sweet One), a photomontage from 1926, Höch combined a mask from the former French Congo and the body of an idol figure from the Bushongo tribe with an eye, lips, and the legs of a distinctly modern European woman.[12] The obvious incommensurability of the figure's right eye with its mask-face indicates a critical strategy of optical disruption: the image literally looks back at the viewer with two different eyes. The singular and standardized view of the object, a view many scientists sought to secure through an "immediate visual perception" in museum displays, was a significant focus of early German anthropology. Höch's incorporation of asymmetrical eyes physically incommensurable with the body in her photomontage challenges the viewer to deduce through his or her own gaze, through his or her perception, competing visual claims about the figure on display. In other words, the photomontage challenges what Lorraine Daston describes as the supposed aperspectival objectivity of scientific evidence (111). The figure with its strange eyes demands that the viewer see the evidence of human manipulation of the representation. The viewer cannot conclude through vision alone the truth that the photomontage figure is supposed to represent. Rather, the photomontage calls attention to the failure of all representations to reproduce the complexity and richness of human lives.

Examining Höch's photomontage series in light of the issue of scientific display reveals a new and important dimension for art historical consideration. Maud Lavin suggests that, despite Höch's incorporation of ethnographic objects, the artist was not especially critical of anthropological attitudes during the period, although there is an implicit criticism of racist and colonialist ideas to be found in Höch's work (160). To that end, Lavin makes an important clarification:

> The series' primary referent is not race, however, but the way race is socially encoded in the ethnographic museum. What concerned Höch in these works is the display of culture marked as different—for the Other as well as the self in Höch's photomontages is the modern European woman. (182)

Indeed, although many of the images in the series focus on representations of women, not all of them do. Rather, it is the focus on display in the series that connects the otherwise disparate objects. In works such as *Die Süße*, Höch implicitly questions museological and anthropological politics, as well as the means of display and visual isolation. In other words, the confusion of anthropological artifacts and signifiers of gender in *Die Süße* indicate an awareness of the construction of visual knowledge, of supposedly scientific evidence.

Höch's education at the Kunstgewerbeschule (Fine Arts School) in Berlin, her engagement with anthropological topics as indicated by her extensive collection of photographs and illustrated magazines, and her visits to science centers and museums in Berlin suggest that *Denkmal II: Eitelkeit, Die Süße*, and the rest of the *Aus einem ethnographischen Museum* series can be read as an attempt to appropriate the visual practices of scientific display. Despite the popularity of photomontage among the Berlin Dadaists, Höch's use therefore indicates an important, alternative understanding of the medium's critical artistic potential: an attempt to challenge "immediate visual perception" advocated by Virchow and his protégés in service of a rethinking of the exclusions and constructions that informed such optical immediacy. Thus, in Höch's series, photomontage takes the visual evidence "out of a museum" to reveal the illusory nature of a scientific tradition that depended upon an "immediate visual perception" to try to eliminate any epistemological uncertainty.

Notes

1. Peter Boswell and Maria Makela, eds. *The Photomontages of Hannah Höch* (Minneapolis: Walker Art Center, 1996): 102.
2. Makholm has convincingly demonstrated that two images not previously included among the *Aus einem ethnographischen Museum* series should be. Thus, I concur with her that there are a total of twenty photomontages associated with the series.
3. I explore the issue of artistic intervention and scientific display at greater length in my dissertation, *Grotesque Visions: Art, Science, and Visual Culture in Early Twentieth-Century Berlin.*

4. Although the term *unmittelbare Anschauung* has a complex history and a number of possible English equivalents, the idea of an "immediate visual perception" is closest to the purposes and ideas of figures like Virchow, figures who had an extensive knowledge of developments in physiological optics in the nineteenth and early twentieth centuries and sought to incorporate these developments into scientific practice itself, in both its professional and public manifestations. I thus use the phrase *unmittelbare Anschauung* to refer to the supposed visual obviousness of science's evidence, an obviousness that is paradoxical: an "immediate visual perception" was possible only if the evidence were displayed in the right way, using the most appropriate physical and spatial arrangements, and if the viewer, public or professional as he or she may be, was trained as to how to view the evidence correctly. Indeed, given this lengthy clarification, the idea that this "perception" was by any means "immediate" seems suspect. This is, however, precisely the point.
5. See Joachimides; Köstering; Penny; and Zimmerman, *Anthropology*.
6. See fn. 3.
7. Today the facility is known as the Berliner Medizinhistorisches Museum der Charité.
8. The subtitle of Foucault's book contains the often forgotten qualifier, "An Archaeology of Medical Perception."
9. In many ways Virchow's exchanges with the zoologist Ernst Haeckel in the late 1870s and early 1880s indicate the profound problem that the issue of evolution posed for many scientists in Germany, especially prior to the so-called rediscovery of Mendelian genetics. The well-known exchange between the two began during the Congress of German Naturalists and Physicians in Munich in September 1877. On the surface, it was a difference of opinion as to whether or not they and their colleagues should openly (i.e., in front of the lay public) discuss unproven scientific hypotheses as well as their current unverified research findings.
10. See Penny; Zimmerman *Anthropology*; and Zimmerman "Looking beyond History."
11. J. Berman has pointed out the different affiliations among the Kwakiutl, affiliations that Boas ignored—or was ignorant of—in his work. While Höch probably was not aware of these intratribal distinctions either, her photomontages nevertheless suggest a concern with the homogenizing tendencies of visual strategies and research practices that would erase such distinctions.
12. Boswell and Makela 104.

Section IV

Architecture and Urban Planning in Weimar Modernity

Imagining the New Berlin: Modernism, Mass Utopia, and the Architectural Avant-Garde

Sabine Hake

There are few cities in which the historical encounter between urbanism and modernism found such heightened, and often controversial, expression as in Berlin, the capital of the embattled Weimar Republic, the center of the literary and artistic avant-gardes, and the site of fundamental changes in the organization of urban life. The transformation of the metropolis into the home of the modern masses can be measured by the actual interventions of architects and city-planners into the historically grown cityscape. Yet the reorganization of urban functions can also be examined through architecture's failed opportunities, missed chances, and glaring mistakes. It is in recognition of the overdetermined function of modern architecture as mass utopia that this chapter focuses on visions of the metropolis that, for better or for worse, remained unrealized. Architecture's utopian qualities, I argue, provided a privileged means for exploring the complicated relationship between aesthetic innovation and social progress and for enlisting quintessential urban structures like the highrise (*Hochhaus*) in the representation of modern mass society. The broader implications for the project of urbanism and modernity are nowhere more apparent than in Ludwig Hilberseimer's unrealized 1928 proposal for an office and business complex in Berlin's historical Friedrichstadt (figure 4.1). An examination of his ambitious design confirms the importance of the unbuilt as an integral part of the urban imagination, primarily through the spatial articulation of historical change within the existing cityscape and, secondarily, through the identification of architectural form with new lifestyles and mentalities. Moreover, Hilberseimer's avant-garde position allows me to connect the proliferation of urban utopias to the post–World War I crisis of class society and, in so doing, to affirm the centrality of class to most architectural practices of the times.

Figure 4.1 Ludwig Karl Hilberseimer, "Berlin Development Project, Friedrichstadt District: Office and Commercial Buildings, Bird's Eye Perspective View." 1928. Photocollage of ink on paper mounted on serial photograph. 17.2 x 25 cm. Reproduction. ©The Art Institute of Chicago

Source: Courtesy of the Art Institute of Chicago

Despite its ubiquity as an adjective in cultural debates (i.e., as a synonym for "innovative," "provocative," or "unconventional"), the term "avant-garde" continues to resist easy explanation and classification. From the beginning, the historical avant-gardes have led a peculiar existence as the uncanny double of the modernist movement, articulating its most radical demands and extreme visions, but also highlighting its conceptual shortcomings and ideological failures. Unfortunately, the reassessment of the historical avant-garde in the programmatically interdisciplinary (and transnational) field of avant-garde studies has rarely extended to Weimar architecture with its ambitious social programs and utopian dreams. One might argue that the architectural avant-garde requires very different categories of analysis than the literary and artistic avant-gardes, given architecture's complete lack of autonomy and its very different functions as an industry, technology, and essential part of everyday life. At the same time, no artistic practice would seem better suited to explore the aporias of avant-garde discourse and to do so in both the abstract terms of architectural manifestos and the concrete terms of urban development. Assuming the perspective of architecture would in fact allow us to scrutinize Weimar's social utopias precisely for the elements that are resolved or suppressed in the planning process. These involve the economics of place and space, the politics of the local and the regional, and, most important for my discussion, the role of architectural discourse in making sense of the fundamental transformation of both traditional class society and classical metropolitan culture during the postwar years.

All architectural utopias can be understood as programmatic responses to social, economic, or political crises. Yet when articulated in response to actual cities, even the most ambitious designs submitted to competitions or presented at exhibitions must be situated *ou topos*, which means: no place but still somewhere. In accommodating both tendencies, Weimar Berlin emerged as one of the major sites for the historical compromise between mass culture and modernity and, despite the contentious status of German modernism within the avant-garde canon, remained one of the major crossing-points in the postwar trajectories of Dada, expressionism, and constructivism. "It is not by chance that the metropolis, the place of absolute alienation, is at the very center of concern of the avant-garde," writes Manfredo Tafuri in an influential study on architecture and utopia that includes a long chapter on the Weimar period (*Architecture and Utopia* 1). The revolutionary fervor of the early postwar years, he argues, may have heightened everyone's awareness of the ideological function of architecture, both in the self-representation of capitalist society and the nation-state and as a means of mass mobilization and social reform. However, in Tafuri's analysis, the compromises reached during the subsequent years of heightened building activities also necessitated the displacement of the early socialist rhetoric into what he calls the "ideology of the plan" (*Architecture and Utopia* 48).

From the perspective of today, when public architecture seems to aspire to little more than symbolic functions and nostalgic effects, the revolutionary impulse behind architecture as mass utopia seems doubly anachronistic. First, the use of urban planning as an instrument of social change draws attention to the ambitious experiments in rationalized living that, more than any formal innovations, distinguished architectural culture during the Weimar Republic. Second, the association of architecture with ideology evokes a unique time period when architects in Berlin and elsewhere openly aligned themselves with political causes. Both modernists and avant-gardists believed in the ability of the aesthetic in overcoming the alienation of modern life and in achieving what Bürger calls "the reintegration of art into the praxis of life" (*Theory* 22). Their opposition to bourgeois high culture often resulted in a selective appropriation of modern mass media and consumer culture. However, where the modernists located any liberating potential within the art work itself, thus also defending the bourgeois principle of autonomy and advocating an elitist position of negativity, the avant-gardists extended their critique to the institution of art and responded with a politicization of aesthetic practices that, especially in urban design, called for more radical interventions. Taking an activist stance, the architectural avant-garde turned the process of building into a revolutionary act and endowed individual buildings, especially those used by the modern masses, with the power of reorganizing social reality; for that reason, the avant-garde is sometimes described as a radicalized part of the modernist movement.

In their manifestos, proposals, and designs, avant-garde architects cultivated an aggressive gesture of *tabula rasa*, of making room—even if that meant destroying historically developed streets and neighborhoods and opposing all ornamentation as a manifestation of bourgeois individualism. Searching for alternatives, some architects embraced the principles of massification and quantification that, in their view, still represented modern society as a totality. Accordingly, social conflicts and contradictions were to be resolved through the transformative effect of new urban spaces and structures, and the problems of alienation, fragmentation, and differentiation were to be overcome through the rational principles holding together the city economy of the future. The barely concealed hatred of difference, diversity, and, in the most general terms, of history is nowhere more apparent than in the public rhetoric that aligned the avant-garde ethos of social change with an aesthetic of destruction. In the words of Alan Colquhoun, "the city was seen diachronically, as a linear development over time, each period canceling the one before in the name of the unity of the *Zeitgeist*," (116), an indication of the avant-garde's deep suspicions toward the contingencies of urban life.

In Weimar Berlin, the interventions of the avant-garde threw into relief the tension between the international, cosmopolitan orientation of architectural modernism, as represented by groups like DeStijl, Bauhaus, and CIAM (*Congrès Internationaux d'Architecture Moderne—International Congresses of Modern Architecture*), and the pressures of local, regional, and national politics that, in the context of *Neues Bauen* (New Building), made architecture an agent of change and a defense against change. Under these difficult conditions, German architects had to confront the fact that their rearticulation of the relationship between the social and the spatial would more often than not remain limited to the meanings inscribed in architectural form. The utopian impulse—that is, the anticipation of the future in the present—only intensified the inevitable dilemmas resulting from the inherent tension between the avant-garde's belief in the liberating effect of historical rupture (i.e., the revolution that gives rise to the ideal city) and its problematic relationship to the end of history (i.e., everyday life in the ideal city). For that reason, the architectural avant-garde was able to preserve the purity of its vision only to the degree that it avoided all references to the reality of Weimar Berlin, from the social and economic inequities implicating the modern metropolis in the global money economy to the political developments that confirmed the centrality of class even to the organization of everyday life. This problematic erasure of the bad present is most pronounced in the almost fetishistic belief in formal solutions, with the conditions of lack, chaos, and uncertainty inspiring fantasies of perfect order that come to stand in for the original promise of peace and plenitude.

Far from being limited to dreams of revolution, the utopian tendencies within the avant-garde played a key in the enlistment of architectural discourse in giving form to a new social class, the white-collar workers, and in articulating their position vis-à-vis the traditional bourgeoisie and the industrial proletariat. Some critics hailed the white-collar workers as the vanguard of a future capitalist economy driven by mass consumption rather than industrial production; others saw them as the avatars of a homogenous middle-class society unburdened by class struggle and ethnic strife. The optimistic visions of social equality and mass mobility found symbolic expression in the modern office buildings, apartment complexes, and transportation systems that anticipated this bright future in their formal clarity, simplicity, and transparency. Deeply invested in this new social class, modern architecture sought to complete the difficult transition from the antagonistic class model that prevailed in the nineteenth century metropolis to the more democratic formations introduced by the emerging technocratic and managerial elites during the postwar years. According to Tafuri, these elites shared the avant-garde's assault on tradition and its obsession with innovation as the driving force behind modernization. By marginalizing the educated bourgeoisie, the *Bildungsbürgertum*, a new generation of city managers, developers, and architects succeeded for a brief time during the mid-1920s in establishing more adaptable structures of organizing the circulation of goods and services within the metropolis. Yet as the avant-garde project gave form to the negativity set free in the process, Tafuri concludes, its artistic and critical interventions in the final analysis only helped to sustain the rationality of the system and to set free its seemingly unlimited potential—not for true social change but for economic growth and, later, political domination.

In considering the relationship between avant-garde discourse and urban life, we cannot underestimate the degree to which working-class culture was written out of the new scenarios of rationalization, functionalization, and standardization. But in reconstructing these processes of erasure, we receive little guidance from the advocates of proletarian culture or the proponents of social reform; whereas the latter resorted to the rhetoric of uplift and remediation, the former took an uncompromisingly oppositional stance. In the effort to conceptualize this process of exclusion, we must therefore focus on the destabilized class identities inscribed in the urban utopias of the architectural avant-garde, which also means the most radical positions within Berlin architecture. Notwithstanding the considerable differences between functionalists and rationalists, both groups of architects used the act of building to address two equally formidable oppositions: the class differences that determined everything from the look of the city's residential neighborhoods to the location of commercial, cultural, governmental, and industrial districts; and the historical processes that separated the old structures of commerce and industry from the new patterns of mass consumption, communication, and entertainment. In seeking architectural solutions to urban problems, some architects conveyed typical bourgeois anxieties about massification that found expression in an almost masochistic embrace of serialization, standardization, and functionalization as the new principles of subject formation. Yet by relying on the transformative powers of great design, all of them asserted their belief in the aesthetic and its redemptive powers. In so doing, they ended up practicing, in the bitter words of Tafuri, "architecture instead of revolution."

If Siegfried Kracauer is right to call spatial images (*Raumbilder*) the dreams of society, in what ways can we use Hilberseimer's rationalist designs to uncover some of the contradictions within the project of *Neues Berlin*? Despite his participation in the major architectural competitions during Wagner's tenure as *Stadtbaurat*, Hilberseimer remained on the margins of the changing cast of public officials, city bureaucrats, art critics, local businessmen, and real estate developers that, together with their modernist or traditionalist architects of choice, set out to reconcile the principles of capitalist development with the reformist ethos of Social Democracy. This complicated process of mediation found programmatic expression in the streamlined forms, clear lines, simple materials, and modest proportions preferred by a loosely defined, but unmistakably German group known at the time as functionalists, organicists or, to use Hilberseimer's terminology, elementarists. Interested in the conceptual problems addressed by the young discipline of city planning, Hilberseimer, like Walter Gropius and Hannes Meyer, took a more systematic approach inspired by other European architects; Le Corbusier with his famous 1922 Contemporary City of Three Million remained a major influence. The representatives of the rationalist tendency within *Neues Bauen* were concerned with the basic needs of the urban collective and aimed at the most effective organization of the public sphere. In the words of Gropius, "the necessities of life are the same for the majority of people" (rpt. in Conrads 96). Building the modern metropolis for him meant the pursuit of "simplicity in multitude, limitation to typical basic forms and their serialization and repetition, the structuring of all constructive elements based on the function of buildings, streets, and means of transportation" (Gropius cited by Hüter 91). Welcoming the expansion and mobilization of space through time machines like trains, automobiles, airplanes, telephones, and, not to forget, films, Meyer described this radically expanded city space in very enthusiastic terms: "Pure construction is the trait of this new world of forms. The constructive form knows no fatherland" (rpt. in Hartmann 147).

Hilberseimer's 1928 proposal for an office and business complex in the Friedrichstadt, which exists in the form of a photomontage, explores some of these planning principles in relation to an actual site, the large area near Gendarmenmarkt marked by Unter den Linden, Glinkastraße, Charlottenstraße, and Kronenstraße. The proximity of the proposed site to the famous monuments of the Prussian Enlightenment and to the prewar center of commerce and entertainment only underscores the violent gesture of erasure, but it also suggests a hidden affinity between these two competing topographies of power. In the drawing, the layout of three rows of six eight-story parallel slabs each follows the *Zeilenbau* system, the ribbon development or straight row system, that, during the 1920s, was promoted as an alternative to the dreaded block system of the tenement. The tension between buildings and open spaces, which is heightened by the vertical axes of staircases and elevators shafts, articulates this bold vision of the future against the heterogeneity of the historically developed neighborhood. Assuming a bird's eye perspective, the architect imposes his design on the existing street layout and forces a rigid geometrical order onto the layered topography of the site. In making this aggressive gesture Hilberseimer follows the example of the Dadaists and takes full advantage of the creative possibilities of photomontage in thematizing conflict and rupture. The combination of aerial photograph and architectural drawing simulates the destructive impulse within the avant-garde, with the process of cut and paste illustrating Walter Benjamin's famous observation that "the destructive character knows only one watchword: make room; only one activity: clearing away. His need for fresh air and open space is stronger than any hatred" ("Destructive Character" 301).

The 1928 proposal for the Friedrichstadt offers a variation of an earlier, more schematic model for a highrise city. First published in 1924 in *Die Form* as a response to Le Corbusier's City of Three Million, Hilberseimer's two sketches for a city of approximately one million inhabitants feature fourteen-story parallel slabs shown from a bird's eye perspective in north-south and east-west orientation. Designed in the typical minimalist style, the structures follow the *Zeilenbau* system above ground but retain the traditional perimeter block system underground. As in the sketches for a residential city published later in *Großstadtarchitektur* (1927, Big City Architecture), the buildings are simple upright boxes, with the grid-like pattern of window and facade reminiscent of New Objectivist painting. In U.S.-American exile, Hilberseimer would later describe his 1924 highrise city as "more a necropolis than a metropolis, a sterile landscape of asphalt and concrete, inhuman in every respect" (*Entfaltung einer Planungsidee* 22). At that point, he had already applied the same rationalist principles to the very different project of suburbanization that implicated his teaching of city planning and regional planning at the Illinois Institute of Technology in the rapid postwar expansion of the Chicago area.

Conceptually, the first highrise city and its later variants were designed to resolve urban problems (e.g., traffic congestion, unsanitary housing) by eliminating all potential points of congestion or malfunction and by reorganizing all urban relations along a vertical, rather than horizontal, axis. As in the medieval city, this vertical organization of urban functions was meant to have an integrative effect, with commerce located on the street level, with housing available "above the store" as it were, and with individual and mass transportation banned underground. Unlike Le Corbusier, Hilberseimer in his 1924 layout of buildings and streets did not assume total motorization and, instead, resolved the problem of commuting by distributing the various functions within one architectural structure. By 1927 and 1928, respectively, this bleak vision of total control had given way to an equally frightening, but very different model of social organization: one that used the same principles of repetition and duplication to promote the complete separation of urban functions into commercial, administrative, and residential districts. Significantly, in all cases, the metropolis of the future included no designated spaces for labor and industry, and the solutions offered were only systemic, not substantive ones. For these reasons alone, Hilberseimer's urban designs from the 1920s must be read above all as the product of repression and denial.

The architect's critical writings shed an important light on his contradictory views on the relationship between modern metropolis and late capitalism and on the enlistment of mass architecture in the cause of socialism. In *Großstadtarchitektur*, his main treatise on the principles of rationalist city planning, Hilberseimer describes the metropolis as "a creation of all-powerful big capital, as an expression of its anonymity, as a city type with specific economic-social and collective-psychic foundations, allowing at once for greatest isolation and closest association of its inhabitants" (1–2). On the one hand, he sees the modern metropolis as a product of capitalism in the imperialist stage—which means, a period of increasingly violent confrontations over contested resources and territories both globally and locally. On the other hand, he separates the problem of urban growth (e.g., the building of satellite cities) from all external factors and limits available solutions to the structural relationships between elementary cells and the city organism as a whole. The heavy reliance in his writings on terms like "centers of energy," "force fields," and "total organism" suggests a corporatist, if not biologistic model of these centers of capitalism; but his architectural solutions point to the exact opposite, the containment of urban life in rigid structures and mechanical processes. What cultural critics like Siegfried Kracauer, Joseph Roth, and Franz Hessel praise as the most redeeming feature of the metropolis—namely, the experience of differences and contingencies and the pleasures of the quotidian and the ephemeral—Hilberseimer attacks as a deplorable state of disorganization that can only be overcome through a comprehensive building plan. For him, this means planning new residential neighborhoods on the periphery and limiting the center to commercial and governmental uses. Only big cities designed according to a rational plan, Hilberseimer insists, are able to respond adequately to the problems of modernization. Consequently, he condones the leveling of historical structures and neighborhoods. Questions of style should be considered only in so far as "the general case, the law, will be honored and emphasized, the exception by contrast will be put aside, the nuance be eradicated—the rule becomes master, and chaos is forced to become form: logical, unambiguous, arithmetic, law" (Hilberseimer, *Großstadtarchitektur* 103). To achieve this goal, the modern city-planner has to eliminate everything irregular, inefficient, and inadequate. Only then, Hilberseimer concludes, will architecture become the "expression of a new mentality that is not of a subjective-individual, but objective-collective nature" (*Großstadtarchitektur* 98). Another name for this mentality would be the ideology of corporate capitalism.

Hilberseimer's avant-garde credentials must be evaluated in light of this revealing insight into the discursive function of negation as part of all aesthetic practices. Involved with leftist causes, he was an early member of the radical artists' group Novembergruppe and the association of progressive architects known as Ringgruppe; he participated in the 1928 founding of CIAM in La Sarraz, Switzerland. Living and working in Berlin, he submitted proposals to the 1927 competition for a central train station (now Lehrter Bahnhof) and the 1929 competition for the remodeling of Alexanderplatz. Total commitment to architecture as a profession also meant writing for an avant-garde journal like *G*, published by Hans Richter as a forum for avant-garde art, architecture, and design, as well as teaching, like Mies van der Rohe, at the Bauhaus during its final years (1929–1933).

Of course, establishing Hilberseimer's avant-garde credentials requires much more than reconstruction of the real and imaginary topography of the New Berlin; such a discussion must always extend to the politics of class and nation. Depending on one's mapping of the historical trajectories of modernism and the avant-garde, Hilberseimer's proposal for an office and business complex in the Friedrichstadt can be read either as a case study on the death (or death wish) of the avant-garde or a radical formal and conceptual response to the crisis of bourgeois subjectivity and those notions of space and place that organize classical Enlightenment binaries such as interior versus exterior, public versus private, and so forth. According to the first reading, Hilberseimer's chilling vision of a white-collar city is nothing but compulsive in its belief in quantification, neurotic in its cult of order, paranoid in its fear of diversity, and masochistic in its denial of sensory pleasure. Hilberseimer's standard type of the modern office and apartment building reveals a masculinist ultrarationalism that, in its fixation on total mobility only highlights the underlying horror of femininity, motherhood, and family life. The deliberate exclusion of nature, a trait shared with De Stijl, suggests an almost pathological hatred of the *Lebenswelt* (life world). Finally, the overwhelming sense of megalomania and monomania points to a totalitarian worldview that cannot but confirm recent studies on the affinities between avant-garde and fascist imaginary. For all of these reasons, it would be easy to agree with Richard Pommer who asserts that "Hating the city, Hilberseimer also hated modernity" (36). And it would make perfect sense to conclude with Pommer that the antiurban impulse in Hilberseimer, which utilizes a Nietzschean contempt for the masses in keeping with the pervasive elitism of the avant-garde, made possible the problematic transition during the 1920s "from a social and technical definition of the city to a purely formal vision" (27).

On the other hand, we might take K. Michael Hays' position and read the Friedrichstadt proposal as a radical articulation of the formal principle of negativity that fuels all avant-garde impulses. According to such a reading, the aesthetic principle of serialization allows for a problematization of the forces of late capitalism. Similarly, the rationalization and standardization of building technologies corresponds to the ascendancy of new bureaucracies. Questioning the false alternatives of humanism and inhumanity, Hays introduces his notion of the posthumanist subject in order to conceptualize Hilberseimer's refusal of any reconciliation as a critical, if not subversive force. Describing modern architecture as "a conscious response, whether with applause or with regret, to the dissolution of psychological autonomy and individualism brought by technological modernization" (Hays 7), Hays praises the work of Hilberseimer (and, with different implications, of Meyer) for its consistent reconceptualization of basic humanist concepts such as identity, subjectivity, and individual agency.

The conflicting diagnoses of antihumanism and posthumanism in the critical assessment of Hilberseimer's work leaves out one important aspect in the organization of urban life: that of social class. Both Pommer and Hays link modernism to the disappearance of the autonomous, self-conscious subject and the becoming problematic of bourgeois humanist thought after

World War I; yet it is a subjectivity undifferentiated in terms of class (and, to acknowledge an equally important term, that of gender). The insertion of modernist and avant-garde designs into the contested spaces of Weimar Berlin makes clear that the appearance of an anti- or posthumanist tendency within *Neues Bauen* cannot be explained solely through generalizing references to modernization, urbanization, rationalization, and so forth. A precise historical mapping must also include the functionalization of the modern metropolis as an overdetermined trope in the then contemporary debates on the growing tensions within postwar culture and society. And these debates were as much concerned with addressing urban problems like poverty, unemployment, and homelessness as with displacing the underlying social conflicts into the imaginary relations reproduced by the city as text, which an imaginary city constituted above all through its openness to changing discursive investments and defined precisely through its difference from the material conditions of everyday life.

In order to understand the ideological function of this city text or textual city, we must return once more to the particular conditions in Weimar Berlin and consider the historical factors that contributed to the ascendancy of architecture as metadiscourse. First, the humanist concept of subjectivity began to become problematic with the deterioration of the traditional alliance between urban culture and bourgeois culture that had dominated the Wilhelmine era, a process that was greatly accelerated through the appearance of a new social class, the white-collar workers, which became synonymous with the experience of massification alternately hailed and vilified under the motto of Weimar America. Second, the architectural responses to the ensuing crisis within bourgeois subjectivity took place within a well-established tradition, started by the Werkbund and other life-reform groups, of utilizing art as an instrument of social change and, later, of extending this impulse to new mass media and modes of cultural consumption. Third, the urban utopias that preoccupied artists, architects, and sociologists since the early years of impressionism and expressionism continuously adapted existing bourgeois theories of social reform and aesthetic reform to an urban environment that could no longer be defined in terms of the local and regional and that relied on entirely new strategies of deindividualization and deterritorialization.

Responding to such developments, Hilberseimer engaged with the problem of massification on two levels: through his interest in quintessential urban structures such as office buildings and apartment buildings and through his belief in serialization as a superior formal and structural principle. As the most radical proponent of rationalist city planning, he early on set out to transform all urban elements in accordance with organizational principles that, in typical avant-garde fashion, anticipated the disappearance of social and economic distinctions. Striving toward greatest efficiency, Hilberseimer wanted to "develop the fundamental principles of urban design out of contemporary needs" and to formulate "general rules that made possible the solution of specific concrete tasks" (*Großstadtarchitektur* 13). These rules allowed him to extend the principles of serialization from the module to the modular, with the respective tropes of construction also guiding his conception of the future metropolis. Thus the problem of form, which appeared first through the notion of the type and its debts to industrial production, found full articulation in his famous sketches for a postindustrial, presumably classless society. Hilberseimer's assertion that "what the room is on a small scale, the layout of the big city is on a large scale: the comprehensive organization of reciprocal needs and relationships" ("Der Wille zur Architektur" 139) takes this vision of endless multiplication to its insanely logical conclusion. Needless to say, his proposal not only ignores the most basic problems of scale and size, it also glosses over the social, economic, and political processes necessary to achieve such perfect compatibility among different urban functions. But precisely by excluding all signs of difference and by denying the power of tradition and history, his urban utopias continue to reenact again and again the traumatic experience of massification associated with the Berlin of the war and immediate postwar years.

In closing, I want to return to the significance of the unbuilt for understanding the relationship between urban architecture and mass utopia and for developing a more critical view of the overdetermined role of architectural discourse in Weimar Berlin. Hilberseimer's unrealized projects have not only shed light on the very different views of the modern metropolis associated with *Neues Bauen*, they have also highlighted the different approaches to aesthetic innovation and social change identified with modernism and the avant-garde. The radical otherness of the avant-garde makes it possible to acknowledge the power of utopian thought in Weimar architecture while confronting its shortcomings. More specifically, the function of negation sheds light on a troubling contradiction within the entire avant-garde project, its enthusiastic embrace of massification and leveling and its contemptuous views on the modern masses and big-city life. Situating the avant-garde historically as well a geographically enables us to retrace the emergence of an ideology of architecture and to see the function of *Neues Bauen* both as an articulation of change and a defense against change. Yet such a reading requires not only that we abandon one of the most enduring myths of the avant-garde, which equates its radical gestures with transgressive politics, whether socialist or fascist. It also compels us to recognize the elitist investment in the power of the aesthetic that is most apparent in the architectural avant-garde's deeply flawed views of the modern metropolis and its equally problematic conceptualization of class difference.

Rebuilding Babel: Urban Regeneration in the Modern/Postmodern Age

Janet Ward

Babel, Baudrillard, and the World Trade Center

We still live with the shock of 9/11's mangled steel girders, pulverized cement, and incinerated human bodies, even after all the ashes have been cleared away and the reconstruction phase has begun. But what exactly will this rebuilding seek to replace or to correct? The fallacy being perpetuated, at least within intellectual circles, that the World Trade Center—or skyscraper design in general—was somehow the blameworthy epitome of Western imperialist modernity. It is certainly true that a certain set of "meaning[s] collapsed with the [WTC] towers," as *New York Times* architectural critic Herbert Muschamp wrote a few weeks after the tragedy (AR1): specifically, the meaning that, until September 11, 2001, skyscrapers once had for us. But we should not reductively synecdochize the WTC into an emblem of imperial (or, predictably, phallic) technoid (post)modernity. If we did that, we would be repeating the view of lead suicide bomber Mohammed Atta, who, before hijacking and piloting the first plane to crash into the WTC, had written his urban planning masters thesis in 1994 at the Technical University of Hamburg-Harburg on the Syrian city of Aleppo, railing against what he perceived to be the modern American building form of skyscrapers being inserted as alien intrusions into the Arab cityscape. With his deed, he certainly authored a horrifically enduring addendum to his thesis.

This suggestive architectonics of just rewards is precisely why the essay by Jean Baudrillard, "The Spirit of Terrorism," published in *Le Monde* in November 2001 as an immediate response to the crisis, and now available in extended book form, is so irresponsible. Baudrillard's "terrorist hypothesis" is built upon the seductive Babel-motif of urban rise and fall: he explains the collapse of the double towers as a deserved come-uppance to the "definitive order" constituted by globalization and represented by the World Trade Center. Globalization may indeed be a nefarious form of monocultural domination in need of an adversary of sorts, but Baudrillard's tactic as an essayist effectively discounts the massive scale of harm done by the terrorists in his avant-gardistic remake of the 9/11 event as a kamikaze guilt-wish of the United States in its role as global superpower. By dint of its own "unbearable" strength, the United States "suicided spectacularly," and the inevitability of this event, states Baudrillard, is due to the fact that "power is complicit with its own destruction. [. . .] The West [. . .] becomes suicidal, and declares war on itself" (Baudrillard, "The Spirit of Terrorism") As Foster et al. caution, however, in "The ABCs of Contemporary Design," critics should guard against any proclivities toward a *Gesamtkunstwerk*-reading of 9/11: such a "confusion of art and life abets a conflation between symbolic transgression and mass murder. It is long past time to forego crypto-fascist ideas of sublimity" (*Obsolescence* 100).

Baudrillard's dangerously sublime reading, then, suggests that the WTC's demise was more a self-generated implosion than a terror attack. While New York's cultural elite used to use the WTC as an easy target of nonpostmodern design, referring disparagingly to the twin towers as "the boxes that the Chrysler and the Empire State came in" (Muschamp AR37), there is now a nostalgic recognition that the WTC did in fact serve New York City, for the twenty-eight years of its existence, as the single most important symbol of postwar growth and wealth for the metropolitan region. Indeed, Saskia Sassen's entire global-city theory of the way the contemporary corporate world works is indebted to such structures that center and confirm their urban surroundings as hosts of international finance.

Baudrillard, in his accusatory thesis, leans heavily on the godly nemesis demanded by the Babel myth, and this goes some way to explaining his appeal among those seeking for answers to the tragedy within U.S. society. Yet the millennial destruction of the WTC also glorified its status as the ultimate Tower of Babel of Western culture for those who seek to hold on to the missing structure as a means of mourning. As an absent icon, its void has become, in the words of architect Allan Wexter, a permanent "metaphysical structure" (cited by Bahrampour). This ghostly afterlife was indicated by the temporarily installed substitute in Battery Park, "A Tribute in Light": the nighttime electric sculpture, originally called "Towers of Light" and designed by Paul Myoda, Julian LaVerdiere, et al., was installed in the park near the WTC-site from March to April 2002 (Protech 136–39). The human need for the spiritualization of this site was enormous: when rescue workers uncovered one of the steel girders, broken in the form of a cross, it was immediately sanctified by a priest, and still stands on the site (cf. Steinhauer). Fragments of the exterior aluminum façade of the south tower's bottom half a dozen storeys have been sold worldwide to serve as multiple 9/11 memorials, as if to spread the sacrament of ruin around the globe.

Does, then, the fifty-mile-an-hour collapse of the WTC constitute an end to American/global-city empire building through architecture? Is, in other words, Baudrillard right in his anti-American fatality and his determination not to focus on the agency of the terrorists themselves? Anthony Vidler, who watched the towers fall from the window of his dean's office at Cooper Union, hoped, in an interview for National Public Radio recorded shortly after the attacks, for a new era of institutional architecture that seeks less to demonstrate its might through height than through its accessibility and its transparency. On the other hand, Vidler is, as an advocate of public urban space, far from the Virilian high-tech worldview of posturban decentralization ("A City Transformed"). Particularly in the wake of the WTC-attack, Vidler joins the lifelong effort of urbanists like Richard Sennett and Murray Bookchin in maintaining the heterogeneous public spaces of cities as the truest sites of *democratic* space, where "civilization" itself is hosted not by blood lineage but by the "realm of the citizen" (Bookchin 48). In this chapter I seek to demonstrate that a key part of this spatial configuration of the metropolis that makes the sites of democracy possible is contained within the notion of and need for urban centralization. It can be actualized, I submit, in acts of building high density (and building high).

It would appear that the Baudrillardian thesis was not heeded at all by Daniel Libeskind with his winning design entry for the reconstruction of the WTC-site by the Lower Manhattan Development Corporation. Entitled "Memory Foundations," Libeskind's visionary project found favor because it promised to both commemorate the act of erasure, and yet build decisively up and over it as a regaining of the past in the future. An extension of this logic was Michael Sorkin's design entry of "disaggregation," an "earthen berm" for the entire WTC-site, as a model of resistance and voidedness that took literally the call for a delay in the rush to rebuild and make permanent the memorialization of trauma (Protetch 131). Significantly, Libeskind chose to memorialize the "bathtub" slurry wall holding back the Hudson river, as a way of commemorating, in the form of public space, that which had survived the attacks and been exposed during the phase of rescue work. The very trails of the rescue workers were overlaid by Libeskind onto a regained city street grid that predated the WTC's tenancy of the sixteen-acre site. Furthermore, his intended "spire" on the northwest corner of the WTC-site asserted its metaphysical role as the reclaimed tower of the global city, with the excesses of the International Style that the WTC had summarized now corrected by the architect's signature mystical fractalities. At 1,776 ft., it would be the tallest structure in the world (the WTC occupied only positions five and six in that hierarchy, at 1,368 ft. and 1,362 ft. for the north and south towers respectively). However, with new infrastructural and transportation links being inserted below Ground Zero, an entirely separate 9/11 memorial being designed by Michael Arad and Peter Walker, and not just the Freedom Tower but the WTC-site rebuilding project itself being claimed in practice by architect David M. Childs of SOM (Skidmore, Owings & Merrill, the preferred architectural firm of developer Larry Silverstein), not much of Libeskind's $330 million plus vision will ever become an architectural reality (cf. Giovanni; Goldberger; Golson). His spire that beckoned in a gesture akin to the Statue of Liberty has been remolded in a Childsean corporate practicality. But the symbolism for New Yorkers and beyond of Libeskind's original scheme remains crucial. Babel has been reclaimed, even if the upper levels of the revised Freedom Tower (in the combined Libeskind+Child's design, unveiled in late 2003) remain prudently empty of office workers.

Babel and Modernity

The desire to build towers of Babel (or experience a Jacob's Ladder to the sky) can be seen, of course, as the single most primal building urge next to that of constructing basic shelter (the *domus*). For a mythic precursor to this debate, we can consider Pieter Bruegel the Elder's painting, *The Tower of Babel* (1563), the early modern paradigm of mankind's ultimate, imaginary building of self-deification and demographic concentration. Intriguingly, the Babel that Bruegel depicts is one that incorporates God's interruption of the building process in Genesis with a scattering confusion of tongues—whereas the Bible story of *Genesis* xi.1–9 has the latter following upon the former as God's punishment. Contained in Bruegel's picture is the very opposite of a monolingual monolith: namely, innumerable composite labyrinthine parts, presenting behind the façade of outer monumentality an unstable dynamism of pending collapse and growing motion around an inner core.

Following on from *Genesis* and Bruegel, one could say that the inhabitants of industrialized cities in the West became, in the late nineteenth and early twentieth centuries, the components of a mechanized Babylon of modernity, one that is yet more confused in its relations and activities than its mythical precursors, forcing people to adjust to the "shock" of increased population density, technologized tempo of activity, and mass industrial and cultural production. This is also the Benjaminian definition of the perceptual experiences of film and city alike. The tensions of modern city-dwelling were first indicated, of course, by Georg Simmel in his seminal essay of 1903, "Metropolis and Mental Life" (Die Großstädte und das

Geistesleben). The modern city, according to Simmel, is organically structured such that it functions according to both the code of self-immortalizing order and the code of self-destroying chaos: it is *babelesque*, but creatively so.

Out of the condition of this modern city, then, arose the New York and Chicago skyscraper of the early twentieth century. This "*Automonument*" building form, as Rem Koolhaas terms it (100), gave rise to the imagined towers of the German avant-garde of the 1920s. After the Great War, the image of American skyscrapers began to figure in the German architectural imagination, taking over from Paris and London and their monuments left over from decades of international trade exhibitions, as the embodiment of what a city could and should aspire to be: in short, the "New Babylon." Competitions for skyscrapers, arising alongside an artistic tectonics of the new building materials (namely steel, reinforced concrete, and glass), became a new variant of the late-nineteenth-century crystal palaces boasting of capitalist capability. But it is fair to say that the German variety added a metaphysical, mystical, namely expressionist twist, as in the entries for the 1921 Berlin competition for a skyscraper on the Friedrichstraße, which gravitate all the way from their American precursor models to more expressionist innovations. In the wake of World War I, the ambitious scale and innovative scope of the 140 designs for the Friedrichstraße competition were more visionary than practical. No Weimar-era skyscraper exceeded seventeen stories (the height of the Hansa-Hochhaus in Cologne); no skyscraper in 1920s Berlin was taller than the Tegel borough's Borsig tower of eleven stories; and the financiers of the Turmhaus-Aktiengesellschaft never raised the money to build any tower on the Friedrichstraße site at all. Nonetheless, while Ludwig Mies van der Rohe's design for the competition exceeded the era's ability to build, his glass-sheathed three-part prism, minus setbacks of any kind, transformed the history of skyscraper building.

This dream image of Mies' radical skyscraper is still there as an invocation for today's New Berlin, as the latter builds itself afresh in the image of the Weimar era's aspirations. In 2001, boosterist plans arose all over again for a Miesian type of glass tower to fill the empty patch of the Friedrichstraße Spreedreieck, this time at twice the height of Mies' originally conceived twenty stories. The return of Weimar-era "skyscraper fever" (Hochhausfieber) as an emblematic regaining of capital city worth is already evident in the Potsdamer Platz's three modest skyscrapers by Renzo Piano, Hans Kollhoff, and Helmut Jahn's architectural firm. But whether post-Wall Berlin's most ambitious skyscraper project, namely Kollhoff's thirteen towers for the Alexanderplatz, will actually get built remains an open question for the currently bankrupt regained capital.

Taut's Expressionist Babels

The national loss of empire as a result of losing World War I had negated the Imperial German era's spate of Bismarkian monument building. German expressionist architecture arose in and around this void of monument and nationhood, and sought to fill it with cultural renewal for the denizens of the modern metropolis. Even the Weimar German *Amerikanismus* was hardly American, but had a definite infusion of a metaphysical substructure. The ziggurat-fantasies and skyscraper-(paper) realities of expressionist architecture were conceived of as serving an ideal far higher than that of the "functionality" (*Zweckmäßigkeit*) that was to follow in the later Bauhaus years. They are the early twentieth century's reflectors and deflectors of the modern human condition of technologization and commodification. These towers strategically adapted Zarathustran spirituality for the city, in a will to overcome the *Angst* and alienation of the metropolis through rising above it, thereby turning the city's negative conditions into a positive material embodiment. The spiral organics and conjectural deformations of the ziggurat in expressionist architecture unconsciously echo this double condition of technologized life, as depicted in Erich Mendelsohn's Einstein Tower at Potsdam (1917–21), Vladimir Tatlin's design of 1919 for the Third International, or Bruno Taut's Glass House built for the 1914 Cologne exhibition.

For all its antiurban rhetoric, German expressionist architecture was intrinsically a design of and for the city, infusing it with a postwar program of new communal identity. The neo-Nietzschean visionary architects of this movement such as Hans Scharoun and Taut saw themselves as artists with an absolute right to recreate the city site of Babylon for the glory of its inhabitants after the spiritual apocalypse of war. Their aim was to streamline the machinic confusion of the metropolis into lines of purer expressivity. Such architects, notably Peter Behrens and Taut, consciously worked with the metaphysical and social power that monumental architecture can literally express and harness in the viewing subject through the effect of its construction. As socialist pacifists—and naively unaware of their own hypostatizations of the new technologized building materials—they wished to make a monumental center out of the pluralized Babel. In addition to the skyscraper, they realized that industrial buildings were among the most potent Babel-symbols of the modern age, and so they sought to apply a new monumentalism to factories, gas works, railway stations, water towers, and war memorials—not by decorating, but by letting them be "pure skyscraper" (*eben Hochhaus*)—such was the heavy dialectical sublation involved therein, in which building for eternity became superimposed over building for life. In his photo-book *Amerika* (1925), Erich Mendelsohn worshipped the functional essences of both the skyscraper and the grain elevator. The expressionist tower of Babel, especially as it evolved in its most programmatic form under Bruno Taut's guidance, was hence far from "babbling"—in the sense given by Derrida, in "Des Tours de Babel," to translation. Rather, it evolved toward the monolingual, or even the silent. That which Nietzsche had defined as "monumental history" was being represented as a mythic-organic building format.

Bruno Taut was essentially *the* publicist (or tower, so to speak) of the expressionist architectural group in Germany, becoming the first leader of the "Working Council for Art" (Arbeitsrat für Kunst) in 1918 (that is, before Walter Gropius' tenure), and instigating a messianic exchange of chain-letters among like-minded friends called *The Glass Chain* (*Die Gläserne Kette*, 1919–20), and editing the architectural magazine *First Light* (*Frühlicht*, 1920–22). Taut designed, in effect, the first civic centers, or *Volkshäuser*, that would serve people's needs via massive doses of light and color. The ultimate building in these projects was a tower-like "crown of the city" to hover over the utopian metropolis. After all, the *Stadtkrone* was the very thing that Berlin lacked, as Taut's teacher Bruno Möhring stated in 1920: the German capital was a "stone desert," a "flat city" (Neumann 38). The corrective enterprise of German architectural expressionism as a whole was a cosmic approach, promising an imminent globality of formerly scattered souls, hence a correction of what Taut perceived as mankind's present babelesque (urban, decadent, burnt-out) condition. To some degree this is, of course, an obvious and often satiated architectural urge: in his unfinished *Arcades Project* (*Passagen-Werk*, 1927–40), Walter Benjamin notes how the rebuilding of Paris by Baron Haussmann in the mid-nineteenth century likewise planned such dominant towers or feudal monuments for each *quartier*.

For Taut, the architect is no less than a world builder of the *Gesamtkunstwerk. The World Masterbuilder* (*Der Weltbaumeister*), for example, was the megalomaniac title of Taut's stage play of architectural scenes and music that he endeavored in vain to have filmed. Taut and company saw themselves as servants or media of a future paradise, enablers of a new worldview—"mediators" rather like the final intertitle for Frieder, whose task it is to rebuild society in Fritz Lang's sci-fi film of 1927, *Metropolis* (itself a Babel allegory). Taut's most sustained effort in this mediatory role is his most utopian picture book, *Alpine Architecture* (*Alpine Architektur*, 1919)—inspired by his late friend Paul Scheerbart's poetics of glass architecture (such as the latter's *The Gray Cloth* novel about a glass tower of Babel in Chicago). Here, Taut's fantasy designs of Babel strategically combine three building elements: mountain, glass, and Gothic. He sketches a technological-cum-Zarathustran topography, worthy of the natural monument setting of the Alps, to recreate the city's ideal image of itself, far above its lowland swamp locations that Zarathustra also avoids. There will be in this land, he states, manmade mountains of glass, a godlike "crystal house" ("Kristallhaus"), and the icecaps will be sculpted into a prismatic clarity of form that is suggested by the Matterhorn itself (Taut, *Alpine Architektur* 3, 20). Glass represents, reflects, and encourages the new collective, public transparency of crystalline purity—suggestive of an extreme form of Heideggerian being-in-dwelling. The paths to the Alpine towers and the interiors thereof indicate a secularized sacredness inclining the traveller/reader toward a purpose-free worship. In these self-reflecting, self-reflexively constructed glass temples, architecture expresses its own sublimity to itself through its own transparencies.

Another particularly stunning example of the essentially cinematic viewing experience that is proposed for Weimar architecture by Taut is his fantasy design of 1919 for a "Monument of the New Law" (*Monument des neuen Gesetzes*) (White 24). This diagram bears Taut's hallmark of combinatory written and designed (expressive and visible) text. Despite his call for an architecture of dynamism one finds an increasing obsession with the creation of stasis: the picturized letter is to be a text to be read first by his fellows in the chain-group, and subsequently by the viewing public of this ideal monument as an architectural hyper-reality. Taut's paper monument contains the tension of a universalizing, proselytizing mission, with the multitextual, citational presentation of a series of new inscribed "tablets," as in *Thus Spake Zarathustra* (Nietzsche, *Sämtliche Werke* 4: 278–81). The rotational effect of the law-giving tablets is suggestive of the necessarily intermittent projection and motion of film images. Taut apparently wishes the pedestrian readers of the monument—the first letter-cum-tower of Babel, so to speak—to read and feed upon the messages on the transparent, colored glass tablets against the light of the sun ("one reads against the sky"). The tower is to be electrically lit by night, as if beckoning to an audience who crane their heads upward in a respectful position before flickering of the screen light with its silent filmic intertitles—a concept that Taut repeated in his 1924 design for hospital patients to watch a film from a supine position ("Plan for Reclining Spectators"). No matter how apparently babelesque, Taut is intent on creating a "new law" of cinematic perception with his heavenward text.

Redemptive City Building

A cultural kinship between the German expressionist building urge out of the ashes of World War I and today's crisis in the wake of the WTC-destruction is discernible in the extent to which both moments can be seen as a desire to turn to the skyscraper-form as a redemptive path, albeit from different chronological directions (i.e., at its modern inception and after its postmodern collapse). As architectural theorist Manfredo Tafuri summarizes of the modern German avant-garde's obsession with towers, they sought "within the depths of the 'great alienated one' the promise of a collective catharsis" (*The Sphere and the Labyrinth* 174). Likewise, we find ourselves yearning, after the fact that the WTC unwittingly contained, namely the nation's anchor or framework for urban density and national economic strength: this image was swapped, in the moment of destruction, for that of the indelible grave of almost three thousand people. Now we must seek such structuring comfort in other (less conspicuous) building forms, or rebuild in the hope of reconnecting what was lost (and risk challenging the terrorist mentality again). German expressionist architects, before they transformed their dream-like ideologies in the later 1920s into the more practical functionalist application of the housing developments (*Siedlungen*), tried to deny the skyscraper's double function as both labyrinth and monolith in one and concentrate instead, as Tafuri indicates, on the skyscraper's purported "purifying" power, the new cathedral of Gotham (*The Sphere and the Labyrinth* 174). The lost WTC is regarded, too, as a lost purifier of and for urban identity.

Both positions, however, while powerful in their emotional content, are based on faulty ground. The skyscraper per se cannot ever live up to its image, both at its point of modern historical conception and of its contemporary possible demise or more cautious phase, as the granter of a spiritual *genius loci* for lost souls (Tafuri, *The Sphere and the Labyrinth* 174). Neither can redemption come in the form of a mediator like Lang's Frieder. The process of post-Babel yet heterogeneously babelesque rebuilding is more complex than that.

In his magnum opus *The Arcades Project*, Benjamin gives perhaps the most refreshing antidote to date to the German expressionist dilemma of redemptive monumentalism. He effectively inverts Haussmann's monumental plan for the city of Paris, by showing that the voiding effect intended by the Second Empire to rid the city of the danger of future barricades by the working classes did not remove the innate metropolitan tendency to recreate itself as babelesque organism (Benjamin, *Gesammelte Schriften* 1: 56). As in Bruegel the Elder's painting, Benjamin's Paris is full of allegorical holes. In the final analysis, as Benjamin points out, the 12,000 monadological iron pieces that were put together under the name of the Eiffel Tower, a monument built to glorify and boost the host city for the 1889 world exposition, are the same materials as those used in the arcades (*Gesammelte Schriften*, 1: 223).

Nazism, effectively, collapsed the expressionist architectural project of redemption. The plan of Hitler and his architect Albert Speer for Berlin, in contrast to, say, Benjamin's metaphor of allegorical building for the arcades of Paris, would have emptied out the city center in order to purge it into a *unicum* of itself; thus a stage of destruction was required in order to pave the way for an antimetropolis, Germania. As Holocaust historian Raoul Hilberg has noted, the Nazified *Volk* viewed Hitler as the "*den Erbauer des deutschen Reiches*, the Architect of the Third Reich. For Hitler everything was architecture," one that required, states Hilberg, the destruction of the Jews as a redemptive "edifice" in the urban planning process: Auschwitz, like the Germania to be created out of Berlin, was regarded as a purifying act, the ultimate consequence of teutonic *Lebensraum* ("living space"; cited by van Pelt 348).Hitler's regime put this urban purging into practice at Potsdamer Platz, when it removed the Kempinskis' Jewish family ownership from the entertainment center Haus Vaterland (Balfour 67, 126–32). Such acts of purging led, not surprisingly, to the opposite of authentic urbanism. The false densification of the concentration camps with their international babel of languages, as experienced by Primo Levi, can be contrasted as in a reflecting mirror to the regime's emptying of Berlin. Robert van Pelt finds that the death camp system "marks the actual caesura that has ended architectural history as such [. . .] Auschwitz recapitulated the city which it completed" (348).

The expressionist concept of the "city crown" (*Stadtkrone*) was thus expanded by Hitler into a "world crown" (*Weltkrone*), intended to unify a far larger stage than just the nation. The "Great Hall" (*Grosse Halle*) at the top of Germania's North-South Axis was to be constructed in time for a world exposition in 1950; at 1,000 feet high, its Pantheon-inspired dome was going to contain the volume of St. Peter's sixteen times over (Balfour 94). When contrasted with such plans, Benjamin's piecemeal version of the city as multitudinous "trace" (*Spur*) seems thwarted. The sense of the Nazi program for renovating the modern Babylon is alluded to in the film footage of Hitler and Speer during their comparative urban planning "visit" to an empty Paris in 1940, just to compare themselves auratically as colonial masters alongside the monuments (Benjamin, *Gesammelte Schriften* 1: 560). In face of the reified staging of Hitler measuring (or merging) himself with the Eiffel Tower, Benjamin, who was forced to flee Paris toward a tragically preventable suicide, leaves his readers with the minor triumph of the montage-monument built only on the "yardstick of the 'smallest' " (*Gesammelte Schriften*, 1: 233).

Urban Cycles of Destruction and Renewal

Such errors of needing to redeem the metropolitan *mélange* periodically feature in modernist conceptions of urban planning. And yet alternative patterns are also discernible, including that of the Tower of Babel myth as a natural life cycle of cities. In early 1931, when Germany was still reeling from the stock market crash one and a half years previously and when its democracy had only two more years to go, Siegfried Kracauer, in a *Frankfurter Zeitung* article, "Destruction and Rebuilding" (Zertrümmerung und Aufbau), emphasized the inevitability of the cyclical nature of urban destruction and renewal. He saw how the two processes often operate in simultaneous cohesion so that the latter can serve in a compensatory fashion with the former. Looking around him at the radically collapsing sales prices, he recognized clearly the presence of a "will toward destruction" [Vernichtungswillen] in late Weimar political, economic, and commercial-urban life alike; and yet, Kracauer also stressed, the former disaster was nonetheless being balanced, in equal measure, by a "will to build" [Aufbauwillen]—most obviously at the Alexanderplatz, a building site of radical changes on the level of the U-Bahn system below ground and new office buildings above, such as those by Peter Behrens. It was as if the Freudian "circuitous paths toward [urban, social, democratic] death" on the cusp of Nazism were being matched, come what may, by persistent urban self-reformulation—or, as Kracauer puts it, Berlin's ineffable "courage for life" (Lebensmut).

Out of the ruins of the Babel myth we can identify a revolutionary urge that humankind has long expressed to recreate the city and the denizens within. Those who would tear down Babel were, in architectural modernism, not so much dictators as would-be democratic reformers, at least in their intentions. Ludwig Hilberseimer's visions in *Architecture for the Metropolis* (*Großstadtarchitektur*, 1927), or Le Corbusier's plans for both Le Marais in Paris or for Manhattan, were intended to raze first, then regenerate a new metropolitan hygienic openness, an urgently rational master plan of cellular high-rises imposed on top of the *tabula rasa*. Not that the revolutionary building urge is always destructive: sometimes it can be reconstructive to a fault, in a persistent case of attempting to put Humpty-Dumpty back together again. Today, in the post-Wall era, we find ourselves witnesses of a new age of rebuilding Babel-Berlin as the repaired German capital. The psychological underpinnings to the critical reconstructionist tenets of making "Berlin look like Berlin" aim to put back the city center as a healing form of reparations for the wounds that destroyed or demolished more than 80 percent of the downtown core over the course of the twentieth century. As Hubertus Siegert's recent documentary film *Berlin Babylon* suggests, the current boosterist effort to recreate the spatial "closure" that the intact pre–World War II Berlin possessed is, then, an understandable, if imperfect, ongoing repair-response to the bombed-out cityscape ruined by war.

This revolutionary-cum-reconstructive motion is, perhaps, the truer meaning of the cyclical dynamics of the Babel myth, and it moves us usefully beyond the extremist paralysis of Baudrillard's view of the World Trade Center destruction as the self-imposed death wish of the globalizing West. The Babel myth endures because of an anthropomorphizing need to stage the life of cities according to a quasi-human, hence limited lifespan. Baudrillard's aesthetics of nihilism has attempted to deny the inevitable last stage in the process of temporal-spatial rise, fall, and rebirth. He has omitted the one that Kracauer saw enduring in an economically depressed late Weimar Berlin, and the one that Libeskind originally designed for tomorrow's downtown Manhattan: an end stage that forces and forges resilient rebeginnings—a "pleasure principle" not of mute voids or monuments that nullify in their attempts at redemption and purification, but of heterogeneous structures for a living, democratic city. Babel continues to speak.

Section V

The Politics of Visual Culture: Weimar, Exile, and Postwar

Politicizing Painting: The Case of New Objectivity

Maria Makela

In the September 1922 issue of Germany's leading art magazine, *Das Kunstblatt*, editor Paul Westheim published the results of a questionnaire that he had circulated to contemporary writers, artists, critics, and historians of the time regarding the existence and status of a new trend in the visual arts: Neonaturalism. In his introduction to the article, Westheim wondered whether this new naturalism was just a passing fashion or, in fact, it was a necessary development that would supersede expressionism (369). Not surprisingly, there was no consensus of response. Somewhat myopically, E. L. Kirchner professed to see no evidence of a new naturalism in the visual arts (Westheim 375–76), while the dramatist Georg Kaiser and architect/critic Adolph Behne acknowledged its existence but questioned its validity as art (Westheim 383–84, 406). Other respondents, including Alfred Döblin and Fritz Wichert (director of the Mannheim Kunsthalle—the Mannheim Hall of Art), welcomed Neonaturalism as a healthy antidote to tired and worn-out aesthetic idioms (Westheim 371–73), while Ludwig Meidner waxed rhapsodic about the new trend toward detailed figuration, proclaiming his allegiance no longer to the expressive graphic mark but to "the object" (Westheim 382). Ultimately, though, it was George Grosz and Gustav Hartlaub who defined the terms of the debate for years to come. Grosz distinguished between politically engaged "objectivity" and that of reactionary "neoclassicists" who looked back to Poussin, Ingres, and Corot (Westheim 382–83), while Hartlaub similarly divided the movement into two groups: the right-wing "classicists" who sought calm after the chaos of the war and early postwar years, and the left-wing "verists" who tried to depict the true face of the times (Westheim 389–93). Soon after *Das Kunstblatt*'s survey appeared in print, Hartlaub, in fact, began preparations for the exhibition that would canonize this division of the new movement into left and right, though he would title the survey not "Neonaturalism" or "postexpressionism" (another term used by some to describe the different aesthetic path now taken by many artists), but "New Objectivity."[1] The exhibition opened in June 1925 at the Mannheim Kunsthalle, where Hartlaub had succeeded Fritz Wichert as director. From there it traveled for a year and a half to Dresden, Chemnitz, and other cities in Germany.

Though the parameters of this chapter do not allow for an extended analysis of the subsequent critical response to New Objectivity in the visual arts, some general comments about the historical reception of the style are nevertheless in order.[2] It is, for example, notable that since Hartlaub's remarks about New Objectivity were published in *Das Kunstblatt*, most subsequent critics and historians have also screened the work through explicitly political lenses, pigeonholing artists into the left or right wing of the movement according to the kinds of subjects they represented or to the political party with which they were affiliated. Like Hartlaub, most later commentators have also adopted the designation "New Objectivity" to refer to nonexpressionist representational art of the interwar period in Germany, however much they may qualify their usage of this term. This, I want to suggest, has proved problematic, because New Objectivity has a different historical trajectory as well as dissimilar sociopolitical and aesthetic valences in the fields of architectural and general cultural history than in art history. Indeed, the tendency of many cultural critics to downplay the sociopolitical diversity of the movement's practitioners and to define the style homogeneously as *either* right/reactionary *or* left/liberal can be related in part to this semantic confusion. In this chapter I examine briefly this critical phenomenon and its problematics, so as to suggest an alternate way of conceptualizing New Objectivity in the visual arts, one that would avoid the polarizing terms of "left" and "right," of "progressive" and "reactionary," and allow us instead to see the commonalities in the work of what was in fact a politically, aesthetically, and socially diverse group of artists.[3]

First, however, some preliminary general remarks about the meanings that have accrued to the term itself. Unlike any "isms" that preceded or succeeded it, New Objectivity has been used to describe much more than a particular aesthetic direction or style. It is usually identified with the period of stabilization between 1924 and 1929, when America was taken as a model for the social, political, economic, and cultural life of Germany. At this time, the messianic utopianism of the expressionists fell into disfavor, to be replaced instead by a soberly "objective" outlook on life that rejected the noble and grandiose in favor of the pragmatic. Indeed, the German word *Sachlichkeit* can be translated as "practicality" or "straightforwardness." It can also mean "objective," in the sense of not being distracted by irrelevant emotion or matters beyond the object in question, and contains within it the word *Sache*, which can be interpreted as "object" or "thing," but also "matter at hand," as in "*zurück zur Sache*" or "back to the facts."[4] In the field of literature, this equated with works that tended toward extreme realism, documentation, and a kind of journalistic reporting of facts, while in architecture it translated into radically streamlined buildings made of glass and steel. Façades became permeable by means of the newly important display window, which cultivated consumer attention through innovative presentations of the many commodities now produced by the recently rationalized factories. Walter Benjamin was famously struck by these windows, noting that their insistent electric lighting exposed all secrets and drained the buildings of their "aura," leaving behind what was, in effect, an architecture of pure surface.[5]

This concept of "surface" is also important in the two-dimensional visual arts, but here the term "New Objectivity" does not refer, as one might expect, to the abstract work of the Bauhaus painters, graphic artists, and photographers usually associated with the radically pared-down architecture of Benjamin's façade culture. Rather, it is used to describe the *over*-loaded surfaces of postexpressionist figuration in the interwar period, the essential characteristics of which were outlined in a schematic list drawn up in 1925 by the art historian Franz Roh (119). Though now clichéd by its frequent re-publication and somewhat overstated in its attempt to draw too clear-cut distinctions between expressionism and postexpressionism, the list nevertheless remains useful as an entry point into the issues here at hand. Roh noted that postexpressionists were drawn not to the sketchily rendered ecstatic and religious themes favored by expressionist artists, but to carefully delineated quotidian objects and secular subjects. And while the expressionist painters favored warm colors, dynamic compositions, and impastoed surfaces, postexpressionists preferred their palette cool, their compositional structure static, and their pigments thinly applied. Indeed, the rough surfaces of expressionist canvases (which Roh compared to "uncut stone") preserved clear traces of the work process, while the smooth postexpressionist surfaces effaced, "like polished metal," all marks of the artist's hand. This, for Gustav Hartlaub, was also paramount. In his catalogue of the 1925 Mannheim exhibition, he made explicit note of artists who had become disillusioned with the "unbounded, nearly apocalyptic" hope and belief that they had placed in themselves. No longer was the mark of the brush or pencil equated with the very soul of the subjective artist. Rather, it was now understood as a metaphor of something more objective, something more "certain" and "durable": craft.[6]

The expressionists were concerned little with craft, if at all. Careful attention to the way an object was made was antithetical to their enterprise, which usually entailed working quickly so as better to render their emotions visible on the surface of their chosen medium. Time-consuming reproductive media like etching and engraving or bronze-casting were thus spurned in favor of those like lithography and wood-carving that were more direct and immediate. But in the aftermath of the war, the notion of the well-made object was revived among the avant-garde. Max Doerner's 1921 handbook *Malmaterial und seine Verwendung im Bilde* (The Materials of Artists and Their Use in Painting) was in this regard especially noteworthy, for it became one of the most popular painter's manuals of the twentieth century. Over four hundred pages in length, it was published in four editions by 1933 and contained a wealth of knowledge on all stages of painting, from the preparation of grounds for easel pictures to the grinding of pigments and the use of different binding media for oil paints. Doerner, a long-time teacher at the Münchner Kunstakademie (Munich Academy of Fine Arts), also presented detailed information about oil, tempera, pastel, watercolor, and mural painting, including fresco, secco, and oil painting on walls, as well as about the techniques of the Old Masters, from the van Eycks and Dürer to Titian, the Venetian school, Rubens and Rembrandt.[7]

New Objectivity artists studied the manual carefully. Georg Scholz, for example, derived from it the mixed oil-on-tempera technique that he began to use in the early 1920s, the details of which he published in his own instructional essay of 1924, "The Rudiments of Attaining Effects in Paintings," illustrated with three of his own works (77–80). It was perhaps this article that prompted George Grosz to inquire about Scholz's technique. "I would be interested to know," Grosz wrote his friend in August 1924, "what technique you are working with: tempera underpainting or all oil, and which dilution, linseed oil? Do you make careful preliminary studies? [. . .] It would be interesting to exchange technical knowledge" (Crockett 57). Otto Dix, too, was fascinated by the Old Masters and their craft, so much so that Grosz affectionately referred to him as "Otto Hans Baldung Dix" because of his friend's interest in and study of the German Renaissance painter Hans Baldung Grien. The artist began his studies of the Old Masters in 1921, captivated not just by the work of Grien but also by that of Lucas Cranach the Elder, Albrecht Dürer, and Matthias Grünewald. This led to his use of an Old Master glazing technique in 1924 and, after 1926, of the oil-on-tempera technique that was considered authentically old German. Moreover, many of Dix's paintings from mid-decade on not only employ the formats and compositional devices of Late Gothic art, they abound with quotations of specific gestures, expressions, and figures from German Old Master paintings in particular.[8] Indeed, the interest in art of the past was so widespread among New Objectivity artists that already in the spring of 1921 Munich art dealer Hans Goltz assembled an exhibition in which he made the connection explicit. Before visitors to his galleries reached the work of the contemporary artists Heinrich Maria Davringhausen,

Carlo Mense, Georg Schrimpf, and Tommy Parzinger, they had to pass through two rooms displaying reproductions of Old Master works that situated the recent interest in clarity of form, glazed surfaces, and perspectival spatial construction in Medieval and Renaissance art (Crockett 111).

The paradox here is that while New Objective designers and architects subverted tradition and elaborated surfaces by adopting a functionalist language of pure form stripped of ornament, New Objective visual artists wholeheartedly embraced it, overloading their compositions with carefully detailed representational imagery and references to their own history via the art of the past. It is as if they wanted to reinvest the artwork with traces of themselves, but since they could no longer do so with the now discredited emotive gesture they chose the path of precisely rendered figuration instead.

In any case, detractors had an easy target in the multivalent New Objectivity, since they could attack it from any one of many different angles. Left-leaning critics were particularly tough on the movement. Art historians honed in on the issue of tradition, interpreting the widespread interest in the art of the past as reflective of an insidious political conservatism. Already in 1940, Alois Schardt, erstwhile director of the *Nationalgalerie* (National Gallery) in Berlin and passionate supporter of expressionism, criticized New Objectivity for seeking refuge in the history of art, depending on "technical facility and colorful effects" to invoke the authority of the Old Masters. According to Schardt, the "new" in "New Objectivity" implied a return to the past that was dangerous in and of itself. Hitler, he asserted, supported this artistic movement at least in part because of its reliance on tradition, especially on German tradition (O. Peters, "Eine demokratische Kunst" 21). Writing some forty years later, critic Benjamin Buchloh concurred, referring to the mimetic painting of the post–World War I era as the product of an "ideological backlash" characterized by an "idealization of the perennial monuments of art history and its masters, the attempt to establish a new aesthetic orthodoxy, and the demand for respect for the cultural tradition." Inextricably linked to authoritarian, conservative political cultures, the representational idioms of the 1920s were, he wrote, "treacherous" because they provided "aesthetic pleasure as false consciousness" (Buchloh, 222–38). Other commentators who also spoke from the left were made nervous not so much by New Objectivity's interest in tradition as by its fascination with the quotidian objects and aspects of everyday life, in particular those that gave visual form to the commodity culture of the stabilization period: the gramophones, radios, and numerous other electrical appliances that were now produced and consumed in large quantities. Siegfried Kracauer saw this as leading both the artists and the public away from a critical awareness of contemporary events and political change. "Reality," he wrote in 1947, "is portrayed not so as to make facts yield their implications, but to drown all implications in an ocean of facts" (Kracauer, *Caligari to Hitler* 166). Some fifty years later Jost Hermand concurred, noting that the commodity culture of New Objectivity was "based no longer on values like love of other human beings, time-consuming higher education, the capacity for intellectual criticism, high culture, and comradely solidarity [. . . .];" it was, rather, a reifying culture of pure surface, devoid of substance, that fostered "selfishness, entertainment, change, mobility, the avoidance of frustration, and the release of sexual and psychic pressure" (Hermand 63). Walter Benjamin was similarly put off by what he believed was New Objectivity's proclivity to divest objects of their real meaning and thus politically neutralize them,[9] and it was to this as well that George Lukács alluded when he noted that "the realism of the 'new objectivism' is so openly apologetic, and leads so clearly away from the artistic reproduction of reality, that it can find a place in the fascist inheritance" (112). Ernst Bloch, too, disliked the movement, mocking the "puritanical" New Objectivity that sought to establish a world of "classicist calm" and "noble simplicity" for the Weimar capitalists (199).

New Objectivity as proto-fascist? However trenchant in some respects, such interpretations do not account for the fact that both America and France also had strong traditions of figurative art in the interwar period that obviously did not lead to fascism. They also do nothing to explain why it was that in Germany most of those visual artists who initially embraced tradition and figuration were not members of a right-wing or even centrist political party but *Communists* who were motivated to reject modernist abstraction because of their dissatisfaction with expressionism's allegedly apolitical narcissism.[10] During the war many artists on the political Left had already begun to distance themselves from expressionism, but an incident occurred in March 1920 that crystallized their contempt. At that time the army attacked striking workers on Dresden's Postplatz, killing 59 and injuring 141 others. During the battle, a stray bullet entered the nearby Zwinger Palace, hitting Peter Paul Rubens's painting *Bathsheba Receiving David's Letter* (ca. 1635). The following day, Oskar Kokoschka, newly appointed professor at the Dresdener Kunstakademie (Dresden Academy of Art), published an appeal to those "who intend to use firearms in order to promote their political theories" to take their battles outside the cities so as to avoid endangering "human culture."[11] In the overheated atmosphere of the moment, those artists who sympathized with the political Left took his words to mean that human culture was more important than humankind. Many responded, none more bitingly than Grosz and his colleague John Heartfield, who together published a scathing indictment of expressionist artists under the title of "The Art Scab." Taking aim at Kokoschka's statement that the German people would later "find more joy and meaning in these preserved pictures than in the collected view of the politicized Germans of today," the authors proclaimed:

> He who wishes his business with the brush to be regarded as a divine mission is a scab. . . . The deification of the artist is equivalent to self-deification. The artist does not stand above his milieu and the society of those who approve of him. For his little head does not produce the content of his creation, but processes (as a sausagemaker does meat) the worldview of his public. (Heartfield and Grosz 485)

In the aftermath of this controversy, left-wing artists and critics began to issue statements calling for the creation of an artistic style and syntax that the masses would understand. In September, Grosz and Heartfield together with their two colleagues Rudolf Schlichter and Raoul Hausmann—members of the KPD, every one—wrote "Die Gesetze der Malerei" (The Laws of Painting), an essay that celebrated craft, technique, and mimesis as means of eliminating expressionist individualism and creating an art of the people. "Materialistic" painting, as they termed it, would be based on "plasticity and tenacity of perception and not on the indecisiveness of subjective impressions or spiritual excursions." The rules of perspective should be rigorously followed so as to "raise the optical impressions of the masses toward clarity of meaning. We reject the standpoint of abstract art or likewise that of *l'art pour l'art*. . . . Painting is collective." (Grosz et al. 696–98) In November of that year Grosz wrote "Zu meinen neuen Bildern" (On My New Paintings),[12] which likewise proclaimed that individualism was meaningless and that "stability, construction, functionalism" would now be the watchwords of an art that would "give an absolutely realistic picture of the world. I am attempting to be understood by everyone [. . .] to create a clear and simple style [. . .]." (14)

For radical artists of the early 1920s, then, part of what this return to representation and tradition initially offered was its imagined accessibility to the masses. Put differently, it might be argued that the roots of New Objectivity in the visual arts are not proto-fascist, but quintessentially democratic. This, in fact, is exactly what other interpreters of the style have suggested. Günter Metken, for example, asserted that "New Objectivity was perhaps the *only* real democratic and widely accessible art of the interwar period" since both its style and subjects were comprehensible to the newly large and diverse middle-class audience that, for example, now owned radios and gramophones and went to the cafés, cinema, and theatre (114). In this conceptual framework, New Objectivity is said to be an exclusively Weimar-era phenomenon, which, according to Metken and others like Wieland Schmied, came to an end in 1933 with the Nazi accession to power, thus sharing the fate of modern art in general (Schmied 69–71).

Yet such interpretations that would cast the style as uniformly democratic are as limited as those that would define it as homogeneously protofascist. In fact, numerous painters and graphic artists associated with New Objectivity went on to prominence in the Third Reich, not least because the style of their paintings corresponded in many ways to that which was officially sanctioned by the Hitler regime. The smoothly articulated surfaces and detailed figurative imagery of the work of Alexander Kanoldt, Georg Schrimpf, Carlo Mense, Franz Lenk, and Carl Grossberg provided no cause for offense in the Nazi era, nor did the chosen subject matter of these artists or their interwar political affiliation. They were consequently awarded professorships and exhibited frequently and successfully up until the onset of World War II. That even erstwhile leftists could sometimes use the New Objective style in the service of fascism is evident in the career of Rudolf Schlichter, an author with Grosz, Hausmann, and Heartfield of the programmatic "Laws of Painting" essay that proclaimed in 1920 representational art to be *the* style of the masses. Schlichter, who joined the Communist Party in 1919, was throughout the early twenties involved in the KPD, and his work of this time often reflects this political engagement. A decade later Schlichter was still using representation to address the sociopolitics of his times, most notably in *Blind Power* (1932–37), a painting that has always been interpreted as a statement of the artist's dismay about the Nazi terror. In it, a muscular warrior wearing a helmet that obscures his vision clutches sword and hammer, leaving behind him a legacy of fiery death and destruction. Though Bosch-like beasts consume his flesh, the giant remains as yet invincible, giving no indication that he will succumb to the attacks.

What has escaped notice until only recently is that this painting was actually made in 1932 under the title of *Greatness and Destruction* and reworked in the mid-1930s.[13] Although we can only speculate about the exact changes that were then made to the painting, the cover to Schlichter's 1932 autobiography, *Obstinate Flesh* (Das widerspenstige Fleisch), suggests what the original version may have looked like. Notably, the book jacket reflects the artist's pronounced move to the right in the late 1920s, when he critiqued in both print and image Weimar's liberal democracy and forged close ties with leading representatives of the conservative revolution like Ernst Jünger, whose portrait Schlichter painted in 1929. Of special note are the parasites that attack the body of the warrior on the book cover; here they are not the generic beasts in the painting, but a lascivious female nude and a pot-bellied male figure with Semitic features wearing a red Phrygian cap. For conservatives who equated the liberal republic with Jews and sexualized women, this image connoted the devastation of the nation by the democratic ideals of 1789 and their supposed incarnation in Weimar Germany.

When the Nazis assumed power in 1933, Schlichter wrote his friend and fellow Nazi sympathizer Franz Radziwill, "Heil and Sieg. Finally everything has been cleared away, just as we have wanted for so long." (O. Peters, *Neue Sachlichkeit* 105) Though the artist would change his mind about the National Socialists by the mid-1930s, at the end of the Weimar Republic and on into the early Nazi era he would put his representational style in the service of his now pronounced antiliberalism.

In short, New Objectivity in the visual arts connoted different things at different times, even within the career of a single artist. Interpretations that would characterize the style as *either* left- or right-wing, radical or reactionary, do not acknowledge the many different positionalities from which it spoke. More interesting to me than any retrospective attempt to typecast the movement politically is the tendency of its practitioners themselves to typecast, and this they did not from one but many different sociopsychic viewpoints.

The origins of physiognomic typology lay, of course, in the Swiss clergyman Johann Kaspar Lavater's *Physiognomische Fragmente* (Essays on Physigonomy). Published in the mid-1770s, Lavater's Enlightenment-era handbook taught the classification of the human visage as an exercise in appreciation of God's creations, and put forth the belief that a person's characteristics, subjectivity, or even soul could be read in the physiognomic features of the face. The idea that a person's outward appearance signifies inner character has had its devotées since then, but at virtually no other time or place did it have the immense popular currency that it did in 1920s Germany.[14] Germans of the Weimar era were fascinated by taxonomies of all kinds, from the sort of physiognomic typecasting practiced by now popular nineteenth-century criminologists like Cesare Lombroso and Hans Kurella, whose goal was to identify a person's potential for deviant behavior in the way she/he looked,[15] to contemporary characterologists like Emil Peters and Gerhard Venzmer, whose observations about personality and physiognomy were drawn from a general rather than specific population.[16] The mass media participated in the discourse as well, publishing numerous articles on, for example, classification systems that allegedly cracked the code of body posture.[17] Indeed, virtually everything, from handwriting and hair color to sexuality, was now elaborately categorized and classified in scholarly books as well as popular periodicals.[18]

In the visual arts, one artist in particular has been noted for his interest in physiognomy: the photographer August Sander. His "People of the Twentieth Century"—a monumental project that comprised some forty-six portfolios of twelve photographs each–has been described as a "topographical pictorial atlas" of professional and class types in Germany from the 1910s through the 1930s (Honnef 2). Although many of his subjects were friends, the artist never identified them by name, preferring to call them merely "artist," "musician," "architect," "working-class mother," "bourgeois family," and so on. Some he photographed in settings suggestive of their origins, while others he framed against neutral backgrounds. Otherwise, Sander standardized the conditions in which he presented his subjects, establishing the rules of lighting, composition and framing in such a way that the differences *between* them are highlighted. He used an overall, even light in all of his photographs, thus minimizing pronounced dramatic effects, and, like the contemporaneous physiognomists whose books he collected, Sander captured his sitters always either frontally or in profile.[19] In addition, they are all more or less the same size, and occupy more or less the same amount of space within the frame of the photograph. Such consistency allowed contemporary viewers to identify at a glance differences in clothing, hairstyle, and physical features, all of which provided clues about the profession and worldview of the sitters. To quote Alfred Döblin, Sander's photographic apparatus produced a kind of "comparative anatomy" of "the cultural, class, and economic history" of the late Wilhelminian and Weimar eras (Döblin 58), one which allowed viewers to pin down more firmly the changing "face of the times" (the title of a1929 selection of Sander's photographs) than they could through everyday perception.[20]

Though doubtless the best-known of the New Objective artists to construct a social physiognomy of Germany in the 1920s, Sander was certainly not the only one, a fact that has been little noted in the literature on this movement. Unlike their counterparts in France, England, Italy, or the United States, New Objective painters and graphic artists in Weimar-era Germany created countless images of professional and social *types*, and this they did from widely varying perspectives. At times the depicted subject is cited by name, as in Otto Dix's famous 1921 portrait *The Urologist Hans Koch*, or his *The Journalist Sylvia von Harden* of 1926, but as often as not the sitters are identified only by profession, as they are in Sander's photographs. George Grosz's numerous satirical portraits of "profiteers" and "producers" are, of course, well-known, but there are many other New Objective artworks that depict both big- and small-time capitalists, such as Heinrich Maria Davringhausen's *The Profiteer* of 1920/21, or Grethe Jürgens *The Cloth Merchants* of 1932. Some of those portrayed, like Otto Griebel's *Ship Stoker* of 1920, were laborers who worked with their hands, while others—to use the terminology of Fritz Lang's *Metropolis*, a film that also relies on taxonomic classification—work with their brains, like Wilhelm Scharrenberg's 1923 *Portrait of an Architect*. Prostitutes were depicted time and again, usually by male artists, but both men and women were captivated by the image of the lone female in a café, inscribing this most popular of Weimar-era subjects with different valences of meaning depending on their own perspective. Even the objects represented in these typological portraits are rendered with a taxonomic exactitude that is virtually encyclopedic in scope; in Walter Schulz-Matan's *The Faience Collector* of 1927, the plates, vases, and statuary crowding the surface of the composition each occupies its own discreet space in a "comparative anatomy" not of professions but of porcelain. This "classification mania," to quote Helmut Lethen, has been explained largely as a mechanism of control (*Cool Conduct*). Typologies, it is said, operate as behavioral guides that regulate both self and other, providing structural security and giving contours to a society in disarray. This observation has particular resonance in turbulent Weimar-era Germany, which arguably experienced more change within a short period of time than any other contemporary European or North American country. Even after the economy stabilized in 1924, the nation's psychic terrain was disturbed not by its financial health but by its newly indistinct *social* shape. While the androgynous "New Women" not only acted but looked more like men, thus blurring once distinct gender boundaries, the nation's socioeconomic base continued to shift from the country and the small town to the big city, and the old crafts were ever more replaced by service-related professions that were indistinguishable by dress. Postwar developments in reconstructive and cosmetic surgery added to the confusion. Having honed their techniques on disfigured war veterans, Weimar-era plastic surgeons soon began to attract other sorts of clients interested in changing their appearance. The Berlin doctor Jacques Joseph, doubtless the most influential plastic surgeon of the nineteenth and early twentieth centuries, pioneered a scarless procedure of removing bone and cartilage from within rather than from without the nose, and drew a huge patient population from the Weimar-era Jewish population and from people afflicted with syphilis whose facial structure had been ravaged by disease. Both groups wanted to change their profile so they could better blend in.[21] Those who could not afford the operation could resort to "noseformers" that were regularly advertised in the popular press of the period, which allegedly would alter the shape of one's nose painlessly over time.[22] Indeed, cosmetic surgery became an increasingly accepted manner of dealing with bodily deviations from the "norm"; in Berlin, the city even authorized a department of "social cosmetics" at the University of Berlin's Institute for Dermatology, whose task was to deal not with the mutilated former soldier, but with the uninjured who were set apart by their appearance (Gilman "Das Gesicht wahren" 171). Cosmetic surgeons could also return old, "unerotic" bodies to some semblance of youthfulness through surgical procedures like face lifts, while "rejuvenation cures" of various kinds, widely discussed in the Weimar mass media, were alleged to transform the aged body into a youthful one. Beginning in 1921, even "sexual reassignment surgery" was performed regularly at Magnus Hirschfeld's Institute for Sexology in Berlin, where men were castrated, had their penises amputated, and were implanted with artificial vaginas and labia. In short, not only were signs of one's profession elided in the Weimar era, so, too, were traditional markers of gender, ethnicity, health, age, and even sex.[23]

Anton Räderscheidt's provocative *Self Portrait* of 1928 eloquently speaks to such slippages of identity. Like other New Objective paintings, it is precisely rendered and carefully composed, as if its sharp contours and aesthetic of *order* could somehow contain the unsettling dissolution of gender boundaries that is pictured here. Indeed, the visual vocabulary of this painting and of so many other figurative artworks of the period bespeaks the era's pervasive concern with capturing and rendering inert qualities that then seemed transitory and fleeting, just as its representation of a professional *type* also helped to pin down such slippages. Hanne Bergius once suggested that the "objectivity" with which 1920s artists regarded the world around them was apotropaic; "sober observation," she wrote, "girds itself against fears, phobias, emotions" (22). This insight pertains as well to the many typologies that were constructed at the same time. That is, if the style of precise figuration offered painters and graphic artists the promise of mastery over their chosen media and techniques in a way that expressionist abstraction seemed not to, together with typology—both physiognomic and social—it also gave them control over the uncertain landscape of Weimar Germany itself.

But, lest I impose yet another overarching interpretive paradigm on New Objectivity that will ultimately collapse from its own unwieldy weight, a final cautionary comment is perhaps in order. Surely not *all* of those New Objectivity artists who spoke in the precisely rendered visual language of typology did so to impose structural security on their destabilized social landscape. In *Weimar Surfaces*, her recent study of Weimar-era Germany's "surface culture," Janet Ward has countered strict Marxist viewpoints on, for example, consumerism, with more affirmative ones that allow for a pleasurable interest in fantasy and festival. This seems particularly relevant for certain New Objectivity photographers, who time and again pictured the newly intensified visual stimuli of the stabilization years: the commodity display windows, advertising, nighttime illumination, and so on. Otto Umbehr, better known as Umbo, clearly took great delight in the visual phantasmagoria of his era, drawing on the language of typological discourse in photographs like *Masters in Wax* of 1928/1929 (see cover illustration of this volume) to comment playfully on mass-merchandising. Similarly, documentary photographers now used the new close-up lenses and hand-held cameras to access plant and animal worlds previously invisible to the human eye, publishing their taxonomic photographs in mass media articles on, for example, the biological characteristics of bugs.[24] More than any other style it was New Objectivity, with its penchant for classification and its vocabulary of smooth surfaces, precisely rendered form, and static compositional structure, that exactly and enduringly captured the physiognomy of this most visual of cultures.

In 1984, Andreas Huyssen published a now-canonical essay on postmodernism that also had important implications for readings of modernism. Huyssen argued that the critical potential of postmodernism's ambivalent meanings could not be measured against modernism, accounts of which had been formulated in times of extreme crisis (totalitarianism and the Cold War) and were consequently based on clear-cut, dichotomizing categories like "progress vs. reaction, left vs. right, present vs. past, modernism vs. realism, abstraction vs. representation, avantgarde vs. Kitsch" (*Great Divide* 217). These categories, he later suggested in an essay written together with David Bathrick, were largely arbitrary, their parameters defined in the postwar period so as to establish a politically tenable version of high modernism. In fact, Bathrick and Huyssen argued, the largest truth about modernism itself is "the heterogeneity of its response to the maelstrom of modernization" (Bathrick and Huyssen 8). The continuing importance of this insight is demonstrated by the case of New Objectivity, a term that is used to describe the rigorously pared-down façades of functionalist glass-and-steel architecture *as well as* the overloaded surfaces of Old Master-inspired figurative art of the interwar period. For this and other reasons that I have tried to present here, polarizing descriptors like modernism/realism or progressive/reactionary only work to limit our understanding of the movement. By removing such semantic straitjackets, the common responses of this heterogeneous group of artists to the shared experience of modernity become more clearly evident. Typology, in particular, offered postexpressionist artists a means to address a world that was both more and less visual than before. As clear markers of identity (ethnicity, health, gender, age, profession, and sex) became less visible, commodity culture—with all its eye-catching displays of consumer goods—became more pronounced. The continued viability throughout the interwar period of New Objectivity in the visual arts, which initially evolved out of disgust with expressionism and a desire to create a clear and simple style that the masses would understand, was related to its remarkable ability to *describe*, typologically, both that which was *dis*appearing as well as that which was appearing.

Notes

Regrettably, it has proved impossible to secure permission to publish illustrations of the works discussed in this chapter. Copyright holders were unwilling to grant the press "non-exclusive world rights in all languages, all editions including electronic, and for promotional material," as was required.

1. The exhibition was accompanied by a catalogue. See Hartlaub.
2. For this I refer the reader to the excellent survey of the early years of New Objectivity by Crockett, *German Post-Expressionism*. By grounding New Objectivity within the inflationary era of 1918–1924 instead of, as is more common, in the stabilization period of 1924–1929, Crockett is able to call attention to the left-wing origins of figuration in Germany.
3. This chapter is a revised and expanded version of " 'A Clear and Simple Style.' " My thanks especially to Jay Clarke, Stephanie D'Alessandro, and Gregory Nosan for their input on this.
4. For a more extended discussion of the various meanings of the term, especially in architecture and design, see F. J. Schwartz.
5. Ward, *Weimar Surfaces*, 45–91, provides an excellent analysis of the concept of surface in Weimar-era architecture and of the reaction of Benjamin and other contemporary critics to this austere façade culture.
6. See the introduction to the unpaginated catalogue by Hartlaub.
7. Crockett elaborates at some length on Doerner's book and on the revival of tradition in Germany of the postwar period.
8. For specific examples see B. Schwarz.
9. See, for example, Benjamin's critique of New Objectivity photographers in "The Artist as Producer," 774–75. See also Benjamin, "A Small History of Photography," in which the critic praises August Sander's "extraordinary body of work" (252), but critiques "the posture of a photography that can endow any soup can with cosmic significance but cannot grasp a single one of the human connexions in which it exists, even where the most far-fetched subjects are more concerned with saleability than with insight" (255).
10. Crockett is particularly succinct on this in his *German Post-Expressionism*, in which he outlines in detail the origins of New Objectivity.
11. Kokoschka's appeal, as well as the response described later, is published in Heartfield and Grosz. The controversy and its impact on Otto Dix in particular is described in some detail by Weitz.
12. Although Grosz wrote the essay in November 1920, "Zu meinen neuen Bildern" first appeared in *Das Kunstblatt* in 1921.
13. The following discussion is based on O. Peters, "Rudolf Schlichters *Blinde Macht*." On the complex topic of New Objectivity and National Socialism, see also O. Peters, *Neue Sachlichkeit*, a condensed version of which is his "Die Malerei der Neuen Sachlichkeit."
14. This phenomenon has been recently and thoroughly examined in Schmölders and Gilman. For a more wide-ranging study of physiognomic thought in Germany from the age of Enlightenment to the Nazi era, see Gray.
15. On the methods of Lombroso and Kurella and their use by Weimar-era police, see D'Alessandro.
16. E. Peters, *Menschengestalt und Character*; and Venzmer, *Sieh Dir die Menschen an!*
17. See, for example, "Neue Wege der Charakterforschung. Was die Beinhaltung enthüllt," *Berliner Illustrierte Zeitung* 38 (1929): 517.
18. Frame provides an excellent and provocative overview of the issue of typecasting in general and as regards women in particular.

19. Birgit Bernhard in *Zeitgenossen. August Sander*, 56, lists a number of the books on characterology that were in Sander's personal library.
20. On Sander's *Antlitz der Zeit*, see, especially, Hake, "Faces of Weimar Germany."
21. On Joseph and the slippage of ethnic identity in the Weimar era, see Gilman, "Das Gesicht wahren."
22. See, for example, the gadget that was pictured in many issues of the *Berliner Illustrierte Zeitung* in 1919 and 1920.
23. Gilman, *Making the Body Beautiful*, discusses the rejuvenation cures and sexual reassignment surgeries of the interwar period. For cultural responses to such developments, see Makela, "Grotesque Bodies."
24. See, for example, "Gelbrand und Kolbenwasserkäfer."

Modernism from Weimar to Hollywood: Expressionism/New Objectivity/Noir?

Richard W. McCormick

"The German cinema of the Weimar Republic is often, but wrongly identified with Expressionism," writes Thomas Elsaesser (3). He also problematizes another favorite cliché in film history that has to do with the legacy of Weimar cinema: namely, that so-called German "expressionist" directors in Hollywood exile created the film style there that we now call "film noir." For of the famous directors of the Weimar Republic who could arguably be connected to expressionism, only Fritz Lang made any films in Hollywood that are now considered to be in the style of film noir. And Fritz Lang always denied that he was an expressionist filmmaker, even in the early 1920s when the German film industry liked to market its big-budget art films with that label (Elsaesser 145).

Among the other famous directors in Hollywood who came from Germany or Austria, Ernst Lubitsch had little to do with expressionism and made no film in America remotely resembling a film noir; F.W. Murnau, the director of *Nosferatu* (1922), certainly can be connected to expressionism, but he died in 1931, long before anything like film noir was produced, soon after finishing *Tabu*, a poetic but also quasi-documentary film set in the South Seas. William (Wilhelm) Dieterle, who had acted in some films usually called expressionist (such as *Hintertreppe*, or *Backstairs*, of 1921), directed no films in America that were "noir."

Of others who started in the film industry in Weimar Germany and did go on to make American films now considered noir, directors like Billy Wilder, Robert Siodmak, and Edgar Ulmer started their film work in Germany for the most part after the heyday of expressionism in German film. The German work of Wilder and Siodmak is much more easily associated with *Neue Sachlichkeit*, the "New Objectivity," the artistic sensibility that follows expressionism in the Weimar Republic from about 1923 or 1924.[1]

Another filmmaker who made only one film in Hollywood, G.W. Pabst, did so in 1934, long before film noir. Yet some of Pabst's famous films during the Weimar Republic might be considered precursors to noir, although those films are usually categorized with what Siegfried Kracauer called the "New Realism," which he associated with New Objectivity.

In this chapter I want to question and to complicate some standard narratives about the relationship of German cinema and modernism in the Weimar Republic and then the legacy of that relationship in American exile. The story is often told this way: expressionism was the ultimate German modernism, and thus modernism in the classic German cinema of the Weimar Republic meant expressionist film. Expressionist film then manages to survive in a revised form in Hollywood when directors in exile from Nazi Germany create a new film style and/or genre in the 1940s that we now call film noir, an island of European modernism in the sea of American mass-cultural kitsch produced in Hollywood.[2] When I formulate the narrative in such a reductive caricature, its flaws seem obvious, yet I would assert that this narrative remains the dominant one. I attempt to explore some of the problems with the standard narratives, first with regard to expressionism and to other modernist, avant-garde tendencies in the Weimar Republic, and then with regard to the relation of expressionism to the origins of film noir in Hollywood. Then I look specifically at three directors who first became prominent as film artists in the Weimar Republic and whose work can arguably be related to the subsequent development of film noir in Hollywood: Fritz Lang, G.W. Pabst, and Billy Wilder. As it happens, all three were born in what was then Austria-Hungary, and then later moved from Vienna to Berlin, where they all worked in the German film industry.

Expressionism, New Objectivity, and Film Noir

First of all, how accurate is the wholesale equation of modernism with expressionism in Germany? Expressionism begins in Germany in painting around 1905, emerges in literature around 1910, first in poetry, and then on the eve of World War I begins to flourish in the theater, increasing in prominence throughout the war. At the end of the war, expressionism is briefly associated with the revolutionary hopes of 1918, as evident in pieces like the Bauhaus's "Cathedral of Socialism." Those revolutionary hopes were however soon dashed. In the early Weimar Republic, expressionism was already exhausted in many artistic media—and it is only then, when it had arguably lost its revolutionary edge and had started to become a fashionable, ornamental style, that the film producer Erich Pommer decided to try to adapt it for the German cinema. The international success of this experiment in *The Cabinet of Dr. Caligari* (Das Kabinett des Dr. Caligari), which premiered in early 1920, caused it to become a formula imitated in a number of German art films produced primarily for international export in the next three or four years. Obviously some famous techniques, such as the expressive use of shadows created by lighting techniques borrowed from the expressionist theater, the "chiaroscuro" effect that Lotte Eisner made so much of in her famous book on Weimar cinema, continued to be part of the stylistic repertoire of the Weimar art cinema and do arguably show up in American crime films of the 1940s.[3] But such a use of shadows is hardly enough to label a film "expressionist."

Expressionism was dominant in Germany during the teens; by the 1920s it was on its way out. Already during World War I the Dadaists attacked expressionism, and so did the young Bertolt Brecht. While the Bauhaus in the immediate postwar period—the era of the "Cathedral of Socialism"—produced designs that could be called "organic" and/or "expressionist," within a few years a rectilinear functionalism became dominant at the Bauhaus, and this of course is the style that made the Bauhaus internationally famous. The modernist avant-garde in the Weimar Republic is characterized more by a number of tendencies other than expressionism: leftist Dada, Bauhaus functionalism, the influence of Soviet constructivism, New Objectivity, and documentary theater, as well as the experimentation with technology in the theater of Erwin Piscator. What these movements or tendencies have in common is a much more positive engagement with the modern metropolis and modern technology—and mass culture and film in particular—as opposed to expressionism's more romantic, antimodern, inwardness, which was combined with a horror of technology and modern mass culture and an almost religious belief in the power of art ("high art"), an attitude famously and brutally parodied by the Dadaists.

In his 1994 book on Weimar culture called *Verhaltenslehren der Kälte* (which in 2002 was published in English with the title *Cool Conduct*), Helmut Lethen places a great deal of emphasis on the break between expressionism and these other avant-garde movements, stressing the "coldness" or "coolness" of the newer sensibilities, the concentration on surface as opposed to depth, and the related importance of façades and masks to conceal interiority in opposition to what he considers the cult of emotional authenticity associated with expressionism. Of course, any time one emphasizes a binary contrast between two artistic movements or sensibilities such as the inward, romantic expressionism and the supposedly "objective" concern with surfaces of New Objectivity, one has to become suspicious: obviously many expressionists concerned themselves not only with their own feelings, but wanted rather to transform the world (through a new kind of art); New Objectivity in turn protested a bit too much its coldness and "objectivity" as it set about documenting social reality. As Kracauer wrote in his 1929 study of white-collar workers, *Die Angestellten*, the secret of New Objectivity is that lurking behind its modern façade is often nothing but bourgeois sentimentality (287). In many ways New Objectivity and expressionism were just two sides of the same coin: what they had in common was an ambivalent response to modernity. Indeed often the same modernist artists went through both phases, first indulging in excessive expressionist enthusiasm for art as a medium of authentic emotional expression in the face of an alienating modern age and then beating an excessive retreat behind the façade of the cool "sobriety" of New Objectivity, which either "neutrally" documented modernity or celebrated it—but also frequently presented it critically in a social-realist style.[4]

Above all we should remember that the modernist avant-garde of the 1920s cannot simply be labeled expressionist. With regard to the cinema, this is even clearer: one cannot simply adapt a romantic, antimodern artistic sensibility for a modern, industrial mass medium like the cinema without taking note of the rather large contradictions that this move creates. Nor should it be forgotten that the so-called *Autorenkino* or "author's cinema," also known as the art cinema in Germany—out of which expressionist cinema emerged—was not really "revolutionary" but rather the calculated strategy of a very large, commercial industry.

The painted shadows and distorted perspectives built into the theatrical mise-en-scene in the film *The Cabinet of Dr. Caligari* did not have a long legacy in the Weimar cinema, but the expressive use of "real" shadows in the (brief) murder scene in that film did. Even more influential was the use of ("real") shadows in Murnau's *Nosferatu*—a film that otherwise is striking for its outdoor cinematography, a cinematic naturalism that enhances the uncanny effects associated with the "unnatural" vampire Nosferatu. Those "unnatural" special effects in Murnau's film were achieved through an impressive display of cinematic technology, and in this way the film would also be very influential.

This trend continued as the 1920s went on; while this technological hubris was often emphasized in a way that arguably lent the films a modernist self-reflexivity in excess of simple realism, there is not necessarily any reason to call this "expressionist," unless any modernist deviation from realism demands such a label. The bold editing one finds in German films of the mid- and late 1920s has much more to do with the influence of the Soviet avant-garde rather than anything reminiscent of German expressionism; by the same token, the virtuoso display of cinematic special effects in these films has arguably more to do with New Objectivity's fetishization of technology than it does with expressionism.

And as for a type of film in the Weimar cinema that could indeed have been influential on the development of film noir in Hollywood, the so-called street film in Weimar cinema would most clearly be a possible precursor to those Hollywood crime films of the 1940s. While the first street film, *Die Strasse* or *The Street* of 1923, is often considered a late expressionist film, as the genre develops over the course of the 1920s in the direction of greater social and even documentary realism, there is much less reason to see it as somehow expressionist. It is rather the development of a gritty urban realism in Germany that might be said to have something to do with film noir.

But of course critics have long tended to associate all the best stylistic and thematic elements of the Weimar cinema with expressionism; the most famous and influential example of this tendency one finds in Lotte Eisner. The opportunism of Eisner's achievement in this regard mirrors the original intention of the German film industry in manufacturing expressionist films in the first place: because expressionism was the main or only modernist movement for which Germany was famous, the idea of marketing German art films as expressionist was a way to create a "high art" brand name associated with Germany without any connection to the Prussian militarism for which Germany was notorious in the wake of World War I.

In contrast to the all-too-typical conflation of all of Weimar art cinema with expressionism, I have tended here to take the polemical tack of minimizing the extent of what German expressionism actually meant in the cinema. While this may be excessive in the opposite direction, I want to make it clear that there was a lot more to the Weimar avant-garde and to the Weimar cinema than what can properly be called expressionist.[5]

And once one starts to talk about the origin of the so-called film noir in Hollywood, there are other even larger problems with the conventional narrative. For one thing, it completely ignores the American roots of the films we call film noir—namely the crime film of the 1920s and 1930s, and indeed the gangster film of the early 1930s, one of the genres banned in 1934 when the industry began to enforce the Hays Code so strictly. Jonathan Munby has argued that it is the elliptical modernist style that exile directors in America had learned in Europe that helps to create what we now call the film noir, in part to disguise the subversive crime film and thus to trick the would-be censors. To the extent that exile directors like Lang, Wilder, and Otto Preminger played a role in the creation of noir, Munby asserts that it was more the result of their embrace of the democratic America of the New Deal (which gave them refuge from fascism in Europe), as opposed to any European disdain for American mass culture. He sees the crime film as a critical and often subversive American genre long before German and Austrian directors from European modernist cinema began to help mold a new variation of that genre—with help from a number of American directors, too, of course, such as John Huston and Orson Welles.

The very term "film noir" was first given to certain American crime films by French postwar critics. In Hollywood in the 1940s these films were called "realistic melodramas" (May 219), a categorization just as reminiscent of the critical, social-realist tendency within Weimar cinema in the era of New Objectivity in the mid- and later 1920s and early 1930s as it is of the stylized expressionist films of the early 1920s.

The Case of Fritz Lang

Fritz Lang was an Austrian born in 1890 who came to Berlin at the end of World War I. At least according to the most common version of the story, he was supposed to direct *The Cabinet of Dr. Caligari* for Erich Pommer in 1919, but he was not able to do so because he was in the middle of filming a two-part adventure film called *Die Spinnen*, or *Spiders*. Lang's attraction to the adaptation of pulp novels for the cinema is clear from the beginning of his career, and this may explain both why his collaboration at the beginning of the 1920s with his future wife, popular novelist and screenplay writer Thea von Harbou, became so important for him, and why, many years later, he would be so well suited to the filming of crime and detective novels in Hollywood during the 1940s and 1950s, the very type of literary source material upon which the films we now call noir were based. This attraction to more popular, low-brow sources is closer to the theory and practice of Dada, the leftist avant-garde, and New Objectivity, all of which worked programmatically to undermine the boundaries between high and low culture and between art and life.[6]

Of Lang's films of the early 1920s, two are most often linked to the expressionist cinema: *Der müde Tod*, or *Destiny*, of 1921, and the two-part *Dr. Mabuse, der Spieler*, or *Dr. Mabuse, the Gambler* of 1922. While *Destiny* is a romantic fairy tale involving the protagonist's intercession with Death on behalf of her husband, which takes her to exotic lands in different historical periods, it is not so clear to me what this has to do with expressionism, other than the fact that it is indeed a fantastic film and not a realist film. As for the Dr. Mabuse film, it clearly cites expressionism—but with ironic distance. The famous quote by the film's title character is as follows: "Expressionism!—it's a game of make-believe!" (cited in Elsaesser 158); expressionist décor in the film is associated with decadent night clubs, not with a revolutionary aesthetic. And for the rest of his life Lang would deny that the Mabuse films had anything to do with expressionism.[7]

Lang's next two gargantuan projects were the two-part *Nibelungen* film of 1924 and the ill-fated epic *Metropolis*, which did not premiere until early 1927. Elsaesser calls the *Nibelungen* film a national epic decorated in a Bauhaus-style medieval architecture; *Metropolis*, often considered the swan-song of expressionism, is more accurately the swan-song of the big-budget German art film, because *Metropolis* went so much over budget that it supposedly bankrupted Germany's largest studio, Ufa. While there are clearly expressionist elements, or at least allusions to expressionism in this film, it is at least as much a futurist, science fiction dystopia. It is just as fascinated as it is horrified by the machines it depicts and by its own technology in representing that world of the future. Andreas Huyssen interpreted the film as the triumph of a futurist, technology-fetishizing New Objectivity over expressionism.

In any case, bombastic epic films like *Metropolis* and *The Nibelungen* have little to do with the films Fritz Lang made in Hollywood that we now consider film noir. The Weimar film of Lang that has the most stylistic and thematic similarity to those later films of the 1940s and 1950s would have to be *M* of 1931, Lang's first sound film, a street film about crime and pathology but also technology and surveillance. *M*, compared to the big-budget films Lang had made for Ufa, was a down-sized production, but the better for it, a New Objectivist look at the metropolis, an urban realism with atmospheric effects that do indeed allude to expressionist techniques, especially lighting.[8]

Lang asserted that "I don't know what I took from expressionism. I may have used it, maybe to get it out of my system" (cited in Elsaesser n. 3 188). His first film in the United States, *Fury* (1936), continued in the vein of *M*; if anything its agenda was even more social realist in its examination of vigilante justice. In Hollywood Lang made crime films and Westerns, but obviously the crime film was the genre in which films later considered film noir belong. During World War II he made antifascist films like *Hangmen Also Die* (1943) and *Ministry of Fear* (1944) that put into play for more overtly political ends the paranoid atmosphere Lang's crime films were so good at creating.[9] In the 1950s, crime films that Lang made, such as *The Big Heat* (1954), also had an implicit political agenda in their exploration of police and government corruption. Munby reads this as related in part to Lang's anger about being blacklisted in the early 1950s, at the height of the McCarthy era. It is the socially critical look at urban reality in the United States that arguably links such a film more with New Objectivity than with expressionism, although of course Lang obviously brought stylistic techniques with expressionist origins to these films, as well as his mastery at creating an uncanny, paranoid atmosphere that also is reminiscent of expressionist films.[10]

The Case of G.W. Pabst

G.W. Pabst was born in 1885; he did not stay in Hollywood long enough to make film noir, and yet the style and subject matter of some of his

Weimar films do in some ways anticipate noir. At the same time, Pabst is the famous director of the Weimar Republic most associated with the more realist style of the New Objectivity. I think it is instructive to examine one of the more striking scenes in the 1925 film that made him famous, *Freudlose Gasse* (Joyless Street), a social-realist film about Vienna during the destabilizing inflation of the early 1920s. The scene depicts in one tracking shot the impoverished citizens of the title street of the film as they stand in line in front of the butcher shop at night, illuminated by the headlights of a car carrying wealthy speculators in search of nocturnal pleasures that the Viennese night life supposedly promises them.

In this scene there is a self-reflexive use of lighting that also alludes to Eisner's expressionist chiaroscuro. But at the same time it puts both this stylistic technique and its modernist self-reflexivity in the service of a socially critical depiction of poverty and exploitation. What is also clear is how there is as much emphasis on gender as well as class inequity: what we see are overwhelmingly women in line for meat at the butcher's. Pabst's *Joyless Street* is a social melodrama that places a primary emphasis on the experience of two women protagonists, so much so that this film's title was used by feminist critic Patrice Petro for the title of her groundbreaking 1989 book *Joyless Streets*, which argues that Weimar cinema cannot be understood without taking into account its appeal to the female spectator so long ignored by critics who focused only on "male crisis" in Weimar cinema.

Two of Pabst's other famous films of the1920s featured American actress Louise Brooks, *Die Büchse der Pandora* (Pandora's Box) and *Tagebuch einer Verlorenen* (Diary of a Lost Girl), both of which were released in 1929. These two films highlight another side of New Objectivity and the middle and later period of the Weimar Republic, namely the emphasis on sexuality that can be interpreted either as emancipated, "decadent," and/or cynical. Certainly Pabst, as a male intellectual (and the director most often associated with New Objectivity), was ambivalent about the sexual freedoms associated with Weimar's emancipated "New Woman," but there was in any case in his films a more forthright look at this phenomenon—or at any rate a more sustained, if perhaps more obsessed look—than in the films of the earlier expressionist period. Nowhere is this clearer than in Pabst's films with Louise Brooks, who steals these two films in spite of their narratives, which try so hard to contain the femme fatale figures she plays. It is this ambivalent obsession with sexually assertive women that reminds one of film noir, although in those later, American films, the femme fatale is more clearly demonized than in late Weimar cinema with its famous vamps Louise Brooks and Marlene Dietrich.

The Case of Billy Wilder

Billy Wilder, who died in Southern California in 2002, was born Samuel Wilder in 1906 near Kracow in a part of Poland that then belonged to Austria-Hungary. Educated in Vienna, in 1926 he left Vienna and went to Berlin from Austria (as Lang and Pabst had before him). Wilder, sixteen years younger than Lang and twenty-one years younger than Pabst, had little connection to the expressionism of the early 1920s. Already then, in the mid- to late 1920s, Wilder was the future émigré most positively disposed toward both America and the Americanism that was the rage during the Weimar Republic—and this Americanism was closely associated with the New Objectivity, and not at all with expressionism. Wilder would also eventually become the most successful of the émigrés in America, indeed the most successful émigré director from Germany since Lubitsch.

Wilder never got the chance to direct while in Berlin; he was a screenplay writer. His first screenplay was cowritten with Curt Siodmak; the resulting 1929 film was directed by Curt's brother Robert Siodmak and Edgar Ulmer, with cinematography by Eugen Schüfttan and Fred Zinnemann. All of these young men would end up in Hollywood within a few years. The1929 silent film that resulted from their collaboration was *Menschen am Sonntag* (People on Sunday). For polemical reasons I may too often be minimizing the influence of expressionism in this essay, but it is nonetheless indisputable that *People on Sunday* has nothing at all to do with expressionism. Indeed, it may be the ultimate example of cinematic New Objectivity as an accessible, democratic art for a modern urban society; it is a proto-neorealist, quasi-documentary that looks at the weekend of some simple office workers in Berlin, almost completely shot on location in Berlin and the lakes on its western edge and acted supposedly by "amateurs."

At the center of the film is a montage of close-ups of supposedly "ordinary people" posing for a photographer in a park. This sequence is self-reflexive in its mirroring of the project of the film: capturing ordinary Berliners with affection, whimsy, and democratic egalitarianism. Of course, at the same time one can also read the scene as characteristic of New Objectivity in some of its less positive traits: the fixation with documenting and/or classifying faces, and also a humor that tends to be mostly at the expense of women and the working class.

Wilder had of the three filmmakers I am discussing in this chapter clearly the least to do with expressionism, yet one of the first few films he directed in Hollywood, after some years there as a screenwriter, was *Double Indemnity* in 1944, one of the most classic crime films now considered a film noir. Toward the end of the film, Walter Neff, the character played by Fred MacMurray, murders Phyllis, the femme fatale played by Barbara

Figure 5.1 "Walter (Fred MacMurray) Shoots Phyllis (Barbara Stanwyk)." Billy Wilder's *Double Indemnity* (1944). Still Photo from DVD

Stanwyck. The scene is notable for its use of shadows and its overall ambiguity: the two are embracing, and the cold femme fatale has her most sympathetic moment just as Neff shoots her (figure 5.1). It is thus reminiscent of the death scene of Schoen with Lulu in Pabst's *Pandora's Box*, in which the struggle for the gun between the two of them is blocked by Schoen's body in front of Lulu's, the two bodies in such close proximity that when smoke is seen as the indication that the gun has been fired, it is not completely clear who has fired the gun and who has been shot (figure 5.2).

Like Lang, and unlike Pabst, Wilder was Jewish. Indeed, he lost his mother in the Holocaust. Wilder is paradigmatic for the ambiguous relationship many of the German- and Austrian-Jewish émigré directors had with Europe as well as with America. They escaped Europe, where they had always been to some extent outsiders, and they embraced a New Deal America that seemed to accept them only to find that in the postwar era of "McCarthyism," their enthusiasm for the New Deal (and antifascism) turned them again into outsiders.[11]

Wilder's postwar films like *Foreign Affair* and *The Emperor's Waltz* (both of 1948) could be scathing in their critique of fascism (or proto-fascism) in both Germany and Austria, but Wilder could also be very critical of

Figure 5.2 "Struggling for the Gun, Lulu (Louise Brooks) Shoots Schoen (Fritz Kortner)." G.W. Pabst's *Büchse der Pandora (Pandora's Box)*, 1929. Still Photo from DVD

American society, as his treatment of the Jean Arthur character in *Foreign Affair* demonstrates. Wilder made all sorts of films in the United States, by no means only film noir. In his comedies he liked to skewer America's puritanical obsession with sex and its sexual hypocrisy. In such films one is reminded of the sexual frankness—and perhaps also the sexual cynicism—of Weimar Berlin and the New Objectivity with the blurring of sexual boundaries and the breaking of sexual taboos—an important part of the emancipatory legacy of Weimar.

This questioning of traditional ideas about sex and gender is nowhere more clear than at the end of Wilder's 1959 film *Some Like It Hot*, a comedy about gangsters and cross-dressing that undermined the sexual conservatism of the 1950s. Joe E. Brown plays a millionaire who finds out at the end of the film that the woman he has been courting is actually a man, played by Jack Lemmon. Taking off his wig to prove that they cannot marry, Lemmon exclaims, "I'm a man!" The millionaire responds simply, "Nobody's perfect," and continues to drive the motorboat carrying his beloved off into the night.[12]

This frank depiction of sexual transgression and emancipation is very much a legacy of the middle and later periods of the Weimar Republic and not at all of the expressionist cinema in its early years—much more a characteristic of the films of someone like Pabst as opposed to Murnau. The same can be said of Wilder's populism and Americanism, something he championed long before coming to the United States, and certainly much more connected to New Objectivity than to expressionism. The same cannot be said for the Weimar work of Lang, whose dystopia *Metropolis* was inspired by his first glimpses of New York. But once the fairly apolitical, elitist Lang went into exile, he became much more concerned with politics, and while always concerned about mobs and demagogues, he embraced the New Deal.

What we now call film noir had in any case deep American roots in gangster films and "fallen woman" films, the two types of films that had been banned in 1934. The émigrés from Europe who contributed to the development of film noir brought their own stylistic and political concerns to it, but their interest in it was just as much the result of their allegiance to a New Deal America they saw becoming endangered over the course of the 1940s. Along with the stylish modernism (including chiaroscuro lighting) they brought to film noir, the émigrés also brought a commitment to a socially critical realism that had its roots in New Objectivity.

Notes

1. Ulmer did begin as an assistant to Murnau. On Siodmak, Lutz Koepnick writes that his work "prior to 1943 shows no expressionist predilections whatsoever" (166); the same is true for Wilder.
2. See Koepnick's critical take on this cliché: 166.
3. In fact, Koepnick cites research that argues that this lighting style can be found in the American cinema long before expressionism is adapted for film in Germany: 170; 297, n. 10.
4. On New Objectivity, see also Lindner; Ward; and McCormick.
5. See also Hake's nuanced discussion of this issue in "Expressionism and the Cinema"; she maintains that expressionism's legacy is undeniable if only because critics have continued to use the term (however broadly or loosely). I do not deny that this legacy exists, but I would insist that Weimar modernism was more than merely "expressionist."
6. Hake in "Expressionism and the Cinema" maintains that expressionism had the same "hybrid" project of using pulp materials for its "high art."
7. Bernd Widdig contests Kracauer's reading of the first two Mabuse films as expressionist (115–16).
8. While the Berlin streets of the film were entirely constructed in the studio, the film's depiction of the various types of Berlin milieu and dialects was very realistic. See Kaes and Gunning.
9. On Lang's troubled collaboration with Brecht on *Hangmen Also Die*, see Gemünden.

10. Another reason why the Hollywood films of Lang and others have the "look" of Weimar films is of course the fact that émigré technicians worked in Hollywood—the most famous example would be the cinematographer Karl Freund (who by the 1950s was working on the *I Love Lucy* sit-com on television). But there were of course American technicians who worked on films we now call noir.
11. For a discussion of how the situation of exile specifically affected the films of the émigrés, see Dimendberg; and Gemünden and Kaes.
12. Wilder had bought the rights to a 1950 West German film, *Fanfaren der Liebe* (Fanfares of Love). That original German film had cross-dressing musicians but no gangster plot. The latter "Americanizes" the story in Wilder's film and adds (darker) humor; also, the German film's cross-dressing plot ends much more conventionally, with both male protagonists restored to "normal" male heterosexuality.

Clement Greenberg and the Postwar Modernist Canon: Minimizing the Role of Germany and Northern Europe

Matthew Rohn

Clement Greenberg played a leading role in constructing a canonical narrative of modernism, and his views helped push German and Nordic contributions to the peripheries of many accounts of modern art.[1] Even though he started his career in 1939 as a literary critic who advocated German modernists to an American audience, his enthusiasms for modern poets and artists linked to Germany waned as World War II progressed. By the end of the war, he had gravitated to the emphatically formalist, French and cubist-centered aesthetic that he would make famous over the next decade. Greenberg always claimed that this aesthetic made use of a process that freed anyone employing it from social and cultural prejudices, but recent analysis of his writing has uncovered mounting evidence that mainstream, post–World War II, American, cultural values colored his judgments. Scholars in a number of fields have documented how his responsiveness to anticommunism and the postwar intensification of masculinist values in society helped shape his judgments. This chapter examines how Americans' disquietude about German and Northern culture following World War II also informed his thinking and became a fixture in the modernist canon he played such an important role in forming.

Though he initially wrote for an American audience, his own ambitions and the American government's use of his ideas through its Cold War propagation of anti-leftist, apolitical, modernist, artistic culture after World War II helped him contribute globally to what Jürgen Habermas has defined as the "modern project." This was begun, as Habermas relates, in "the 18th century by the philosophers of the Enlightenment [. . .] their efforts to develop science, universal morality and law" but found its greatest fulfillment in the twentieth century ("Modernity—An Incomplete Project" 9).

Greenberg's formalist criticism aspired to the scientific objectivity of the Enlightenment project. But modernists, as Michel Foucault has demonstrated, have often used scientific objectivity to disguise the traditional moral and hierarchical imperatives governing their practices. This proves true with Clement Greenberg, who never shed his early Marxist desire to reform society. He at most tempered and sublimated that inclination following his encounter with Stalinism in the 1930s. Formalism helped him cloak reforms his writings supported and camouflaged his attraction to seats of power. Formalism provided his judgments with a mantle of scientific objectivity that often prevented even him from seeing the extent to which personal and social values informed many claims he made about art. By the end of the war, Greenberg, who was Jewish, a veteran, and the child of central European immigrants, had many reasons to be leery of German culture and its influence on American thought. Until then, German culture had deeply impressed and influenced him. He would not turn his back on it easily, and his post–World War II writings show him seeking to reform German culture itself by using its Enlightenment resources to guide European and American art and thought. Conscious of it or not, he set out to steer American culture away from overt Germanic influence and to reform Germany itself from what he viewed as its less desirable traits.

He advanced his position through his reading of early, twentieth-century modernism in the visual arts and by minimizing the influence of German and Nordic art on painting created in the United States during what proved for the consolidation of canonical modernism to be an important, post–World War II decade. His views about Germanic qualities and his love for abstract expressionism produced jarring contradictions, but the social, moral, and aesthetic force of his views sustained his position. He expressed a widespread postwar American worry, stated in an important 1947 essay "The Present Prospects of American Painting and Sculpture" that "the dominant creative tradition in America during the last century and half, as in England and Germany, has [. . .] been Gothic, transcendental, romantic, subjective" (O'Brian 2:164). This essay introduced Jackson Pollock for the first time as a major painter to an international audience, yet Greenberg fretted about the "Gothic-ness [. . .] paranoia and resentment" in Pollock's art, and warned that these very qualities, which most people have long viewed as central to the artist's vision, "narrow" his art (O'Brian 2:166). Greenberg repeatedly sought to steer Pollock and other American artists away from Germanic influences (along with other sources of the "Gothic" and romanticism), contested Germanic elements others saw in their art and frequently questioned the importance of Germanic contributions to modernism. He did so for complex reasons, and the story of Greenberg's problematic response to Germanic art reveals much about modernist narratives and the equivocal role German and other Northern artists have played in canonical accounts of modernism.

Early in his career, Greenberg showed himself to be an unusually knowledgeable advocate of German-derived modernism. His first published essay was a review of an English translation of Bertolt Brecht's *Dreigroschenroman* (the novelized version of his "Three Penny Opera"). Reviews of volumes of poetry by Brecht, Anna Seghers, and Stephan George followed, and these included commentary on other modern, German poets. Greenberg collaborated with Willa and Edwin Muir to translate two collections of Franz Kafka's writings that Schocken Books published in 1947 and 1948 respectively. His very first commentary on art, penned in 1941, included a review of a Wassily Kandinsky exhibition, and his second article was a relatively lengthy obituary paying tribute to Paul Klee. In it Greenberg had high praise for Klee's work and spoke at length about the value of Klee's Germanic roots and what he viewed as its liberating provincialism. Greenberg claimed it an "asset [. . .] that [Klee] had been born and brought up in German Switzerland in the presence of a provincial [rather than Mediterranean] [. . .] art [. . .] which had something relatively new to contribute to the main stream of Western painting [. . .]" (O'Brian 1:65–66). Following the war, however, Greenberg wrote less and less about German modernism and began speaking about it having a lesser stature in the visual arts relative to what he most often called "School of Paris" and "cubist" art.

Trends in Greenberg's writings are sometimes difficult to ascertain with precision. As a working critic, with some justification, he asserted that he did "not prescribe to art, and [was] willing to like anything, provided [that he] enjoy[ed] it enough" (O'Brian 2:205). He believed that his personal response to work initiated his evaluations and those operated free of socially conditioned expectations or fixed aesthetic criteria. He sometimes praised a body of work by an artist and critiqued the same artist's work on another occasion. A number of instances exist in which he changed his views about Germanic artists. But when his writings are read collectively, as John O'Brian's four volume edition of Greenberg's complete writings has allowed, overarching values that shaped his thinking emerge between his prewar and postwar thinking on Germanic and Nordic modernism. Over time, he increasingly spoke unfavorably of Germanic artists' work in comparison to the work by artists centered in Paris. When he did speak well of individual Germanic artists, as readers will learn, he increasingly rationalized his praise by commenting on how those particular Germanic artists embraced French modernism more fully than others. At the same time that he and many of the New York intellectuals turned increasingly politically conservative during the Cold War era, they also grew more influential. His pronouncements became more authoritative over the period of time when he progressively made fewer references to Germanic modernists. They, in part, became less important through exclusion. When in 1961 he compiled a set of revised essays in his highly influential anthology titled *Art and Culture*, he minimized the role Germanic art had previously played in his own thinking. Greenberg always believed that he rendered judgments based on relatively pure aesthetic criteria, but his treatment of Germanic artists reveals how societal and personal biases informed his canon. By 1961, Greenberg had become a leading figure defining modernism in the United States, and within a decade his views became highly influential in other nations and in fields other than art.

Paul Klee and Max Beckmann provide examples that document the complex response Greenberg had toward Germanic art and the way he strove to winnow Germanic qualities out of modernism after World War II. Greenberg went back-and-forth throughout his career about the value of Klee's work, and his changing attitudes help chart the trajectory of his thinking about German contributions to modernism. The praise Greenberg had for Klee in 1941 turns to skepticism soon after the war. By 1947 he suddenly writes: "doubt persists whether Klee's art, as compared with the still unexploited potentialities of the cubist heritage, has enough carrying power to support a school of major importance" (O'Brian 2:150). But by this time, Greenberg increasingly worried that the cubist masters had grown decadent, and he considered whether other strands of modernism that interested artists working in the United States at that time might provide new blood to rekindle excellence in modern art. "The problem for criticism is to explain why the cubist generation and its immediate successors have [. . .] fallen off in middle and old age, and why [. . .] even the German expressionist, Max Beckmann, so inferior to Picasso in native gifts, should paint better today than [Picasso] does" (O'Brian 2:212). As this quotation reveals, Greenberg did not believe that an artist with a Germanic heritage would be likely to generate the high quality he sought in art. He used Beckmann in this instance as a competitive model. But his tactic also helps point toward the dialectical solution Greenberg eventually constructed to rationalize how he would occasionally praise a few Germanic artists.

He would contend that the value of their art derived little from Germanic roots (even when it showed otherwise) and drew most from a proximity to Paris. This affinity was crucial, he believed right up to his last published comments made in 1969: "If you weren't in Paris or in touch with Paris you were condemned to be a more or less provincial or minor artist. Even Munch, the Norwegian, was Paris-oriented, and [. . .] spent five years there in his young manhood. And Paul Klee, who stayed in Germany most of his life [. . .] broke through his art only after he made contact with cubism in Paris in 1912. There you are" (O'Brian 4:305–06).

Paul Klee briefly resurfaced in Greenberg's writings around 1950 as one of the rare Germanic artists whom Greenberg held up as a model to others. He praised Klee only occasionally and less vigorously than he would artists who lived in Paris. He justified his admiration in good measure by grafting on to the German heritage of Klee's that he had celebrated in 1941 a French lineage. "And yet Klee did succeed in going to the 'Mediterranean' and possessing it as no other Germanic artist has. Perhaps it was his French mother [. . .]" (O'Brian 3:5). French blood, Greenberg would have us believe, could redeem a Germanic artist.

References to Germanic artists relative to French artists important prior to World War II dropped off significantly in his reviews and essays after 1949. He never mentioned in print again a number of the writers and artists he had commented on through 1949, including Arp, Benn, Brecht, Kollwitz, and Seghers. Others he wrote about after 1950 only in passing and generally as foils to artists he came to contend had French leanings, such as Paul Klee, whom he would claim in 1950 "unlike Marc and the later Kandinsky [. . .] was able to transcend and subordinate [an unproductive Art Nouveau] formation [. . .] [and] is unique among artists of the Blaue Reiter group in the success with which he overcame Art Nouveau" (O'Brian 3:6). Greenberg made a number of praiseworthy comments about the German sculptors Barlach, Kolbe, Lehmbruck, and Gerhard Marcks, but in reviews that have never received much attention—writings where one sees him schooling himself about modern sculpture, a topic he did not handle as well as painting until late in his career. More significantly, he continued to brood about the value of select Germanic artists. This group consisted entirely of individuals who had attenuated relationships with Germany: Paul Klee, who was Swiss; Wassily Kandinsky, who was Russian; Hans Hofmann, who was recognized by Greenberg and others as an American artist; Prague-native Franz Kafka, who, Greenberg would contend, "unlike Heine [. . .] surrenders nothing of his Jewish self-possession in order to possess German" (Greenberg 266); and the Romanian-Jewish poet Paul Celan, living in Paris, whose "Todesfuge" Greenberg translated and published in a 1955 issue of *Commentary*.

This small group of individuals plus Bertolt Brecht (but minus Paul Celan) are the only Germanic artists and writers who received sustained commentary in Greenberg's own 1961 collection of essays, *Art and Culture*, that for a generation would be the major source of his writings and the primary text for his canon. His construction of this anthology is as illuminating as his choice and treatment of Germanic artists and writers. He revised essays and attempted to present ideas he thought would be of special importance. As his commentary in the "Preface" makes clear, *Art and Culture* was "not intended as a completely faithful record of my activity as a critic [. . .] [for] I see no reason why all the haste and waste involved in my self-education should be preserved in a book" (Greenberg vii). Germanic visual artists constitute a segment of what he eliminated when cutting "haste and waste." Klee receives repeated mention in the anthology, but Greenberg included none of the reviews or essays he had written about Klee. Kandinsky is the only decidedly Germanic visual artist to whom Greenberg dedicated an essay, and its placement in the anthology and the perspective he shares about Kandinsky sharpens the contrast between French art and what he wanted readers to perceive as a flawed German modernism—a contrast that he had for over a decade increasingly propagated. Greenberg divided *Art and Culture* into sections such as "Culture in General," "Art in General," "Literature," "Art in the United States," and what should have logically been "Art in Europe." Instead of titling that section "Art in Europe," he called it "Art in Paris." Paris now encompassed all that was important in European art, he would have his readers believe. As he wrote in an *Art and Culture* essay he titled "The School of Paris: 1946":

> Paris remains the fountainhead of modern art, and every move made there is decisive for advanced art elsewhere—which is advanced precisely because it can respond to and extend the vibrations of that nerve-center and nerve-end [. . .] Other places (Weimar Berlin, for example) may have shown more sensitivity to immediate history, but it is Paris over the last hundred years that has most faithfully conveyed the historical essence of our civilization. (Greenberg 120)

It was into the "School of Paris" section of *Art and Culture* that Greenberg slipped his "Kandinsky" essay, using the artist to help prove his point about the superiority of French art. Kandinsky provided Greenberg with a difficult case. Many Americans and others proclaimed him to be a great artist—the originator of pure abstraction and a major influence on later artists. On very rare occasions Greenberg acknowledged a possible importance of Kandinsky's early abstractions, but always only momentarily. Most of Greenberg's writings about Kandinsky dwelled on why he was not as important as so many contended. The essay he chose for the anthology (originally written in 1948 and revised in 1957) employs one of his famous, pithy, opening statements and sets forth how Kandinsky's early association with German art and his early remove from Paris led, in Greenberg's view, to his downfall: "Picasso's good luck was to have come to French modernism directly, without the intervention of any other kind of modernism. It was perhaps Kandinsky's bad luck to have had to go through German modernism first" (Greenberg 111). This patently false assertion about Picasso, given the importance of Munch and other northern European expressionists on Picasso's initial, modernist formation when he was in Barcelona and continuing on into his first Parisian years, would become a signature position on modernism for Greenberg and his followers.

One of the reasons Greenberg expended the energy he did on Kandinsky was because of the artist's influence on American abstract expressionists. Greenberg constantly tried to minimize this influence, even when the evidence contradicted him, and he worked hard to steer American artists away from Kandinsky. Greenberg's position, which proved influential for later critics and art historians, was particularly problematic in the case of Hans Hofmann, and it was in Greenberg's writings on Hofmann that he asserted his view most boldly. Greenberg briefly studied painting with Hofmann and wrote one of the rare books that he penned about any artists plus several articles and reviews, one of which he included under the "Art in the United States" section of *Art and Culture*. It is one of the many instances in which he played down Hofmann's German birth, artistic training, and professional life from 1918 to his immigration to the United States in 1931.

> [Hofmann] has been called a "German Expressionist," yet little in what is known as Expressionism, aside from Kandinsky's swirl, predicts him. His color and color textures may be "Nordic," but one clutches at this adjective in despair at a resolute originality to which the "Mediterranean" is assimilated. [. . .] Hofmann would have arrived at the same place had Kandinsky never painted [. . .] Rather than being influenced by Kandinsky, Hofmann [. . .] converged with him at several points on the way to abstraction—a way that in this case was much broader, since it ran through the whole of Matisse and the whole of Cubism. No one has digested Cubism more thoroughly than Hofmann [. . .]. (Greenberg 190–92)

In a 1992 exhibition and catalog curator Gail Levin debunks Greenberg's claim about Kandinsky not significantly influencing Hofmann or other American artists and worries that "Hofmann scholarship has not deviated substantially from Greenberg's [mistaken] assertion" (197). What led Greenberg to make such a claim and why did it and his other views about German modernism prove so persuasive? I hope that by now it is evident that Greenberg's recourse to quality as a defining feature does not adequately explain his position. However good art centered in Paris may have been, Greenberg had to rationalize a French connection in order to make certain claims about quality, and he constantly sought to narrow thinking about modernism in order to sustain his position. Philosopher David Carrier has noted that a power of most influential modernist criticism derives from its capacity to make compelling narratives for the abundance of art surveyed, and he cites Greenberg as an exceptional example of this:

> One commonplace objection to *Art and Culture* is that in it Greenberg gives a prescriptive history, a story in which Cézanne's art inevitably leads to

> cubism and on to Pollock's paintings. The only necessity I detect in [Greenberg's] text, however, is a narrative necessity; like any gifted historian, he represents what happened as if it were inevitable. (23)

Greenberg's propensity to contrast cubist-inspired art with German-inspired tendencies bolstered his evolving philosophical leanings, while also helping him with the arduous task he faced of selling, both literally and aesthetically, modern art to a largely uncultured, upwardly mobile, middle-class, American audience.

Greenberg began his professional life among the American intelligentsia around 1935, and he found his values pummeled by world events throughout the almost twenty years it took him to become known as a leading modernist art critic. This son of Lithuanian-based, Polish Jews came of age as an ardent Marxist. He believed that newer, often German-derived thinking would transform the world. Within a few years, he became one of those known as New York Intellectuals—thinkers who continued to embrace modernism but distanced themselves from International Communism once evidence mounted about Stalinist purges. Still, he and other editors of *Partisan Review* opposed American involvement in World War II. They treated early claims about the Holocaust as propaganda meant to elicit support for the war, and only toward the end of the war faced the grim reality of what Germans had done to Jews and others.

This realization, and other aspects of the war, subsequently encouraged him to rescue his own vision of modernism from any taint of association with stereotypical German propensities (especially Gothicness). While many commentators have investigated how he contributed to the American, anticommunist, Cold War, propaganda efforts, attention should also be paid to how his project steered Western culture clear of numerous Germanic values and propelled American art in what he deemed a proper direction so that its practitioners could shed most vestiges of America's own Germanic heritage. As America's role in the world grew more important, Greenberg worked hard to see that its advanced art assumed a position of leadership. In his eyes America's newer artists needed to create responsibly and lead culture along what he and others viewed as the proper direction. Largely unconsciously, he advanced a position pointing modern art increasingly away from Germanic influences, even as he mined Kantian thought in doing this.

Inwardly and philosophically Greenberg embraced more fully after the war than he had previously the Kantian side of German modernism. As Donald Kuspit has observed, Greenberg began around 1949 to employ "dialectical conversion" in such a way that he could wrest from dialogical debate principles of unity. Kant's aesthetic provided a philosophical key to his conception of unity. Cubism, moreover, became for Greenberg its stylistic and pictorial embodiment. Kuspit notes that "Greenberg acknowledges many 'principles of unity' in art, but [. . .] singles out Cubism as 'that purest and most unified of all [. . .] since Tiepolo and Watteau' " (30–31). Evidence of grids in cubism helped Greenberg see in that style marks of rationalism and a systematic unity in the way that it contended with the welter and chaos of modern life, and nationalistic prejudices drew Greenberg to cubism and what he and others called "School of Paris" art. His emphasis on French-derived art allowed him to scrub modernism clean of what for him increasingly within his adulthood became a problematic German culture. He would redeem only those Germanic artists whom he might claim baptized themselves in Paris's cosmopolitan world and the source of cubist values. At the same time, he conveniently sharpened the contrast between French and Germanic qualities by designating certain individuals as lesser artists—often as too expressionistic or, in the case of Neue Sachklichkeit, too "academic."

A number of late-twentieth-century art historians, beginning with Rosalind Krauss, have explored how Greenberg's canonical view of modernism falsely imposed ideas about grids and orderliness on cubism and much modern painting. T.J. Clarke recently characterized this as "the Achilles' heel of [Greenberg's] account of modernism as a whole" (424, n. 18). But in recognizing the accuracy of their analysis, we should not lose sight of the longstanding persuasive power of Greenberg's vision. Greenberg thrust himself into the mainstream of international thinking that emerged after World War II, and his narrative helped him sell modernism and abstract expressionism to a skeptical, American audience.

After the war, a wave of Francophilia swept American intellectual circles when French Existentialists, a number of whom had been resistance fighters, emerged as cultural as well as intellectual heroes. America made powerful allies both politically and intellectually with freed France, while Germany figured as a discredited culture and an occupied power in ruins. Greenberg was one of the few intellectuals in the abstract expressionist circle who showed almost no interest in Existentialism, yet his championing of French art won him entry into leading circles of thought both in this country and abroad. It also helped him with the difficult task of selling abstract expressionism.

Americans have long been skeptical about the value of art. Anything that reinforces their skepticism can have devastating results. Those who have sought financial or intellectual support for modern art have had to thread their way carefully, and Greenberg's spirit of reform made him eager to advocate abstract expressionism, to win for it monetary as well as critical support. He saw at the very beginning of his career how the social revolutions that had led to the rise of middle-class culture destroyed what had been "the inevitability of its particular forms, [this shift in power broke] up accepted notions upon which artists and writers [had had to] depend" (O'Brian 1:6). This provided the opening for avant-garde culture, but also for reactionary swings to what he called "Alexandrianism" or a pluralistic play of tastes most frequently producing what he branded as "kitsch." "The true and most important function of the avant-garde," he would write in his famous, 1939 article "Avant-Garde and Kitsch," "was not to 'experiment,' but to find a path along which it would be possible to keep culture *moving* in the midst of ideological confusion and violence" (O'Brian 1:8). Bifurcation of modern art into cubist and expressionist, French and Germanic, and other oppositional terms provided Greenberg (following a long line of critics, art historians and philosophers) with one means in his own uncertain postwar time to help him chart what he thought this proper aesthetic and moral "path" was. Indeed, it helped him assure those to whom he was selling this art, whose support he knew was crucial to its success, that modernism championed values they could embrace. The more he stripped abstract expressionism and modernism of Germanic qualities and stereotypical values and the more he allied modernism with rational thought and a French heritage, the more he won acceptance for modernism itself among his fellow, Cold Warrior, cultural elite in the United States and the emerging business class, who played such an important role in financing newer art in America.

Greenberg was one among many of his generation who, as Jürgen Habermas has noted, grew uncomfortable with how "Modernity [in its most essential form] revolts against the normalizing functions of tradition" ("Modernity—An Incomplete Project" 5). In reaction to this notion of modernity, as Habermas has observed in "Modernity—An Incomplete Project," "Our sense of modernity [in the twentieth century] creates its own self-enclosed canons of being classic" (4). Greenberg's Cold War time frame, his association with what Frances Stonor Saunders, the author of *The Cultural Cold War: The CIA and the World of Arts and Letters*, has grouped as the more militant anticommunists among the New York Intellectuals and his excellence as a critic helped him develop a powerful, self-enclosing canon for modernism. His career as an art critic through World War II had immersed him in the late phases of an ongoing modernist revolution in the visual arts. Criteria were largely not yet established; each year appeared to produce new artistic possibilities. Greenberg's exceptional powers of perception and his sensitivity to revolutionary art and culture made him a superior critic who had the capacity to sort out major trends and promising possibilities. And because his career coincided with the late phase of modernism proper, his views had an unusually strong influence on postwar art historians and curators in the United States who began to chronicle modernism as a historical phenomenon and export those ideas throughout the world. As Donald Kuspit asserted at the beginning of his 1979 book on Greenberg, "[His] significance [. . .] cannot be overestimated. He is the designer and subtle manipulator of modernism, which is the single most important and influential theory of modern art" (3). Art historians' and curators' accounts often simplified Greenberg's views. In covering a broad sweep of artists, they would because of space limitations drop artists the earlier Greenberg thought readers should know (even if he had qualms about their art). These omissions further rendered Germanic artists less visible.

Even in his lifetime, Greenberg faced frequent charges that he was prejudicial and dogmatic. He constantly defended himself against accusations of prejudice but usually declined to move against complaints about dogmatism. Dogmatism could be a risk worth taking when it led in the direction of defining modernism. He would assert a number of times, including in a review of the 1944 "Art in Progress" exhibition at the Museum of Modern Art, that "The extreme eclecticism now prevailing in art is unhealthy, and it should be counteracted, even at the risk of dogmatism and intolerance. Inevitably, the museum makes enemies. Let it make them for good reasons" (O'Brian 1:213). What he never understood was the degree to which personal and social biases entered into what he wanted to imagine were pure and free aesthetic judgments. Careful reading of his writings reveals that Greenberg harbored prejudices shared by many Americans after World War II against communism and its advocacy of politically engaged art, aspects of German culture, and so on. These assumptions led to his questioning Germanic art (sometimes in complex and convoluted ways) and to his valorizing what he called French-based modern art and cubism. This thought process produced a narrow, canonical reading of modernism that pushed the contributions of artists with Germanic connections to a problematic periphery in Greenberg's and many of his followers' influential accounts.

Note

1. All Clement Greenberg quotations are from O'Brian unless Greenberg's own *Art and Culture* provides a version of the text not in O'Brian's comprehensive compendium. I would like to thank Charlotte Melin and Randall Van Schepen for valuable contributions that they made to this chapter.

Section VI

The Politics of Visual Culture in the Third Reich

Framing Sight: Modernism and Nazi Visual Culture

Lutz Koepnick

I

Seminal theorists of the visual from Walter Benjamin to Jonathan Crary have defined modern visual culture in terms of a dialectic between physiological structures and newly emerging methods of social engineering. In general, these theorists consider the rise of modern visual culture as a development that produced fundamentally unstable, differential, and contested ways of how people saw, how they were able to see, and how they saw this seeing. Epistemologically speaking, it was only after the advent of the modern that we were able to make conceptual distinctions between vision and visuality in the first place—between sight as a biological datum and sight as a social fact. More specifically, however, the modernity of modern visual culture is seen, on the one hand, as the decentered unified models of disembodied looking. It is traced as a process that lodged vision in the interiority of a corporeal, mobile, and essentially distracted viewer, stressed the spatial and temporal contingencies of visual perception, and hence elevated the problem of attention to the hallmark of individual experience. On the other hand, however, what makes modern visual culture modern is understood in regard to the advent of various techniques of power that have come to exploit, discipline, reframe, or recontain the aleatory practices of embodied viewing, techniques whose primary purpose was to close out human agency and the transformative energies of subjective looking. It was one of the defining trademarks of modern visual culture that within its own rhetoric, representations, and modalities it often sought to disavow its constitutive multiplicity and make—in Hal Foster's words—"its many social visualities one essential vision, or to order them in a natural hierarchy of sight" (*Vision and Visuality* ix). Though we cannot think of modern visual culture without thinking of all the machineries that mediated and decentered vision ever since the early nineteenth century, we therefore have to pay equal respect to how these machineries often turned vision into something measurable and calculable, and thus homogenized the fractured field of modern visual perception. For every modernist attempt to position the individual as an active and autonomous producer of visual experience, there were as many practices, techniques, and institutions that made use of subjective vision to subject the individual to improved measures of power, Benjamin's aestheticization of politics, Foucault's panopticum, and Debord's spectacle being only the most salient examples. To speak of the modernity of modern visual culture, then, does not only mean to speak of how the human eye encountered the accelerated temporalities and unfixed spaces of industrial life. It means to tax the different ways in which modern societies implicated visual perception in a double history of subjectification and subjugation—a history that at once enabled distracted ways of seeing the world and refocused the viewer's sight and attention.

Theorists of modern visuality have repeatedly resorted to the conceptual model of architecture in order to elucidate the double history of modern looking. Think, for instance, of Walter Benjamin's discussion of vision in the age of mechanical reproducibility. What structures our perception of built space, Benjamin wrote in 1935, is habit rather than contemplation, tactile appropriation rather than distanciating observation: "Buildings are appropriated in a twofold manner: by use and by perception—or rather, by touch and sight. Such appropriation cannot be understood in terms of the attentive concentration of a tourist before a famous building" (*Illuminations* 240). In Benjamin's understanding, vision crosses the threshold of the modern whenever the architectural model becomes the order of the day and whenever, in our conceptual understanding, sight—somewhat ironically—ceases to be purely optical. Though tactile and haptical forms of vision have of course always existed, modern visual culture renders explicit our need to negotiate touch and use, institutional frameworks and transitory movements as the very condition for the possibility of seeing what is around us. In a modern world in which mediated images allow us to get hold of distant objects at very close range, sight is no longer merely about how and what we see. It becomes deeply entangled with nonoptical domains of sensual perception and signification. In Benjamin's age of mechanical reproduction, then, the study of visual culture and perception cannot be separated from the study of how we—by negotiating the relation of technology and the human—construct, inhabit, transform, and patrol space. What makes vision modern is that we cannot speak about it without speaking about the organization of our cultural geography in general, that is to say, examine (1) the codified ways of producing space that order social relations from above, (2) the peculiar patterns by which people inhabit certain places with their bodies, and (3) the shifting symbols, experiences, and unconscious associations that people draw on in order to understand existing spaces as meaningful.

Whereas sight, for Benjamin, becomes modern by becoming embodied and architectural, architecture's modernity—according to Beatriz Colomina—can be measured by the extent to which it engages with the rise of modern media. With the rise of the modern, architectural configurations cease to be bounded structures juxtaposing interior and exterior spaces, the public and the private. Modern architecture disrupts such boundaries, recasting the inside as outside, the private as public, and night as day. It upsets older hierarchies such as the ones between surface and depth, street and interior, and the near and the far. If perception for the modern city dweller becomes tied to transience and mobility, it also does for the inhabitant of the interior spaces of modern architectural structures. The house here no longer serves as a protected and transparent window onto the world. Instead, it produces this world as an assemblage of fleeting impressions in the first place. Modern architecture transforms the house into a mechanism to see the world as a sequence of shifting images. Its windows turn the outside world into a source of consumable images, display the interior to the gaze of outside, and thus urge us to tailor our domesticity to the shifting expectations of the public. Similar to what we experience in a movie theater, in modern architecture the point of view is never a fixed one. With modernity, the window is no longer a hole in the wall granting the dweller stable, distanced, and Olympian viewing positions. Rather, windows and walls themselves become transitory and moving images. They become the media that destabilize early modern models of disembodied vision and linear perspective, and in this way they take over the role of what in contemporary parlance we call interfaces: meeting-points between dissimilar realities that reconstitute and transform whatever we may find on either side of their common boundaries (Manovich 62–115).

This section examines the way in which Adolf Hitler's legendary Berghof retreat at the Obersalzberg referenced the omnipresence of media in modern society in order to convert built space into an interface producing moving images and offering models of seeing the world. The Third Reich has often been described as a society using and abusing modern visual culture so as to stage totalitarian power as an auratic presence. Nazi Germany, so the argument goes, embraced modern machines of reproduction and image making in order to transform the state into a fascinating attraction. One of the tasks of the following pages is to assess the political dimensions and normative underpinnings of Nazi visual culture and modernism. How, I ask, did the Berghof calibrate what Benjamin defined as the hallmark of modern vision, namely touch and use? To what extent did its window designs allow for what Colomina considers as the defining moment of modern architecture, namely mobile perception? And last but not the least, how can we develop adequate measures in order to assess the mingling of old and new, the archaic and the technological, the natural and the mediated, in Nazi architecture and visual culture?

The purpose of the following remarks is not to argue that Nazi culture historically succeeded in reducing the competing strands of modern visual culture to one single and unified regime of looking. Other modes of modern seeing and visual pleasure clearly existed aside from the model suggested by the Berghof and were of essential importance to integrate Nazi society as a society of the spectacle. What I am tracing in this chapter instead is the material dynamic of an ideological aspiration, namely the desire to contain the multiplicity of modern embodied vision in order to discipline the body and fortify imperial points of view. And yet, Hitler's Berghof is emblematic of larger segments of Nazi visual culture, including commercial entertainment cinema, in its embrace of the modern even when it intended to escape it. The larger question raised by the Berghof regarding the production of visual space during the Nazi period is not whether Nazi visual culture was modern or not, but rather whether and how we can identify meaningful criteria in order to distinguish between different and competing projects of visual and spatial modernization. A few comments about Marcel Odenbach's 2001 video installation *The Big Window* concludes my discussion. Odenbach's installation, I argue here, explored the extent to which structures such as Berghof embraced modern media in order to engineer spontaneity and mobilize romantic myths of natural beauty for the purpose of domination. But even though Odenbach's project rejected the totalitarian possibilities of modern seeing, it did not desert the hope for alternate models of modern vision, models coupled to ideas of transformation, critique, and emancipation.

II

In his preface to the 1935 edition of Heinrich Hoffmann's coffee table book, *Hitler wie ihn keiner kennt* (*The Hitler Nobody Knows*), Baldur von Schirach wrote:

> To be popular means to be photographed a lot. Adolf Hitler has always resisted becoming an object of photography. In particular twelve years ago, when his name emerged for the first time from the darkness of anonymity, he was a declared enemy of the camera. Back then, the illustrated press of the whole world tried to obtain a picture of the Führer. Without success. In spite of monetary offers of all sorts, Hitler categorically refused to have his picture taken for the sake of reproduction. (Hoffmann xi)

Considering the millions of Hitler fan pictures and coffee table books that circulated throughout the 1930s and early 1940s, not much seems to have remained of Hitler's initial camera shyness. Contrary to the Führer's media politics of the 1920s, Hoffmann's und Leni Riefenstahl's Hitler images of the 1930s clearly presented the Führer as an exhibitionist of first rank: a statesman eager to showcase his ideological beliefs and moral values in front of the camera. And yet, as if wanting to return to his early "darkness of anonymity," Hitler in the course of his rule, became ever more eager to escape the media's windows of publicity. He withdrew from sight and reproduction. His remote Obersalzberg domicile allowed Hitler to inhabit spaces that seemed to shut out public visibility. This structure provided a site at which one could look at things without being looked at by cameras, a site at which Hitler could withdraw from his role as a charismatic leader. And yet, in occupying this sanctuary, did Hitler really break away from the burdens of the camera? Did this place, for Hitler, really restore a sense of privacy and interiority, untouched by the interfaces of modern reproduction?

In the summer of 1935, Hitler decided drastically to reshape his unassuming country house at the Obersalzberg into a more stately domicile, known as the Berghof (see Schaffing et al.). Hitler's renovation plans resulted in what Obersalzberg locals experienced as a fundamental modernization of their natural surroundings. In order to secure both the privacy and magic of Hitler's mountain, the Führer's aides not only had to confiscate forests and tear down existing farm houses, but also construct new networks of roads and promenades, as well as to engineer a complex system of escape tunnels and underground shelters. According to Albert Speer's memories, Hitler himself designed the ground plans and cross-sections for his new country residence—much to the dismay of the Third Reich's master architect:

> A huge picture window in the living room, famous for its size and the fact that it could be lowered, was Hitler's pride. It offered a view of the Untersberg, Berchtesgarden, and Salzburg. However, Hitler had been inspired to situate his garage underneath this window; when the wind was unfavorable, a strong smell of gasoline penetrated into the living room. All in all, this was a ground plan that would have been graded D by any professor at an institute of technology. On the other hand, these very clumsinesses gave the Berghof a strongly personal note. The place was still geared to the simple activities of a former weekend cottage, merely expanded to vast proportions. (86)

Speer's disdain for the Berghof exposes some of the central elements, not only of Hitler's interest in architecture, but of Nazi aesthetics in general, including Speer's own designs. Hitler's passion for built space privileged the stimulation of certain effects in the viewer over a building's structural integrity. He deliberately designed the new Berghof as a mechanism to collect sublime visual sensations and to open up monumental views of the surrounding landscape. In fact, Hitler conceived of this panorama window as a self-effacing interface between exterior and interior spaces, between the landscapes of nature and those of civilization. House residents may have smelled the fumes of cars, but their visual perception was entertained with the illusion of dwelling in nature, of inhabiting a clearing within the surrounding forests and mountain landscape. Professional architects may have given Hitler a failing grade, but the Berghof's structural failings were extraordinarily systematic. In so many ways, they resulted from Hitler's overriding ambition to disguise architecture as nature and spontaneity; to engineer a dreamlike semblance of natural authenticity. Hitler's Berghof was not simply meant to rest safely in its environment, but to embody an organic extension of that very landscape in which it rested.

Speer's comments about the Berghof are intriguing and to the point. What they ignore, however, is the intrinsic modernity of Hitler's design, that is, the way in which his new Berghof accessed nature, not in strict opposition to urban culture and technological sophistication, but in secret engagement with the modern, especially the modernity of twentieth-century mass media. Hitler's panorama window allowed residents and visitors to behold the surrounding landscape from the Berghof's most emblematic room: the so-called Great Hall. It was here that Hitler welcomed his guests, took his meals, spent hours having conversations, and last but not the least consumed the latest UFA and Hollywood products with his associates. At a right angle to the impressive picture window, a huge tapestry—showing three equestrian figures in a natural setting—concealed a private film screen. What is striking, of course, is the curious similitude between tapestry and picture window. Both could be removed to open up views on gripping attractions; both relied on advanced engineering in order to entertain the viewer with illusions of wholeness and utopian reconciliation; and both encouraged horizontal over vertical views, the screen at the classical aspect ratio of 4:3 and the picture window at the—shall we say: widescreen—ratio of roughly 2.1:1 (a little less than Cinema Scope's 2.55:1). No matter whether we think that the window replicated the screen or that the screen copied the window, what is important to note is the fact that Hitler's Great Hall at the Berghof was deliberately designed as a viewing machine to gather views, as a lens taking and projecting moving pictures. It was camera and screen at once, an architectural structure simultaneously able to frame natural settings as moving pictures and naturalize cultural products into elemental forces.

The curious modernism of Hitler's Berghof design, as well as its limitations, become the clearest when compared to the window designs of avant-garde architects such as Le Corbusier. In the course of the 1920s Le Corbusier developed a number of residential projects whose primary function was to illustrate the power of horizontal windows to refashion how residents viewed urban and natural landscapes. Unlike his French colleague Auguste Perret, who maintained that vertical windows reproduced most realistic and complete impressions of exterior space—impressions giving a "natural" sense of perspectival depth—Le Corbusier in his designs polemically favored the horizontal window because it cut out both the visual foreground and the sky and thus undermined illusions of spatial depth. In the viewpoint of Le Corbusier, a window was not meant to open transparent views onto the world. Instead, it was supposed to show landscapes as if they were planar projections adhering to the windows' screen itself. The horizontal window's point was to break the connection between being in a landscape and seeing it, to explore and emphasize the window as a site of visual production and nontransparent mediation. Furthermore, operating like cameras, Le Corbusier's houses and windows were supposed to extend a sense of transience and mobility. They were designed like a "box in the air, pierced all around, without interruption" (Le Corbusier 132), as the architect explained in 1930, and they could be moved to any place—to Paris or the Saharan desert, to Biarritz or Argentine. As viewing apparati to collect views, Le Corbusier's box houses were in some sense immaterial. According to Colomina, these structures were:

> no more than a series of views choreographed by the visitor, the way a filmmaker effects the montage of a film. Significantly, Le Corbusier [. . .] represented some of his projects [. . .] in the form of a series of sketches grouped together and representing the perception of the house by a moving eye. As has been noted, these drawings suggest film storyboards, each of the images a still. (312)

In Le Corbusier's designs of this period, the house's window collapsed former boundaries between interior and exterior, the public and the private. Rather than framing the resident's body or simply guiding the user's eye, Le Corbusier's windows became mechanical substitutes for the resident's body—interfaces charged with transformative powers.

Like Le Corbusier, Hitler intended his expanded Berghof as a viewing machine projecting the landscape and screening magnificent horizontal views. His new domicile was drawn with a moving picture, a film-like impression, in mind. It was designed as a frame for that impression, one that converted mere acts of looking into sublime experiences of seeing. Unlike Le Corbusier, however, Hitler was of course not concerned with building a house that could be moved to other places. Considered an organic extension of nature, the materiality of the Berghof instead was to root its inhabitants firmly in the ground, in nature's clearing. For Hitler, the Berghof provided a space of calm and recluse, a space where he could at once relax from and gear up for his public appearances. Rather than encouraging the viewer to become a film editor whose task was to splice different viewing angles into one montage construct, Hitler's house favored the autarky of the frame and the stability of uncut spatial perspectives. Whereas Le Corbusier's house urged its residents to synthesize individual frames and create their own narratives of movement, Hitler's panorama window unified different perspectives and unfettered visual perception from the viewer's narrative drive. Hitler's Berghof presented natural surroundings as display and attraction. Rather than producing detached contemplation or absorbing the viewers, the window appealed to their curiosity. This window seemingly confronted the viewers' senses with the aim of producing not a self-contained world of startling representations, but lodging seductive equations of power and sight directly in the beholders' senses. Le Corbusier's storyboard house, by contrast, positioned the occupant as a moving observer whose pleasures were directed, not at the individual displays themselves, but at their (ever-changing) narrative sequencing. Le Corbusier's windows opened a fragmented image space in whose discontinuities the user was meant to insert the possibility of meaningful narration, understood here as an open-ended activity that in establishing connections—connections between people, objects, sites, and different temporalities—allows us to establish a sense for the aleatory and transitional nature of historical time.

III

Both Hitler's and Le Corbusier's designs (re)presented surrounding space in direct engagement with the omnipresence of mass media and technologies of recording in twentieth-century culture. The difference of their designs, however, resulted from different conceptions of spatial coherence and articulation, of the relationship between visual pleasure and narrative temporality, of why and how picture makers should create impressions of continuity. Far from allowing Hitler to escape the burdens of mechanical reproduction and publicity, then, the Berghof incorporated the inevitable presence of modern mass media in order to conjure impressions of privacy and the elemental. Industrialized perception here situated architecture as a symbiotic expansion of sublime landscapes. It engineered reciprocal relations between the spaces of nature and those of civilization, between the archaic and the historical.

It is this particular modernization of sight—the naturalization of Hitler's rule as one of and over the whole array of modern media—that was at the core of a 2001 video installation by Marcel Odenbach, entitled *The Big Window* (Das große Fenster). This installation consisted of six widescreen television sets positioned in front of the window panes of Germany's perhaps the most spectacular exhibition site: the gallery on top of the Zugspitze, which opens magnificent views on Alpine landscapes close to the former site of Hitler's Berghof. All six video screens showed one and the same twelve-minute-nineteen-seconds film, an assemblage of fiction and nonfiction footage shot by Odenbach himself. In its main sequences, this video offers breathtaking images of a wintry mountainscape, at times seen through the grid of a horizontal window, at times seen without any further framing device. Every now and then, a hand will move a curtain across the screen in order to block our gaze temporarily and mark the beginning of a new chapter. In addition, Odenbach will periodically turn curtain and panorama window into projection screens themselves, displaying moving images that—as we see in the moment—trouble our impression of pristine landscapes and unadulterated looking. A seventh monitor, situated in the rear of the gallery, plays a second video of equal length called *The Spectacles* (Die Brille). Though the images on this second video screen are of much less interest than the exhibit's main attraction, they do serve an important function, namely to simulate the position of the installation's viewer within the perimeters of the show itself.

Ever since the mid-1970s, Odenbach's video installations have investigated the role of photography, film, and video in competing constructions of memory and history, of race, ethnicity, and sexual identity. For Odenbach, to engage with political and social issues—and, more specifically, to recall the burdens of Germany's history of violence and extermination—is always also to engage with the vicissitudes of industrialized perception and mass-mediated representation. A bricoleur par excellence, Odenbach assembles images of the past so as to explore and reframe their impact on the present. His installations picture history as a layered process whose meanings are shifting and unstable in spite of all historical attempts to contain multiplicity and to order conflicting perspectives into one essential model of understanding the world. Again and again, Odenbach wants to put agency and difference back into history even where historical conditions and existing strategies of political representation seemed to deny any sense of difference, subjectivity, and sensual experience. In Dan Cameron's word, Odenbach's work is thus first and foremost dedicated to "uncovering the hidden nature of power: how it is practiced unthinkingly, the way its symbols permeate social behavior, and the degree to which its significance is minimized by those who are its most ardent practitioners" (15).

Odenbach's *The Big Window* continues this line of inquiry. The video begins with two different shots of workers shuffling soil and moving construction materials during the renovation period of Hitler's Berghof in the mid-1930. We cut to a close-up of Hitler. Positioned in front of his refurbished domicile, he allows his gaze to wander slowly across the landscape around him. Next, we cut to what according to classical editing rules must be understood as a subjective point-of-view shot. The camera pans across a majestic mountain panorama as if permitting the viewer to watch natural surroundings through Hitler's imperial eyes. What follows is the video's brief title sequence, interspersed first by two consecutive shots showing Hitler as he walks up the stairs to the Berghof and, second, by a medium shot of Hitler taking position in and possession of the Berghof's interior while turning his gaze silently from right to left. In these first seven shots, Odenbach thus already lays out for us the major themes and premises of this installation: the relation of physical movement and visual perception; the reciprocal blurring of boundaries between interior and exterior spaces, between the subject and the object of looking; the work it takes to enable visual pleasure and awe-inspiring viewing positions; the mediated nature of what strikes the viewer as the mountain's magnificent immediacy. In this opening sequence, acts of panoramic looking are unmistakably marked as enactments of power. Hitler's gaze in fact is that of a film camera, one that renders movement and power, aesthetic pleasure and authority, form and domination, as mutually exchangeable. Modern techniques of building and representing space here are shown as actively constructing the countryside as a site of wonder and enchantment. They subject human bodies and remodel natural topographies in order to produce nature as image—as a sublime experience of first rank.

After the end of this opening sequence, we cut to the video's signature shot: the image of snow-covered mountains as seen through the grid of a panorama window. This footage is shot by Odenbach himself, as much as the recurring shots that show a hand drawing a curtain across the screen. For the next ten minutes, this window and curtain will serve as a projection screen: a site recalling how Nazi visual culture engineered emotions and produced fantasy, how it used moving images to mobilize people's bodies and anaestheticize perception. We see historical footage of Adolf Hitler greeting various guests at his Berghof compound—diplomats, military personnel, movie stars, master architects, civilians, and local children. We behold images of Hitler visiting an art exhibit at the Haus der Deutschen Kunst in Munich. We witness footage of a 1934 parade of SS and Labor Force members in Nuremberg as captured in *Triumph of the Will*; a clip from the opening of Leni Riefenstahl's 1938 *Olympia*, showing the beautiful forms of well-trained athletes in classical poses; and the sight of Hans Albers in the role of Baron Münchhausen as he sails on top of a canon ball through the air and waves his hat at the viewer. And then, after another curtain, we cut to aerial shots of ruined German cities at the end of World

War II; as well as to footage showing British forces as they visit the damaged Berghof and take a look at and through what is left of Hitler's erstwhile panorama window. Intermittent sounds accompany all these projections: the chirping of birds; Hitler speaking over the radio in 1933 to commend the Nazis' "national revolution"; a brief excerpt from a Hitler speech, which defines true art and the beautiful as the representation of all that is natural and healthy; the voices of Labor Force members identifying their regional identities; party rally drumrolls; the clattering of dishes and cutlery; and finally the sounds of at once tragic and commanding symphonic music.

Fredric Jameson and others have described postmodern visual culture in terms of a paradoxical return of the aesthetic. In so many ways, postmodern art and thought endorses the nearly seamless integration of art, culture, economic, and politics today in order to turn modernism's quest for aesthetic autonomy—the conception of the artistic subject as an autonomous and innocent producer of visual experiences—into a viable commodity. Under the sign of the postmodern, nostalgic glimpses of aesthetic autonomy emerge, not in opposition to, but as an effect of the market and the geopolitical rule of capital. Nothing is more foreign to Marcel Odenbach's *The Big Window* than this attempt to reinvent pure vision and aesthetic autonomy. What Odenbach's layering of images and perspectives, of sights and sounds, exposes is that there is no such thing as an innocent eye, no matter whether we cast our gaze at natural landscapes or sublime artworks. Visual perception, for Odenbach, is a historical product, a result of articulation and negotiation. It is dependent on changing cultural configurations, on competing discursive, technological, and political formations, even if certain visual regimes deny the shifting character of human sight and dictate one essential model of vision. In the last shot of *The Big Window*, Odenbach allows us to cast a direct glance at his Alpine mountainscape. Neither the curtain nor the curiously disembodied hand, neither projected images nor the window's earlier grid seem to block or distort our gaze any longer. And yet, in light of what we have seen during the previous twelve minutes, and as positioned in front of the gallery's own window frame, there is no way not to take the final image on screen for what it is: a product of technological mediation, a special effect. In drawing our awareness to the frames that make perception possible in the first place, Odenbach opens a window onto visual practices that oppose delusions of aesthetic self-sufficiency and imperial control. Sight in Odenbach might have always already lost its innocence. But in contrast to many postmodern neoaesthetes, Odenbach's work endorses the impurity of sight and the irrevocability of historical mediation as necessary conditions to formulate counterhegemonic models of seeing—models of modern seeing that are centered around nothing less than the idea of individual emancipation, mutual recognition, and scopic reciprocity.

A Woman beside Herself: Art and Its Other in Nazi Movies

Linda Schulte-Sasse

I want to recall two moments from two Nazi films two years apart, in which a woman stands literally beside herself. *Venus Before the Court* (Venus vor Gericht, 1941) places a woman in a courtroom next to a nude statue, which she identifies as a representation of her own body. In *Freed Hands* (Befreite Hände, 1939), a young woman sculpts her own stone bust. If the first woman experiences a horror we have all endured in our dreams—standing, for all intents and purposes, naked in public—the second woman is effectively bodiless, since her art rendition has no body and her human body is covered by a clinician's white coat. The statue in the first case is in every sense complete (*vollkommen*—with all its Nazi implications), the bust is in progress. Such differences notwithstanding, it is striking how both movies are obsessed with a kind of doubling, whereby the real, flesh-and-blood woman is diminished by her larger-than-life other, yet arguably enhanced in her very diminution, in her subordination of self to art. And in both, the flesh-and-blood and aesthetic reproduction are the effect of cinema, are *not there*. At a point when National Socialism had clearly consolidated its power, why was it "hammering in" (literally and metaphorically) this preoccupation with art and women in the movies?

Though just two of 1,094 Nazi films are discussed here, these are unusual in using popular genres (courtroom- and melodrama respectively) to think out loud about Nazi art. For Nazism to think about itself *was* to think about art. One could say cynically that Hitler was a more successful artist than his dossier at the Vienna art conservatory suggested; he created history's most impressive art movement, with a *Gesamtkunstwerk* character remarked upon by Nazis and their critics alike. Art in Nazism is of course never "just" art, it is a spiritual-moral force permeating everything and aspiring to what Peter Bürger defines as the goal of the avant-garde, to lead the aesthetic back into life (*Theory* 49). Nazism had no choice but to be obsessed with art, given that its *telos* of a pure racial, organic community can work only in the aesthetic.

A number of recent critics have admonished us against blithely labeling Nazi art, or Nazism itself, anti-modern. This easy categorization relies too heavily on NS rhetoric, on what in fact was a *construction* of a polar distinction that compensated for Nazism's own lack of aesthetic vision and disguised its affinities with modernism. Brandon Taylor has gone a step further in arguing that one can refer to NS art as postmodernist in its self-presentation as the next stage, the art of our times (128–43). I have two aims here: first, to see what happens when those bombastic Nazi sculptures wander into a medium that makes them give up their mass and materiality. What do these films say about Nazi art and its relationship to modernity and life itself, and what does this have to do with women as the "givers of life"? Why the doubling?

Second, prompted by Taylor's use of the word postmodern, I wonder if any of the issues surrounding postmodernism might be relevant in this encounter between two art forms. Obviously a major postmodern theme has been the blurring of boundaries among discourses and media, between high and low culture. As these two films pit "real" Nazi art against its Other, each will strike a precarious balance between celebrating the accessibility and universal appeal of Nazi art and distancing Nazi from mass art. This balance is rendered more precarious by the fact that these are *not* "art films" but decidedly *movies* about art. In this sense we could say the statues *condescend* to costar in the movies. What kind of relationship exists between high art and the mass medium that deals with it; if there is a tension, is it perceptible? Finally, if postmodern art about art is marked by a sense of saturation, a *knowing* that nothing is original any more, is there any such knowing, any reflexivity or self-knowledge in Nazi art about art?

This second line of questioning is the hard part, going beyond ideology critique into questions of discursive cross-pollination, textual rupture, and subject effect. If the first inquiry lets me play Perry Mason, making the film break down on the stand and confess what it is *really* saying, in the second, I am reduced to the film noir detective, always already victimized by the dazzle of what I am trying to investigate. Just when I am proud to have mastered the object (in this case classical cinema, whose whole mode of operation aims at making me *forget* itself), it eludes me or does a number on me. With this forewarning, let me turn to my examples.

Venus before the Court: Hans Zerlett, 1941

In 1930 the nude statue of a woman dug up by accident in a Bavarian village causes a sensation when art authorities declare it to be an undiscovered masterpiece from ancient Greece, a Venus figure over 2,000 years old. The claim of the artist Hans Brake that he made the sculpture and buried it as a prank to show his distaste for fashionable modernist art threatens art dealers, art experts, and Berlin's culture minister, who have staked both reputation and financial gain on the statue being genuine. They arrange to have Brake take his claim to court, knowing he has no reliable witnesses. As Brake is about to be convicted of perjury, Charlotte Böller, Brake's model for the sculpture, steps forward as the decisive witness on his behalf.

Venus before the Court seems to have been produced for the few who did not make it to the (in)famous 1937 Munich exhibition on "Degenerate Art." Its surface antagonism is between an authentic Nazi art and modernist pseudo-art, which we see exhibited in the gallery of the Jewish art dealer Benjamin Hecht; at its worst the film degenerates into a treatise on the Nazi discourse of beauty. Brake testifies in court that he made the statue to prove: "Today not the beautiful but the ugly body is glorified! One is 'breaking ground' in the art world when one paints a woman to look like a gorilla's wife!" With its setting in the Weimar Republic the film has the feel of early NS films that condense under the signifier "Weimar" an exploitative capitalism, Jewishness, democracy, and state-sponsored ugliness. Moreover like early programmatic films, this one refers explicitly to National Socialism as the sole force opposing "Weimar" modernity: Hans Brake's NS affiliation is a frequent topic in the film; moreover his name evokes the name of Nazism's premiere sculptor, Arno Breker.

The film also echoes Nazi art theorists who invoked beauty as a racially grounded principle of exclusion. It is no coincidence that *Venus before the Court* (and *Freed Hands*) feature sculpture rather than painting; sculpture was Nazism's most privileged medium, and considered singularly capable of representing Aryan perfection. While a race "expert" like Karl Weinländer could demonstrate the racial character of Asians, blacks, or aborigines via photographs, he considered only stone sculpture capable of capturing the Aryan (Wolpert 227). And as Klaus Wolpert stresses, the monomaniacal representation of the naked body was one of the few distinguishing traits of NS sculpture; it celebrated the body "untouched by the stigma of decay or 'degeneration,' of the ugliness of everyday life and the sickness of the times" (230). As a measure of *Lebenswert* (the value of a life), beauty *needs* ugliness, just as Nazism needs the Jew as the negative element indispensable to the ideal of racial purity. Beauty provides evidence that all men are *not* created equal, a notion Alfred Rosenberg invokes against "the teaching of democratic human rights, with which European society emerges effectively as the protector of the inferior, sick, crippled, criminal and foul" (169). Hence Venus is charged with saving much more than a natural beauty ideal; she is charged with saving culture itself.

At the heart of the film is a problem of vision: the world of "Weimar" culture needs to learn to see, more precisely to UN-learn, *verlernen*, a perversion of seeing. A taste for modernist art requires a willful violence to the instinct, exemplified by a comic moment in which a museum employee rushes to correct the position of an abstract painting: "The picture goes *this* way," she says, scandalized, as if the "right" position could render the picture intelligible to museum visitors. The problem in the film is not, however, that people do *not* see that "real" art is beautiful, but rather one of recognizing what real art *is*, and the film's pedagogy is based on a deception: Nazi art is recognized as real art only when it is misrecognized as Greek art. Its misrecognition as Greek art allows it to be exploited by "Weimar"; implicitly, then, modernist art is recognized as false only when the first part of the equation is exposed, when "real" Nazi art is proven true by being proven false. The artist Hans Brake undertakes a kind of Brechtian "sociological experiment," he is Professor Sokal *avant la lettre*, planting the fake for the delicious—and somewhat malicious—pleasure of embarrassing the experts.

Real art in the film's terms is by definition *not* cryptic or intellectualized, but highly transparent. Brake just makes "art that is still art." An operative word here is *still*, which brings us to the temporal dimension of Nazi aesthetics and the reference to antiquity that is the precondition for Brake's prank *and* his ensnarement by it. Nazi discourse is not just about going back to the past. It involves several notions of the "new" running parallel to each other. For Weimar modernity the "new" represents an accelerated, instrumentalized "progress"; the "old" makes way for exchange value; for National Socialism the "new" means the utopian perspective of a community transcending egotism, which, however, paradoxically involves a return to "old" values of antiquity. Its project is to *re*-new and render timeless an imaginary "old."

This renewal requires a superhuman effort in face of Weimar corruption, however, and if on the level of story Hans Brake is a Pygmalion "wrestling from the Gods a creature perfect in soul, spirit, and body" (Wolpert 232), on the level of image he is himself a Siegfried or a Prometheus. As if every one of his statues were a self-birth or self-creation, mise-en-scène often allows his body to build a graphic continuity with the superdimensional he-men sculptures in his atelier. Brake is, then, at once artist and art work, transforming the spirit of NS art into human character and agency. But unlike Professor Sokal, Brake is as uncalculating as he is unsubtle, making him easy prey for his adversaries. The film recodes this hopeless naiveté, however, as a positive character trait; Brake's revolutionary prank gets out of hand because he fails to understand the bureaucratized world of political, economic, legal, and linguistic machinations: "I am a sculptor, not a prosecutor," he answers when asked why he failed to preserve evidence that he made the statue. Much like Siegfried, who cannot imagine and thus anticipate the treachery of a Hagen, Brake cannot imagine that not everybody is as forthright as he is; his naiveté is idealized "proof" of his uncontaminated nature.

A similar double role applies to Charlotte. On the one hand she is pure art object, Nazism's idealized *Kulturträgerin* or bearer of culture (Richardson 71). But she literally becomes a *barer* of culture as she intervenes crucially in the story, baring the facts and implicitly herself, redeeming not only the hero but art, whose truth she proves in its falseness—how fitting that the German word *Akt* means both act and nude. While modernists in the film are literally purveyors of pornography, Charlotte's healthy nakedness is integrally linked with social health, recalling the functionalization of the female nude in Nazi art: "[It] was [. . .] used to support the idea that Germany was a 'culture,' a complete whole in which everyone participated, instead of a merely political state, a fragmentary parliamentary democracy" (Richardson 77). Taking Hans Johst's claim that "the NS state and culture are identical" to its logical conclusion, Charlotte's act of baring will ultimately unleash a flood of hidden Nazis in her own small town. Yet identification of and with her naked stone self means a kind of social death and the death of her marriage to a small-town mayor.

By casting Venus as a force of redemption, the film seemingly reverses the romantic tradition of Venus as a cold temptress embodying the lure and peril of desire, of *Entgrenzung* familiar from Tieck's *Runenberg* or Eichendorff's *Marmorbild.* Here we have a Venus domesticated, stripped of her demonic power. While the film wants to show what happens to Venus when she falls into the hands of "parasitic [*herumschmarotzende*] Jewish-Democratic artists and art experts" (we see her caged and commercially exploited), it is National Socialism that wants to *contain* Venus, strip her of her demonic power and domesticate her. You can, it suggests, have the sublime *and* the beautiful, *Be-* and *Entgrenzung,* just as you can have a *state* that is a *völkisch,* organic entity. The contradictory truth it aspires to reconcile lies in the oxymoronic condensation of the nickname "*Venus vom Acker*"; Venus of the acre, of the soil, *Blut und Boden,* just a heck of a nice *Bund deutscher Mädel* Venus—Venus as member of the Nazi "League of German Girls." (And while Brake echoes his statues, in Charlotte's case the contrast is striking between the self-confident nakedness exuded by the statue and her own diminutive, self-effacing presence as she stands in a suit and hat.)

As if it were unable to tolerate its own bombast, *Venus before the Court* alternates its pontification with a bawdy humor directed at authority of all kinds. If seeing is the film's theme, *Schadenfreude* is its subject position, and I want to cite two examples for this register. The tabloid journalist who embodies Weimar's exploitative press ironically counterpoints the film's discourse on beauty. His creation is not art but the "sensation," which he dictates in four short scenes, using his cigarette or smoke to sexually harass his secretary. In the first, a shapely blonde sits in an erotic pose that will anticipate our first cut to the ugliness of modernist art, and, with her disapproval of Venus's figure, first speaks the problem of the film: "Those hips! She couldn't show herself today!" The film counters her word ironically by dissolving to abstract statues in a Jewish art gallery. In each subsequent scene the secretary changes, becoming progressively *less* beautiful and *more* aggressive. The second secretary will interrogate the journalist regarding his sexual harassment, the third will slap him for his advances, and the fourth and final one is as ugly as he is. The sequence thus playfully advances Nazism's purported correspondence between inner and outer beauty; the last pairing serves as counterpoint to Brake and Charlotte as exemplars of the Nordic ideal.

The second example of bawdiness is the film's treatment of Charlotte's moralistic, provincial husband, played by character actor Paul Dahlke, Nazi cinema's most jilted man; he will be ditched by Brigitte Horney in *Freed Hands*, and, famously, by Marianne Hoppe in Käutner's *Romance in a Minor Key* (1943). Dahlke's impotent rage as the man who cannot bear to see his trophy wife bared to the world, and who can only scream "revolution!" when Nazis defend her honor, is almost poignant (though a subversive gaze might see him as a parody of Hitler himself). Certainly both of these examples, the husband and the journalist, reinforce the film's ideological message. But they bring in a slapstick tone, and particularly Dahlke offers an identification with blundering and impotent rage—à la Archie Bunker. The question is whether the very aggressiveness of the humor overshoots its mark, whether ideological "message" and subject effect may be at odds.

Where I find the film on more precarious ground is its relationship to mass culture. Let's backtrack a moment and ask: How threatened is real art by degenerate art in *Venus Before the Court*? On closer examination, the film's trial is a purely performative act pretending to demand a judgment. In fact, real art wins either way: if Brake's statue is a fake it is real, but if it should be declared real and he loses the case, its stature is at least as assured: only an absolute master, we are told, could have made this statue (and the film audience *knows* who the master is, of course). Real art is not as resistant, however, to commodification: the most cinematic of modes, a montage sequence, shows us a mass-produced Venus stripped of her aura, whose nakedness now serves only voyeurism and whose sexualized movement violates the motionless grace of sculpture. A single Venus dances at the Variété, followed by a multiplied Venus in a dance line recalling Siegfried Kracauer's Tiller Girls; this reference to an assembly-line aesthetic gives way to a literal assembly line turning out statuettes of Venus before she crops us as a postcard showing her "from front and rear."

If, as Andreas Huyssen tells us, modernism is plagued by "an anxiety of contamination" (*Great Divide* vii); *Venus Before the Court* displays a contamination anxiety of its own. What unleashes cultural consumption if not "real" art itself? With the tip of a hat, the very transparency and *Völkishness* to which Nazi art aspires, its synthesis of the sublime and the accessible—falls prey to mass frenzy, reproducibility, trivialization, and *Verkitschung*. Of course the film blames this on Weimar, but fails to resolve the fact that the "sensation" would hardly be possible without the very transparency so constitutive of the championed aesthetic, without Nazism's own ambivalence toward the mass and the sublime. Nor does it resolve the fact that the sensation produces *pleasure* for a public in and outside of the movie.

Freed Hands: 1939, Hans Schweikart

The protagonist Dürthen carves wooden figures while tending sheep in East Frisia. She refuses to marry Thomsen, the father of her child Jens, and is in love with the local Junker's son, Joachim von Erken. A successful artisan, Kersten Thomas, visits the estate, and she invites Dürthen to become her protégé. Only when the son Jens dies in an accident does Dürthen head for Berlin to work in Kersten's figurine production. The sculptor Professor Wolfram becomes her mentor, and although Joachim wants to marry her, Dürthen leaves him to sculpt with Wolfram.

The Other of art in *Freed Hands* is not art at all but the mass-produced kitsch objects that mean *business* to Kersten. Again this film will dismiss non-art (referring pejoratively to Kersten's art as *ein Betrieb*, a business), but without *Venus Before the Court*'s belligerence. *Freed Hands* is more a *Bildungsroman*, a tale of internal versus external struggle, of decision versus judgment, of an artist versus an artwork. Here the whole film works on the principle of doubles or, more often, inverted doubles. Dürthen (poor, unsophisticated, gifted) has her inverted double in her first (false) mentor, the glamorous, sophisticated, and untalented Kersten Thomas, who in turn has a more worthy double in the serious sculptor Professor Wolfram. The workaholic Wolfram has another inverted double in *Lebenskünstler* Joachim, whom Dürthen imagines as the ideal father for her child, making him an inversion of Thomsen, the rejected biological father (in this sense we can also speak of family as doubled).

This mirroring culminates in the self-doubling of Dürthen I alluded to: it is marked in stations by a double loss that frees up her two hands. The first loss is literally by accident when her son dies; the second is a willful act, as she abandons her lover and love itself. Note how family is dispatched in this film, too; little Jens's only function is to die and become the lost object. If Dürthen is the only real female genius figure in Nazi movies, she does not lose her mother function, but merely advances to a more sublime form of reproduction, recreating her son and self as more than themselves.

Again, "real" art owes a debt to the spirit of antiquity, but the film will spatialize time through parallel trips Wolfram (alone) and Joachim (with Dürthen) make to Italy. A montage sequence shows Dürthen eating spaghetti, riding a donkey, romping in the surf—until she accidentally runs into Professor Wolfram. Always a barrel of laughs, the professor instantly turns Italy into an art appreciation field trip, snatching Dürthen off on a tour of ancient sculptures that make her recode "the happiest days of my life" as a pathetic waste of time. Italy shifts from a signifier of participation to one of contemplative observation, from recess to school, escape to discovery, and, by implication, from union to celibacy.

In general the effect of art in this film is to *immobilize*, as can be demonstrated by contrasting the first coming together of Dürthen with her two "lovers." Dürthen and Joachim find each other in a frenetic folk dance early on in the film, enjoying a spontaneous loss of self to the other in sensuous movement, bodily harmony, and pleasure. Dürthen and Professor Wolfram find each other in the context of *high* culture, *sitting* in a concert hall listening to Beethoven's Fifth, in which movement is purely emotional, and pleasure is that of pathos, loss, and pain. Not only does art render objects impervious to time, and not only does the experience of great art make one forget time, but time comes to a standstill when art is being created. "Doing" art means entering an autistic world where desire cedes to drive. At the beginning of the film, Dürthen carves in the service of desire (eyeline matches show her watching Joachim ride the horizon on horseback as she carves him), fantasy, and life (she makes toys as gifts). "Serious" art begins the moment she carves death, her son's head (of which the professor ironically says "it is alive!"). It only remains for Dürthen to proclaim that "paradise" (Italy with Joachim) makes her "soft and limp," and to flee to a space where she can carve her own death mask (she recreates herself in progressively harder materials, first in wood and finally in stone).

Professor Wolfram serves as Dürthen's master enunciator, calling to mind the homophonic relation between enunciation and renunciation. We have already seen how he, like the Romantic *Doppelgänger*, is a disrupter of pleasure. He offers a crash course in obsessive compulsive behavior, demonstrating the art process as drive and subjugation, as when he patronizingly remarks that one of his sculptures was being uncooperative, but "now the guy will do what I want." Time is always at a standstill around him, as in the Beethoven concert or when he shows Dürthen his atelier full of giant Brekeresque sculptures. On his way to brew a cup of coffee he grabs a mallet and instantaneously loses himself in a work-induced trance. Dürthen's own pupil status ends only when she, too, becomes sublimely spacey.

Both *Venus before the Court* and *Freed Hands* depict "real" art under some kind of threat, and in both cases this art is connected to woman, her body, her loss, and conscious sacrifice, giving a new meaning to Andreas Huyssen's reference to woman as "modernism's Other" (*Great Divide* 44–62). In giving birth to an artistic perfection that defies modernity and promises eternity, woman pays with her Self. Both films know that to be timeless is to be lifeless; both are consistent with an aesthetic that sought "not the copy but the model" for a perfected, or selected, *humanity* (*ein Auslesevorbild*, Wolpert 226). The ideal subject position, then, is a state of undeadness; modernity is haunted in the films by buried objects that return, the Venus statue, the little boy reappearing in stone. They recall Klaus Wolpert's diagnosis of a beauty ideal that is unachievable (*uneinholbar*) as "the instruction to murder," (*die Anweisung zum Mord*, Wolpert 234).

Can we reach a verdict on how these movies reconcile their Nazi "message" with their own status as classical films? *Venus before the Court* buries its own celebration of undeadness in the false reconciliation of a fairy tale ending where social death becomes liberation. The concluding shot shows the ideal Aryan profiles of Brake and Charlotte gazing lovingly at each other; the irksome wedding photo that hovered between them before is now replaced by Venus, who fills the last image, having salvaged love along with the legal, social, economic, class, and aesthetic system. Yet the movie lets its disavowed violence against life and specifically woman seep through in a striking match on action, in which the camera cuts from an angry Hans Brake in the feminized position of pounding rugs to the same pounding gesture, this time directed at—what else?—the female body, albeit of clay, which he pounds to a pulp or what Klaus Theweleit would call a mass. We have caught Nazism red-handed, acting out its true desire.

But can we cross-examine this reading? What I am calling a Theweleitian moment may be just the most cinematic of moments involving a pleasurable release, a sleight of hand that is the fun of this medium with its distracted mode of reception, with Brake standing in as surrogate for our own aggressions.

Perhaps *Venus before the Court's* pretence *not* to know the brutality that underlies it is its concession to Hollywood-made-in-Berlin; it is a film aimed at *satisfaction*: of closure, of couple formation coupled with sadistic release. Perhaps its own message is, at least partially, contaminated by the unresolved tension between its discourses of bravado and parody, by the potential likeability of its antagonists and the built-in exploitability of its "real" art. The film is more *or less* guilty depending on whether we view the medium as working for or against the message.

Although *Freed Hands* is a harmless E film in Gert Albrecht's classification (E for *ernst*, serious with only latently political implications) while *Venus* is a nasty P for political, we can find no fewer—perhaps more—grounds for a guilty verdict in this case. For being less aggressive and propagandistic, *Freed Hands* is all the more cold-blooded in what it knows, that there can be no reconciliation between life and art, that the highest form of life is to entomb oneself, to dream of the ossification, if not metalization of the human body. It is no accident that one of the statues Wolfram shows off in Rome is Laokoon, with his dead mouth open in silent torture. Art for a *living* and for *the* living is denigrated art. The sensuousness that triumphs is necrophilia, as Dürthen repeatedly strokes dead objects (her dead son's stone head, a huge marble woman's face in Wolfram's studio, her own stone image). Far more chilling than Hans Brake's ejaculatory violence is this film's image of pounding: the relentless tap-tap in the last scene of freed up hands, hands freed of children, men, and life.

Lacking *Venus before the Court*'s boisterousness, *Freed Hands* more strongly disavows itself as mass art that is disparaging mass art to convey the notion of the sublime. It denies the tension between the Nazi aesthetic and mass art, presuming a clear opposition between Nazi art and kitsch—clear to diegetic characters if not necessarily to contemporary viewers who may, like me, fail to see much difference between the art disparaged and celebrated by the film, except in dimension and pretension. If Nazi art is inspired by antiquity, how ironic to see businesswoman Kersten taking phone orders for dashboard figurines from Greek mythology. And if the film takes the hard line in denying the satisfaction of desire fulfilled in the imaginary, it compensates with the melodramatic pleasure of loss. Its very kitsch softens the blow of the Nazi sledgehammer; the tension between the linearity of its *Bildungsroman* story of artistic growth and the circularity of its melodrama discourse were likely what motivated Alfred Rosenberg to complain that the film was "a mischmasch considered real art" (qtd. in Leiser 13), but also its commercial success. The film ends with its own highly cinematic moment of reconciliation as Dürthen's "freed" hand is grasped by Wolfram's in a tableau recalling the end of Fritz Lang's *Metropolis*; the stone replica she confronts balanced by the warm touch of a—however unconvincing—lover, an art lover. One might say this mise-en-scène is over*shadowed* by a shadow, a Promethean figure dramatically bearing a heavy stone behind and echoing Dürthen. Nonetheless, the—in every sense—pathetic image defangs what the ending otherwise is: repetition compulsion and a reversal of the atelier scene in which the professor demonstrated art as catatonic drive.

If we do not find a lot of self-reflexivity in Nazism's brand of postmodernism, we may find a homology between Fredric Jameson's remark that postmodern art is destined to be about art ("Postmodernism and Consumer Society" 155f) and the idea that a movement like Nazism was destined to produce consumer products about consumer products. Texts for consumption that, like what in the good old days they called "trivial" literature, draw strong contours between plus and minus. Like the shadow at the end of *Freed Hands*, the two films shoulder their own burden of and for culture. But they protest too much, as if hoping the language of great art they speak could cover their own roots in poor white trash, their own status as the abjected mass art that their contents dismiss. At the same time this very lowliness may *trivialize* the message itself, which is an ambivalent thing when the message itself is depressing. I have played with legal terms as a reminder that we tend to approach this cinema with the stance of a prosecutor, and that the case for an easy conviction becomes more challenging when we move beyond "pure" ideology to the workings of movies. In what other realm than the latter could kitsch and silliness serve as an argument for the defense? If these factors do not acquit the films as dangerous propaganda, they may be allowed as mitigating circumstances, or in support of "bleeding-heart liberal" arguments that the movies are mere products of their social/medial environment.

Section VII

Modernist Politics Now: Critiques of Liberalism

The Stakes of the Political According to Carl Schmitt

Chantal Mouffe

In this section I would like to bring to the fore the actuality of Schmitt and the relevance of his reflections on the political, which I take to be of crucial importance for an adequate understanding of our current predicament. It is my contention that, by allowing us to grasp the nature of the political, Schmitt can help us to visualize the shortcomings of the liberal framework that informs most political thinking nowadays. My starting point is that the political constitutes the blind spot of the dominant liberal framework that structures the "common sense" in our liberal democratic societies. This blind spot is responsible for our current incapacity to think in political terms, an incapacity that has led to the increasing dominance of a moral or juridical type of discourse. This dominance has proved to have very negative effects on the workings of democratic politics. If this trend is not reversed, the consequences can be disastrous. I first scrutinize the incapacity of liberal thought to understand the nature of the political and to acknowledge the irreducible character of antagonism, showing why this constitutes a real danger for the future of democracy. I then examine some topical issues and discuss how an approach inspired by Schmitt can enable us to see them in a completely different light. To avoid any misunderstanding, I want to stress that my aim is not to offer a history of political ideas or an exhaustive study of Schmitt, but rather to use him, sometimes against himself, as a source of inspiration to bring to the fore several shortcomings of current approaches in liberal democratic thinking.

Schmitt's Critique of Liberal Democracy

I have chosen to draw on Schmitt to examine the reasons for liberalism's blindness to the political because I think that given his brilliant and intransigent critique of liberalism, there is a lot that can be learned from him by those who are committed to the defense of liberal democratic institutions. I also believe that Schmitt provides a reflection on the political in its dimension of antagonism that is of particular relevance today. Specifically, he enables us to comprehend the manifold character of antagonism and its possibility of emerging out of very diverse relations: out of ethnicity, religion, nationality, and many other social relations. His approach is therefore extremely pertinent to grasp the transformations of the field of politics in our post–Cold War world. One of Schmitt's key theses is that liberal thought is unable to apprehend the specific nature of the political because of its deeply individualistic nature. In *The Concept of the Political* he writes:

> In a very systematic fashion liberal thought evades or ignores state and politics and moves instead in a typical always recurring polarity of two heterogeneous spheres, namely ethics and economics, intellect and trade, education and property. The critical distrust of state and politics is easily explained by the principles of a system whereby the individual must remains *terminus a quo* and *terminus ad quem*. (Schmitt 70)

Liberal thought must necessarily be blind to the political because of its individualism, which forecloses access to the mode of formation of collective identities. Yet the specificity of the political is that it deals with the formation of an "us" as opposed to a "them" and is from the outset concerned with collective forms of identification. Moreover, the political has to do with conflict and antagonisms and, by showing that every consensus is based on acts of exclusion, it reveals the limits of every rational consensus. It is no wonder, then, that liberal rationalism is bound to miss its nature. The political cannot be grasped by liberal rationalism for the simple reason that rationalism is predicated upon the negation of the irreducibility of antagonism. In other words, antagonism needs to be negated by liberalism precisely because it reveals the limits of any rational consensus and the inescapable moment of decision.

I submit that this denial of antagonism poses a very serious problem to the rationalist and individualist liberal conception as it renders it unable to envisage democratic politics in an adequate way. The political in its antagonistic dimension cannot be made to disappear simply by denying it. Such a negation leads only to impotence, namely, the impotence that characterizes liberal thought when it finds itself confronted with the emergence of antagonisms that, according to its theory, should have belonged to a bygone age when reason had not yet managed to control the "archaic" passions. This is why I consider of the utmost importance for democratic theory to listen to Schmitt when he states that the phenomenon of the political can be understood "only in the context of the ever present possibility of the friend-and-enemy grouping, regardless of the aspects which this possibility implies for morality, aesthetics, and economics" (*The Concept of the Political* 35).

Liberalism affirms that the general interest results from the free play of private interests. One of its versions, the "aggregative" model of democracy, envisages politics as the establishment of a compromise between the diverse forces competing in society. Individuals are portrayed as rational beings driven by the maximization of their own interests and basically acting in the political world in an instrumental way. It is the idea of the market applied to the domain of politics. The other, competing version of liberalism, the "deliberative" one, reacts against this instrumentalist model and aims at creating a link between morality and politics. Its advocates believe that it is possible to create a rational moral consensus by means of free discussion. In this case politics is not apprehended any more through economics but through ethics. In both cases what is erased is the dimension of antagonism, the ever present possibility of the friend/enemy discrimination that for Schmitt forms the criterion of the political. Liberals hope that by relegating all divisive questions to the sphere of the private an agreement on procedures could provide enough common ground to administrate the plurality of interests existing in society. However according to Schmitt, liberalism's attempt to annihilate the political is doomed to failure since the political can derive its energy from the most diverse sources. As he states, "every religious, moral, economic, ethical or other antithesis transforms itself into a political one if it is sufficiently strong to group human beings effectively according to friend and enemy" (Schmitt, *The Concept of the Political* 37). I take this to be a very important insight. Schmitt rightly points out that the political is linked to the existence of a dimension of hostility in human societies, which can take many forms and manifest itself in very diverse types of social relations. Any serious reflection on democracy should take this dimension of the political as its starting point and examine the types of institutions that could help to defuse this hostility, so as to prevent it from escalating into an antagonistic confrontation.

This is the approach that I have followed in my work, where I have used Schmitt's insights in order to remedy the shortcomings of liberal democratic theory. I have argued that those insights could be enriched and formulated more rigorously through the critique of essentialism developed by several currents of contemporary thought. This critique reveals how liberalism deploys a logic of the social based on a conception of being as presence, which leads it to conceive of objectivity as being inherent to things themselves. Liberalism cannot come to terms with the creation of political identities because it is unable to recognize that identity can only be constructed as "difference" and that any social objectivity is therefore constituted through acts of power. What liberal thought refuses to admit is that any form of social objectivity is ultimately political and must bear the traces of the acts of exclusions that govern its constitution.

I use the notion of the "constitutive outside" to explicate my argument. This term has been proposed by Henry Staten in reference to a number of themes developed by Jacques Derrida around his notions of "supplement," "trace," and "difference." Its aim is to highlight the fact that the creation of an identity implies the establishment of a difference, difference that is often constructed on the basis of a hierarchy: for instance between form and matter, black and white, man and women, and so on. Once we have understood that every identity is relational and that the affirmation of a difference is a precondition for the existence of any identity, that is, that identity is grounded in the perception of something "other" that constitutes its exterior, then we can better grasp Schmitt's idea about the ever present possibility of the friend/enemy relation. What is really at stake here is the ability to envisage how a social relation can become the breeding ground for antagonism.

Indeed as I have already indicated, when we are dealing with political identities, which *pace* individualistic liberalism are always *collective* identities, we are always dealing with the creation of an *us* which can only exist by the demarcation of a *them*. This does not mean of course that such a relation is by necessity an antagonistic one. But it means that there is always the possibility of this us/them relation becoming one opposing friend and enemy, that is, of being structured in an antagonistic way. This happens when the *other*, who up to now had been considered as simply different, starts to be perceived as placing our identity in question and threatening our existence. From that moment on any form of us/them relation, be it religious, ethnic, economic, or other, becomes a political one in Schmitt's sense, that is, it becomes the locus of an antagonism.

It is therefore important to acknowledge that the very condition of possibility of political identities is at the same time the condition of impossibility for a society from which antagonism could never be eliminated. Antagonism is indeed an ever present possibility, as Schmitt has made clear. This is what I call the dimension of "the political," which I propose to distinguish from "politics," by which I refer to the set of practices and institutions whose aim is to create an order, to organize human coexistence, however always under conditions that are conflictual because they are traversed by "the political."

Acknowledging the dimension of "the political" and the ever present possibility of antagonism allows us to pose what I take to be the central question for politics. Its aim is to establish the practices and institutions that would "tame" hostility and contribute to defusing the potential antagonism that exists in human relations. The novelty of democratic politics in this context does not lie in overcoming the us/them relation—which is an impossibility—but rather in constructing it in a different way. The objective of democratic politics is to construct the "them" in such a way that it is no longer perceived as an enemy to be destroyed but as what I have proposed to call an "adversary," those whose ideas we combat but whose right to defend those ideas we do not place in question. This is in my view the real meaning of liberal democratic tolerance, which does not entail condoning ideas that we oppose but treating those who defend them as legitimate opponents. The relation between adversaries is not one of antagonism but of what I have referred to as "agonism." I have proposed to call this new understanding of democracy "agonistic" so as to differentiate it from the other models, namely, the aggregative and the deliberative ones.[1]

Understood in this way, the political cannot be envisaged as being restricted to a certain type of institution or as constituting a sphere or a specific level of society. As Schmitt argued, it must be conceived as a dimension that is inherent in every human society and that originates in our very ontological condition. To use an Heideggerian term one could say that the political is situated at the level of the ontological, while politics is at the level of the ontic.

No doubt, the approach that I am proposing here, which takes its inspiration from Schmitt yet departs from him in important points, is profoundly at odds with the main streams of liberal thought. But, contrary to liberals, I am convinced that we need, and, contrary to Schmitt, I am convinced that we can, reformulate liberalism so as to make it really political. Indeed, the impotence of liberal democratic thought when confronted with the diverse manifestations of antagonism can be fatal for the future of democracy. As we are currently witnessing, the outcome of liberalism's incapacity to acknowledge the political is the articulation of antagonisms through a moral or religious vocabulary, which portrays them as manifestation of evil or satanic forces, often running the gamut of expressions that evokes a crusade of good against evil. Such an articulation needs to be challenged because it is incompatible with vibrant democratic politics.

Politics in the Register of Morality

This moralization of political discourse is worth examining in depth because of the increasing and very negative role it is currently playing. To be sure, such a moralization is not completely new. As Schmitt himself repeatedly pointed out, the United States has traditionally been particularly fond of such vocabulary. But today this phenomenon has taken a new and much wider dimension. For instance it is not limited to the field of international relations but is also to be found in discourses that concern the domestic politics of states.

In this context one should emphasize the link existing between the growth of this moralistic discourse and the multiple theories about the end of politics that flourish today under different guises. A good example is provided by the work of Ulrich Beck and Anthony Giddens who both claim that we have now entered a new stage of modernity; in their view, the first modernity has given place to a second modernity, a reflexive modernity in which the adversarial model of politics has become obsolete and with it the categories of left and right that used to structure the political terrain. According to them we now need to think "beyond right and left," in terms of "sub-politics" and about "issues of life and death."[2] To put it differently, instead of thinking in terms of "right and left," we should be thinking in terms of "right and wrong."

A more sophisticated philosophical version of this conflation of politics with morality is found in Habermas, who affirms that political questions are of a moral nature and are therefore susceptible to rational deliberation. In his view the objective of a democratic society lies in creating a rational consensus through appropriate deliberative procedures aimed at producing decisions that express an impartial standpoint equally representative of the interests of all. According to Habermas, those who question the very possibility of such a rational consensus open themselves up to the following danger:

> if questions of justice cannot transcend the ethical self-understanding of competing forms of life, and if existentially relevant value conflicts and oppositions must penetrate all controversial questions, then in the final analysis we will end up with something resembling Carl Schmitt's understanding of politics. ("Reply to Symposium Participants" 1493)

It is clear that in both cases what is at stake is the possibility of eliminating the political in its antagonistic dimension, as well as the belief that relations patterned on the friend/enemy opposition have been eradicated. This is of course celebrated as a great achievement, a progress for democracy, which is thus declared to have entered a new stage where morality has replaced the old confrontational style of politics.

Upon closer examination, however, it is obvious that this is far from being the case. Politics with is supposedly old-fashioned antagonisms has not been superseded by a higher stage of moral concerns. It is still very much alive, except that it is now played out in the moral register. Indeed, frontiers between us and them, far from having disappeared are constantly being established. However, because the "them" can no longer be defined in political terms, given that the adversarial model has been declared overcome, those frontiers are now being drawn in moral categories between "us the good" and "them the evil ones."

Let us examine what is at stake here. The consensus at the center, the one advocated by the "third way" and that supposedly includes everybody, cannot exist without the establishment of a frontier. Indeed no consensus, or no common identity for that matter can exist without drawing a frontier because there cannot be an "us" without a "them" and the very identity of a group depends on the existence of a "constitutive outside." So the "us of the good democrats" needs to be secured by the determination of a "them." However given that the "them" cannot be defined any more as a political adversary, it is now defined as a moral enemy, as the "evil them." There are of course different candidates to fulfill the function of this "evil them" but it is interesting to note that in Western Europe it is increasingly what is defined as the "extreme right" that provides the "evil them" required to secure the existence of the good democrats. The term "extreme right" has in fact become an undefined notion that lumps together without any discrimination a number of very different movements ranging from neo-nazi and skin-head groups to right-wing populist parties. While it proves utterly useless from an analytical standpoint, it serves the purpose of providing the conditions of possibility for defining the "us" and simultaneously offering a ground for moral condemnation. There is more to say about the current rise of right-wing populism, which in my view is a consequence of the shortcomings of liberal-democratic politics, but this would stray from the focus of this section.[3]

The central point discussed in this chapter is that the type of politics played out in the moral register that we are increasingly witnessing is not compatible with a robust democratic politics. When the opponent is not defined in political but in moral terms, she/he cannot be envisaged as an adversary but only as an enemy. No agonistic debate is possible with the "evil them," because for this discourse they can only warrant eradication. Moreover, since they are usually conceived as the expression of a moral plague, there is no need to try to understand the reasons for their existence and success. This is why moral condemnation replaces a proper political analysis and the counter strategy is often limited to the building of a "sanitary cordon" to quarantine the affected sectors.

It should therefore be clear that the approach claiming that the friend/enemy model of politics has been superseded in fact ends up contributing to the very revitalization of the antagonistic model of politics that had been declared obsolete. Instead of helping to create a vibrant agonistic public sphere in which democracy can be kept alive and deepened, all those who proclaim the end of antagonism and the arrival of a consensual society might in fact be jeopardizing democracy by creating the conditions of emergence of antagonisms that are not manageable by democratic institutions. By constructing the "them" as a moral, that is, as an "absolute" enemy, they do not allow for the possibility of envisaging the conflict as one between "adversaries" in an agonistic confrontation; consequently antagonism cannot be transformed into agonism and a democratic framing of the struggle is made impossible.

A Pluralistic World Order?

Many aspects of contemporary politics can be illuminated by an approach inspired by Schmitt. Here I discuss the aspect that is of particular relevance today.

After World War II, one of Schmitt's main concerns was the dissolution of the "Jus Publicum Europaeum," the interstate European law that for three centuries had made possible what he calls in *The Nomos of the Earth* (Der Nomos der Erde) "a limitation of war" (eine Hegung des Krieges). According to Schmitt this dissolution was accompanied by the decline of the political in its modern form and the loss by the state of its monopoly of the political. The question he kept asking was the following: What happens when the state looses this monopoly of the political? He worried that the decline of the state was creating the conditions for a new form of politics that he referred to as "international civil war." For instance in his book *Theory of the Partisan* (*Theorie des Partisanen*) he presented the partisan as a product of the dissolution of the classical state order structured around the demarcation between what is political and what is not political. He saw this as being part of the phenomenon of a totalization of politics that manifested itself in the development of the "total state."

Could one envisage an alternative to this international civil war? What kind of order could replace this "Jus Publicum Europaeum"? Those questions were at the center of Schmitt's preoccupations in several writings of the 1950s and the beginning of the 1960s where he discussed the possibility of a new "Nomos of the Earth." In an article from 1952 he examined how the dualism created by the Cold War and the polarization between capitalism and communism could evolve, laying out several scenarios.[4] Rejecting the idea that such a dualism was only the prelude to a final unification of the world resulting from the victory of one of two antagonists, which would be able to impose its system and its ideology on the whole planet, he stressed the role likely to be played by a third force. In his view this third force, which he saw emerging in the developing countries, would probably take the form of a plurality of third forces, thereby opening the way to a new dynamics of pluralization. Schmitt hoped that the outcome of this dynamics of pluralization could be the establishment of a new global order based on the coexistence of several autonomous blocs or large spaces (*Grossräume*). This would provide the conditions for an equilibrium of forces among various large spaces, instituting among them a new system of international law.

Such an equilibrium would present similarities with the old "Jus Publicum Europaeum" except that in this case it would be truly global and not merely Eurocentric.

Among all the possible scenarios, this was clearly the one that Schmitt favored because he saw it as the basis for a "true pluralism." He did not believe that the existing dualism could last and held that only a multipolar world order could provide the institutions necessary to manage conflicts and avoid the negative consequences resulting from the pseudo-universalism arising from the generalization of a single system. Of course Schmitt was perfectly aware that such a pseudo-universalism was a much more likely outcome than the pluralism that he advocated. And of course his fears have been confirmed and we are now faced with the consequences of the United States's attempt to impose its system and values to the rest of the world under the pretence of a "true universalism."

Schmitt's reflections about the status of a "poststatist politics" are today of a burning actuality and can provide us with important insights to grasp the nature of terrorism. As Jean-François Kervégan has suggested, they allow us to approach the question of terrorism in a very different way from the one currently accepted, which portrays it as the work of isolated groups of fanatics. Taking our lead from Schmitt, we can see terrorism as resulting from the political features of the world order that is being implemented around the absolute hegemony of a single hyper-power.[5] Schmitt helps us realize that the development of terrorism is a consequence of the absence, at the level of world politics, of a pluralism that would allow for a political form of legitimately expressing conflicts. As for the case of domestic politics that I discussed at the beginning, in international politics the consequences of negating the ineradicability of conflict and proclaiming the arrival of an all-inclusive consensus produce an explosion of antagonisms that cannot be managed, due to the lack of adequate institutions to channel them.

All those who are concerned with the way in which the current "war of terrorism" is being waged should take seriously Schmitt's vision of a multipolar world order and heed his warning about the dangers entailed in the illusion of the universalist-globalist discourse, which postulates that human progress requires the establishment of world unity based on human rights. Schmitt is right to warn us against the delusions of the universalist humanitarians and their dream of a unification of the world that would be achieved by transcending the conflictuality of the political. By the same token, he forcefully reminds us that "the political world is a pluriverse, not a universe" (Schmitt, *The Concept of the Political* 53).

Notes

1. This conception is elaborated in chapter four of my book *The Democratic Paradox.*
2. See for instance their respective contribution in *Reflexive Modernity.*
3. I discuss this issue in "The End of Politics."
4. Schmitt, "Die Einheit der Welt."
5. Jean-François Kervégan, "Ami ou ennemi?"

Sovereignty and Its Discontents

William Rasch

Just when you thought it was safe to go into the water again, the principle of sovereignty, that Great White Shark of liberal polemics, has raised its menacing head one more time and bared its razor-sharp teeth. The reappearance of this beast—or rather, to telegraph in advance one of the points of this section—the staged projection of this holographic apparition is most certainly odd. One would have thought that a century—the twentieth—filled with Wilsonian dreams of international legal and policing organizations that were designed to oversee the gentle implementation of universally acknowledged—or, at any rate, rigorously justified—human rights would have done away with the obstinate and arbitrary exercise of state sovereignty for good. After all, we live in an era when the once longed for withering away of the state is thought to be happening, an era in which the state's traditional functions are optimally taken up by civil society—that is, by law and the economy, do we not? In place of lofty sovereign power, the highest underived power, as tradition defines it, we now have the calculable and transparent self-organization of global society, do we not? Instead of what is traditionally called "authority," in other words, we have law and money—and is that not all we need? The liberal order has triumphed and in that order there is no sovereign head, only a kid-gloved, invisible hand.

Yet, the contemporary critique of sovereignty—and I have recent works by Giorgio Agamben (*Homo Sacer* and *State of Exception*) and Michael Hardt and Antonio Negri (*Empire* and *Multitude*) in mind—is not a liberal critique of sovereignty, though to what extent it may replicate liberal motifs will be touched upon later. Rather, Agamben, Hardt, and Negri *take aim* at the liberal order as the modern instantiation of the principle of sovereignty. What once was thought to supplant the repressive principle of sovereignty is now seen to be planting it firmly in the heart of the modern world. For Hardt and Negri, the history of modernity is a history of the Manichean battle between a positively valued revolutionary plane of immanence, in which the desires and productivity of the multitudes are released, and the negatively valued, counterrevolutionary principle of transcendence, which denies desire and imposes order from above. In their view, what marks the liberal phase of modernity is the translation of the transcendent into the transcendental—that is, the internalization of a formerly external authority. Understood politically, the transcendental subject serves as the functional equivalent of a transcendent God or His monarchical representative on earth. Seen this way, what Foucault calls governmentality is not a move away from the sovereign principle, but a movement within sovereignty itself.

Whereas Hardt and Negri can point to a countertradition within modernity—the tradition of immanence that begins with the radical humanism of the Renaissance and comes to philosophical flowering in the works of Spinoza—Agamben's is a philosophically sophisticated totalizing critique that sees no concrete alternative and therefore longs for a Benjaminian divine violence and the thoroughly new historical epoch that would purportedly follow such a total destruction. Rather like a Heideggerian anti-Pangloss who describes the worst of all possible worlds, Agamben analyzes how the principle of the sovereign self-exemption works, how, in other words, the sovereign is both inside and outside the system it establishes, and thus how the subjects of the sovereign too can be placed both under the law and beyond it, out of reach of the law. Thus, the Hobbesian state of nature, which makes of man a wolf to other men, is not a condition from which we are released when we enter the sovereign state, but rather the condition established by that state, a potentiality waiting to be activated. To attempt, therefore, to reform the political from within the political as it is currently constituted is called "nihilism" by him. If Auschwitz serves him, rather melodramatically, as the appropriate image for modernity, it is because the structure of the camp is the structure of bare life within all of modernity. Like Adorno and Horkheimer before him, Agamben makes a distinction only in degree, not in kind, between the liberal capitalist society—the society of the spectacle—and the totalitarian dictatorships of the twentieth century.

This brief and all too inadequate reference to the works of Agamben, Hardt, and Negri are meant as a prolegomena to the following discussion of Carl Schmitt's critique of the incipient American liberal world order between the two World Wars.[1] Agamben, Hardt, and Negri simultaneously rely on and reject the work of Schmitt. Like Schmitt, they indict the modern liberal order; but unlike Schmitt, they replicate a peculiar liberal desire and perhaps also a peculiar liberal deception—the desire sovereignly and completely to deny the principle of sovereignty. I show in broad strokes how this desire and this deception work in the hopes that their current, more radical and popular replications can at least be made visible.

* * *

The United States has always been accused—and, interestingly, the term is always leveled as an accusation—of having reverted to a form of "splendid isolation" after the end of World War I. The great symbol of this supposed isolation is its refusal to join the League of Nations. This multinational body, promoted by President Wilson, aimed at overcoming the anarchy of a Hobbesian state of nature in international relations, an anarchy based on unchecked state sovereignty that was said to have led to the unprecedented carnage of 1914–1918. But like all things splendid, America's isolationism was blindingly deceptive, for the 1920s and 1930s was also a time of great expansion, especially economic expansion, as American industries, symbolized by Ford and Coca-Cola, penetrated European markets and set up numerous subsidiaries. Indeed, the exemplary American manner of industrial production, the efficiency and rationalization of the so-called Fordism and Taylorism, became the model of industrial production the world over. Except for those who saw in the Soviet Union a great experiment and alternative, the United States represented the modern way of life, and "Americanism," not communism, became the true style and ideological wave of the future. If it did not yet act like the empires of old—the Roman, say, or the more contemporaneous British Empire—by sending troops or warships to all corners of the globe, the United States nonetheless was well on its way to the near-universal hegemony that it currently enjoys. The recent terrorist attacks against the United States and its client states only demonstrates the indisputable success of its twentieth-century economic, political, and, ultimately, military expansion. Currently, there is no industrial or financial power that can compete with the United States, certainly no military power that can challenge it in any meaningful way, and the ideological alternatives that presented themselves in the 1920s and 1930s have lost their credibility and all but vanished. There is resistance to the relentless expansion of American dominance, but this resistance struggles to find a language in which it can express itself, and a means by which it can make its political presence felt. In fact, opposition to the United States cannot be articulated politically, because the United States has effectively outlawed political opposition.

By 1932, Carl Schmitt saw no reason to refer to this economic and legal form of American expansion as anything other than imperialism. His reference point was not Marxist-Leninism; thus, his critique was not explicitly a critique of capitalism, with "imperialism" its putatively highest form. Rather, in a narrow sense, his critique was legal, centered on developments in international law since the end of the Great War. In the 1920s and 1930s, American hegemony was theoretically grounded in the fact that the League of Nations formally acknowledged the primacy of the Monroe Doctrine and thus effectively excluded itself from the affairs of the Western Hemisphere. Yet, through its client states in Central and South America who were members of the League, and through its economic clout, perhaps best represented by the various revisions of the reparations clause of the Versailles Treaty negotiated at times by private American citizens (e.g., the Dawes Plan of 1924), the United States gained an ever more effective control over European and, of course, Asian affairs. By virtue of its legal and economic interventions, American supremacy could present itself as ameliorative and peaceful, and it was precisely this self-presentation that was the focus of Schmitt's critique; for Schmitt took aim at the self-understanding of liberal ideology as such, an understanding that was all too readily adopted, he felt, by those who were conquered by it. Succinctly put, by using economic and especially legal terms that affirmed the universality and even "naturalness" of the liberal order of which it now claimed to be the exemplar, the United States could effectively penetrate and suspend the sovereignty of other nations in order to work its own sovereign will. Thus the superior political achievement of the United States lay in its use of general and open-ended concepts. "With regard to these decisive political concepts," Schmitt wrote, "it depends on who interprets, defines, and uses them; who concretely decides what peace is, what disarmament, what intervention, what public order and security are. One of the most important manifestations of humanity's legal and spiritual life is the fact that whoever has true power is able to determine the content of concepts and words. *Caesar dominus et supra grammaticam.* Caesar is also lord over grammar." (Schmitt, *Positionen und Begriffe* 202; my translation)What Schmitt emphatically pointed to, then, was a form of intellectual and spiritual dominance, not just a material one. "It is an expression of genuine political power," he noted, "when a great people determines the way other peoples speak and even think, [when it determines] their vocabulary, terminology, and concepts" (Schmitt, *Positionen und Begriffe* 202; my translation).

In focusing on the question of who decides, Schmitt quite obviously refers back to his 1922 definition of sovereignty, namely: "Sovereign is he who decides on the exception" (*Political Theology* 5). It is precisely this principle—with its apparent emphasis on agency and will in a time of crisis—that liberal ideology, especially during the early twentieth century, attempts to overcome. Indeed, the liberal battle against the nineteenth-century definitions of state sovereignty takes on the flavor of a classic opposition in Western political thinking, the distinction between the rule of man and the rule of law.[2] Although the opposition is not as absolute as presented—the rule of law can have its origins in the rule of the wise legislator—for polemical purposes it has always been convenient to draw the line distinctly, and even more convenient to equate the principle of sovereignty with the rule of man and thus to elevate the rule of law to a postsovereign position. Simply put, the rule of man is made to represent the sovereignty of contingent will, while the rule of law posits for itself the sovereignty of universal and thus necessary reason.

As we are repeatedly told, we are all ruled by the rule of law. Were we not, we would, it is said, at best all be subject to the paternalistic rule of an absolute if putatively wise and enlightened legislator, or, at worst, to the arbitrary will of an autocratic despot. Whatever faith we may once have placed in the notion of enlightened despotism—as exemplified, say, by the career of Frederick the Great—is surely now gone, replaced by our general fear and loathing of Frederick's more recent cousin, Adolf Hitler, the consummate unenlightened tyrant. Thus, it would seem that the history of this alternative—between the rule of law and the rule of man—can now safely be said to be over, for with the expansion of what Weber called occidental rationalism and thus occidental modernity over most, if not the entirety of the globe, we can celebrate the final victory of the rule of law over its onetime vital opponent. Just as the liberal, abstract, rationalized, and thus calculable economic system does away with agrarian traditionalism and paternalistic mercantilism, so the universality of the general norm—or at least the uniform procedure—triumphs over the particularity of socially and historically interested judgment. Indeed, the two—the modern money economy, with its construction of the entrepreneur and the consumer as cultural heroes, and the modern legal system, with individuals, not collectives or communities, as the holder of rights—are intimately connected. The former could not work without the latter.[3] As rule of law, the bureaucratic liberal state seals its victory over radical democracy.[4] Thus, with the victory of the rule of law, the self-description of the rule of man, as the particular judgment of the wise ruler who is sensitive to historical and communal contingency, or as the judgment of the people gathered together as a whole, is rewritten as the arbitrary will of the tyrant or as mob rule. No longer seen as a viable alternative, the rule of man has become the image of the vanquished foe, even if he lingers as a residual, illegitimate menace. We are all ruled by the rule of law, because the rule of law, unlike the willful rule of man, assures us that it is a thoroughly universalizable set of norms that plays no favorites and knows no exceptions.

One way of characterizing this distinction between the rule of man and the rule of law is to say that whereas the former is founded on an exception, the latter is based on an exceptionless and, as the famous phrase from the

Declaration of Independence has it, "self-evident" truth or norm. The rule of the sovereign, embodied as the figure of the monarch, the personified state, or the people, authorizes the rule of law and then places itself under that rule. That is, the sovereign first exempts itself from rules in order, finally, to include itself within the rule of law that it constitutes. Yet, as constituent power, the sovereign retains the right of self-exemption in order to preserve the rule during crisis. The sovereign is thus both above and under the law. The rule of law, however, understands itself, or has come to understand itself, differently, namely as both the power that constitutes order and the order that is thereby constituted. It therefore sees itself simply as a self-constituting power in need of no prior instauration. The finely tuned logical formulation of neo-Kantian positivism puts it this way: "Not the spirit of the people, the monarch, or the State creates law, but law creates itself, establishes the means by which it is to be changed, and lays down the conditions under which the will of the people, the monarch, or the State is legally valid. Thus the self-inclusive legal system comes itself to be sovereign [. . .] since it is independent, self-determining, and self-evolving" (Emerson 167). For the law or the legal system to declare itself to be sovereign, it must act as if there no longer existed any distinction between what Benjamin called lawmaking and law-preserving violence, that is, between a constituting and a constituted power (*Selected Writings*, 1: 241). Agamben is therefore quite correct in his critique of contemporary liberal positivism. "Today, in the context of the general tendency to regulate everything by means of rules," he observes, "fewer and fewer are willing to claim that constituting power is originary and irreducible, that it cannot be conditioned and constrained in any way by a determinate legal system and that it necessarily maintains itself outside every constituted power" (Agamben, *Homo Sacer* 39–40).[5] In other words, in a political order ruled by law, the inaugural, instituting power is not seen as an act of will that operates by way of self-exemption. Rather, it is presupposed either as the universally accepted, self-evident, and incontestable norm from which law is effortlessly and necessarily derived; or, for those made uncomfortable by radical positivism, legitimacy is provided by the putatively "natural" and therefore equally incontestable power of self-evident reason. Thus, the distinction between the constituent power and the power it constitutes eventually dissolves, for even if law finds it difficult to claim an immaculate conception, reason has not generally had the same problem. For those who have faith in its universality and self-evidence, reason does not constitute its own legitimacy by way of an exception. Reason, like God, simply is.

Accordingly, when Schmitt argues against "false normativity" and "abstract formalism" (*Positionen und Begriffe* 202), he is not arguing against the rule of law per se, but against its effacement of the distinction between constituting and constituted power—which, for Schmitt, means its denial of the principle of sovereignty. The claim that law does not involve sovereign coercion—that it is not a form of violence or "Gewalt," to use Benjamin's famous characterization (*Selected Writings*, 1)—but merely the extension of logically valid, naturally reasonable, or simply human rights, makes of the expansion of the rule of law an unacknowledged but smartly accomplished revolution, one that can be resisted only by "illogical," "unnatural," or "inhuman" means. In other words, for Schmitt the expansion of the rule of law under North American or Western European auspices is not the expansion of a transparent universal normative order, but of a particular legal order attached to a constituent power with historically particular political and economic characteristics. It may be a desired or desirable expansion, but it is no less political for all that. Thus, sovereignty is not replaced with universally recognized normative standards. Rather, as an ordering principle, the rule of law is a form of sovereignty, not sovereignty's implacable other. It is, in fact, the instantiation of an all-powerful and all but incontestable universal sovereign—in the event, the United States of America that decides not only in the case of the exception, but also on what is and is not an exception, what is a rule and when and where it is to be applied, and what is and what is not a state of emergency. When, in Schmitt's eyes, this principle of order is wielded by a political, economic, and military force like the United States, it has to be considered a weapon and therefore has also to be recognized as an instance of imposed hegemony. Ironically, because it is not *seen* to be such, its power lies precisely in its *invisibility*. It is far more difficult to combat the sovereign force of a deceptively and supposedly emancipatory principle than it is to resist the ostentatious despot who arrives as a conqueror with all the visible trappings of power. The very weakness of older forms of sovereignty is their visibility, their ability to be imagined and portrayed in the form of the imperious, willful, arbitrary, and ultimately "unnatural" or "inhuman" tyrant or tyrannical regime.

Indeed, if it is reason and law that separate the human being from its more brutish animal relatives, then it is not a difficult step to demote the purportedly nonrational rule of man, and the authoritarian principle of sovereignty associated with it, to the rule of the beast, the existentially and morally inhuman. Within the history of liberal thought, this demotion has been quite explicitly executed. I examine, briefly, two examples of this rhetorical move; one from one of the Western tradition's foundational texts, John Locke's *Two Treatises of Government*, and one from John Rawls' *The Law of Peoples*, a contemporary justification of the current established order.

Although the concept of natural law plays virtually no role in John Locke's *Essay Concerning Human Understanding*—that is, the concept has no epistemological import for one whose task it is to argue *against* innate ideas—the notion is wielded with an astounding nonchalance as a potent political weapon in his *Two Treatises of Government*. Especially in the *Second Treatise* it is reason and the putative law of nature that lend the air of self–evident necessity to an otherwise disputable political theory that is based on a very contestable supremacy of property. Against the force and arbitrary authority of self-interest, associated with monarchical power, Locke pits the irresistible universality of reason. There is a law that governs the state of nature, he says, and that law is called reason, which is plain and intelligible to all who consult it (Locke II, §6, §12).[6] "In transgressing the Law of Nature," Locke writes, "the Offender declares himself to live by another Rule, than that of reason and common Equity, which is that measure God has set to the actions of Men, for their mutual security: and so he becomes dangerous to Mankind" (II, §10). Those who have renounced reason, he continues, have "declared War against all Mankind, and therefore may be destroyed as a Lyon or a Tyger, one of those wild Savage Beasts, with whom Men can have no Society nor Security" (Locke II, §11).

It is important here to understand an essential difference between Locke and Hobbes. Whereas Hobbes identifies the state of nature with the state of war of all against all, Locke explicitly separates the two. Locke writes:

> Men living together according to reason, without a common Superior on Earth, with Authority to judge between them, is *properly the State of Nature.* But force, or a declared design of force upon the Person of another, where there is no common Superior on Earth to appeal to for relief, *is the State of War.* (II, §19, italics in the original)

For Hobbes, as is well known, the default mode of human existence includes violence or the threat of violence as a matter of course. Society is formed to limit and channel violence, but never to eliminate it completely, for that would be to transform the human species into something it is not. Locke, on the other hand, assumes pacification through inherent reason to be the anthropological bedrock of earthly existence. Violence, then, can come only from a position that is morally perverse because it is nonrational and contrary to the reasonable nature of the human species. Such morally suspect, nonrational violence is to be countered by a physically and morally greater violence, the violence of reason. That is, illegitimate violence *against* reason provokes a violence *of* reason that conducts its perpetual wars in the name of perpetual peace. In this way, the question of who decides is avoided because of reason's transparency and universal accessibility, because reason is "plain and intelligible to all rational Creatures" who are not "biassed by their Interest" (Locke II, §124). Only the willfully perverse individual, he who *can* see clearly but *chooses* not to, acts contrary to reason. Thus, on this view, to question the law of nature or its application is not to engage in political polemic, but to usurp power irrationally and out of self-interest, and thereby to lower oneself to the level of the "wild beast" or "noxious brute." Resistance to the invisible sovereignty of reason leaves one exposed for all to see as exemplary of naked aggression and willful force.

If Locke still relies on an epistemologically suspect natural law, John Rawls has no need for any grounding other than the liberal order itself. In his *The Law of Peoples*, he conveniently divides the world into well-ordered peoples and those who are not well ordered. Foremost among the former group are the "reasonable liberal peoples" (Rawls 4), who, by virtue of their history, possess superior institutions, culture, and moral character (Rawls 23–25). Thus liberal peoples have not only the right to deny non–well-ordered peoples respect, but the duty to extend what Habermas has called "gentle compulsion" ("Kant's Idea of Perpetual Peace" 133) to bring the miscreants back into the fold of the well ordered. That is, Rawls believes that the "refusal to tolerate" those states deemed to be outlaw states "is a consequence of liberalism and decency." Why? Because outlaw states violate human rights. What are human rights? "What I call human rights," Rawls states, "are [. . .] a proper subset of the rights possessed by citizens in a liberal constitutional democratic regime" (81). Because of their violation of these liberal rights, nonliberal, nondecent societies do not even have the right "to protest their condemnation by the world society" (Rawls 38), and decent peoples have the right, if necessary, to wage just wars against them. Thus, liberal societies form the measure against which others are judged. Those found wanting are banished, as outlaws, from civil society. Like Locke's beasts, they are ironically denied the rights that liberal societies are said to provide. As outlaw states, they insist on their autonomy, their sovereignty, but, as Rawls notes, "Human rights are a class of rights that play a special role in a reasonable Law of Peoples: they restrict the justifying reasons for war and its conduct, and they specify limits to a regime's internal autonomy. In this way they reflect the two basic and historically profound changes in how the powers of sovereignty have been conceived since World War II" (Rawls 79).

The point to be made here is *not* that beasts and outlaws, whoever or whatever they may be, are to be cherished and protected like some rare and exotic rainforest species, but that the identification of beasts and outlaws is precisely an identification made by a sovereign decision. What Rawls sees as a postwar development in the notion of sovereignty—that is, its restriction—could not, in fact, have occurred had it not been for the supreme sovereign powers of the victors of that war, especially, of course, the United States. The limitation of sovereignty is an imposed limitation, imposed by a sovereign state that has not given up traditional sovereign powers. What Locke referred to as the sovereignty of reason in his political battle against the claims of an absolutist monarchy becomes in Rawls' hands the sovereignty of liberalism. In either case, it is a silent and virtually unseen imposition of sovereign rights, and not, as is often taken to be the case, the dismantling of the principle of sovereignty.

* * *

All that I have said up until now has been but a preamble to the question I pose, but not answer; and it is with this question I close. In the works of Agamben and of Hardt and Negri, we once again are confronted with a radical philosophical and political critique of the principle of sovereignty. In both instances, the liberal order—for Agamben, the society of the spectacle, and for Hardt and Negri, the neoliberal form of imperialism they simply call empire—stands for the new form of sovereignty. To repeat: they all would, by and large, agree with Schmitt that liberalism, far from overcoming sovereignty, simply reinstantiates the ordering principle that the sovereign exception constitutes. And like Benjamin, they chastise the mythic violence of law and long for a truly new and truly postsovereign historical epoch—whether this new epoch erupts spontaneously as the result of unfettered productivity and reproductivity, or whether it arises as a consequence of a cleansing and total violence. But in so doing, these critics of the sovereign principle seem to duplicate the very gesture of the liberal order they chastise. Like liberal theorists from Locke to Habermas and Rawls, they sovereignly deny the principle of sovereignty in the name of a truly new but unspecified politics that will have as its constituent power not the people but the "multitude," those "singularities" guided not by knowledge or power, but by "desire." If a much discredited reason no longer serves as the unquestioned medium of a naturally ordered society, it is because now "natural innocence" (Agamben, *Homo Sacer* 28) and "an alternative ontological basis that resides in the creative and productive practices of the multitude" (Hardt and Negri, *Empire* 47) have taken its place. The question I ask is the question Schmitt would ask: Who will decide when such a new order has been constituted? And will he, she, or it decide in a sovereign manner? If not, how will the rest of us recognize the new order when it in fact does arrive? Will it, like God, nature, reason, and the liberal order of human rights, be self-evident, clearly intelligible and discernible for all to see? If so, will the political still exist in such a new society? If the political is currently defined by sovereignty, even in its liberal guise, will a totally new politics be recognized *as* politics, or will it come clothed in the purple robes of theology or the black robes of law and morality? Within this new postsovereign domain, will opposition—that is to say: politically legitimized conflict—be possible at all? Or in this new, pacified, immanent realm, will all political opposition be condemned as morally perverse and left to the beasts, barbarians, and outlaws who once again will be banished from human society?

Notes

1. And to be as clear as possible: when I say "liberal order," I refer to an international legal and economic order that serves, by and large, the national and political interests of the United States and some of its client states. And when I refer to liberalism, I have in mind a political theory that philosophically justifies the liberal order by arguing for the universal validity of historically contingent moral and legal norms. That there are other versions of liberalism, ones that value contestation over consensus, and thus ones that keep open the possibility of legitimate political opposition and conflict, is quite clear to me. Indeed, this chapter could be interpreted as an attempt to champion an agonistic or antagonistic version of pluralism—as articulated, for instance, in the work of Chantal Mouffe (e.g., *The Return of the Political* and *The Democratic Paradox*)—over what Schmitt called the monism of a liberal humanism, whose aim, ultimately, was to eliminate dissent by carefully limiting the rules of acceptable political discourse and action.
2. On this classic distinction, see Bobbio Chapter 7.
3. "Historically, too, 'progress' towards the bureaucratic state which adjudicates in accordance with rationally established law and administers according to rationally devised regulations stands in the closest relation to the development of modern capitalism. The main inner foundation of the modern capitalist business is *calculation*. In order to exist, it requires a system of justice and administration which, in principle at any rate, function in a *rationally calculable* manner according to stable, general norms, just as one calculates the predictable performance of a *machine*. By contrast, it finds quite uncongenial what is popularly called 'cadi justice,' where judgements are made on each *individual* case according to the judge's sense of fairness, or according to other irrational means of adjudication and principles which existed everywhere in the past and still exist in the Orient today" (Weber 147–48).
4. "The basic principles on which a bureaucracy functions, however, and its prevailing ethos, are directly contrary to those that prevail in a democratic political system. A bureaucracy is essentially an administrative system that operates according to fixed, antecedently known rules; it is hierarchical with well-defined areas of competence for each functionary. Bureaucrats have access to information and power only conditional upon satisfying strict criteria. Democracy, on the other hand, as a political ideal, and direct democracy as a form of political practice, is inherently anti-hierarchical and egalitarian. Furthermore, in its purer forms, democracy is, if not explicitly anti-nomian, at any rate anti-regularian. That is, democracies do not exist in order to follow existing rules, or even necessarily to give themselves new sets of *rules*, but rather to make *new* decisions. The basic principle of a bureaucracy is: Those with the necessary qualifications and

authorization will meet and follow the rules. The basic principle of a direct democracy is: the whole people will meet and they will do what they want. . . . [B]ureaucracy has outstanding virtues. Some of these virtues are of a kind to make it, rather than democracy, especially attractive to liberals. Thus, the rule of law is a bureaucratic, not a specifically democratic ideal[. . .]." (Geuss 122–23).

5. Agamben does not, however, thereby recognize the necessity of the principle of sovereignty. Rather, he argues for the "difference between constituting power and sovereign power," that is, for a rethinking of constituting power that avoids the "nihilistic" effects of sovereignty. "Only an entirely new conjunction of possibility and reality, contingency and necessity, and the other *pathē tou ontos* will make it possible to cut the knot that binds sovereignty to constituting power. And only if it is possible to think the relation between potentiality and actuality differently—and even to think beyond this relation—will it be possible to think a constituting power wholly released from the sovereign ban" (Agamben, *Homo Sacer* 43, 44). Since the "structure of the sovereign relation" is the cause of the "nihilism in which we are living" (51), it is unclear what we as political beings are to do while we wait the long wait for "a new and coherent ontology of potentiality (beyond the steps that have been made in this direction by Spinoza, Schelling, Nietzsche, and Heidegger)" to replace "the ontology founded on the primacy of actuality and its relation to potentiality" such that "a political theory freed from the aporias of sovereignty" can become thinkable (44). With reference to the resurgence of right-wing thought in France, Gopnik notes: "It used to be said that for evil to triumph it was necessary only for good men to do nothing; in France, historically, for evil to enter it is necessary for good men to tell other good men that nothing is the best thing a good man can do" (50). Indeed, doing nothing while Rome burns would seem to be the only way to avoid the "nihilism in which we live."
6. Citation of Locke refers to paragraph number (e.g., §6) of *Second Treatise* (i.e., II).

Works Cited

Abendroth, Walter. *Hans Pfitzner*. Munich: Langen-Müller, 1935.

Adamy, Bernhard. *Hans Pfitzner: Literatur, Philosophie und Zeitgeschehen in seinem Weltbild und Werk*. Tutzing: Schneider, 1980.

Adorno, Theodor W. "Abschied vom Jazz." In *Gesammelte Schriften*, edited by Rolf Tiedemann. Vol.18. Frankfurt: Suhrkamp, 1982, 795–99.

———. "Einleitung in die Musiksoziologie." In *Gesammelte Schriften*, edited by Rolf Tiedemann. Vol. 14. Frankfurt: Suhrkamp, 1982, 199–218.

———. "Jazz." In *Gesammelte Schriften*, edited by Rolf Tiedemann. Vol. 18. Frankfurt a.M.: Suhrkamp, 1982. 70–73.

———. *Mahler: A Musical Physiognomy*. Chicago: University of Chicago Press, 1996.

———. "Pfitzner's *Palestrina*," *Theodor W. Adorno als Kritiker der Frankfurter Oper, Frankfurter Opernhefte* 5 no. 3 (December 1976), 35; rpt.

———. "Über Jazz." In *Gesammelte Schriften*. Edited by Rolf Tiedemann. Vol. 17. Frankfurt: Suhrkamp, 1982, 74–108.

———. "Zeitlose Mode: Zum Jazz." In *Gesammelte Schriften*. Edited by Rolf Tiedemann. Vol. 10.1. Frankfurt: Suhrkamp, 1977, 123–37.

Agamben, Giorgio. *Homo Sacer: Sovereign Power and Bare Life*. Translated by Daniel Heller-Roazen. Stanford: Stanford University Press, 1998.

———. *State of Exception*. Translated by Kevin Attell. Chicago: University of Chicago Press, 2005.

Albrecht, Gerd. *Nationalsozialistische Filmpolitik. Eine soziologische Untersuchung über die Spielfilme des dritten Reiches*. Stuttgart: Ferdinand Enke, 1969.

Andersen, Jørgen. *Viggo Stuckenberg og hans Samtid: I*. Copenhagen: Gyldendal, 1944.

Bahrampour, Tara. "An Artist's Inspiration Lives on in His Mind." *The New York Times*, October 1, 2001, E7.

Balfour, Alan. *Berlin: The Politics of Order, 1737–1989*. New York: Rizzoli, 1990.

Bathrick, David, and Andreas Huyssen, eds. *Modernity and the Text. Revisions of German Modernism*. New York: Columbia University Press, 1989.

Baudrillard, Jean. "The Spirit of Terrorism." *Le Monde*, November 2, 2001. Translated by Rachel Bloul. http://www.egs.edu/faculty/baudrillard/baudrillard-the-spirit-of-terrorism.html (accessed September 19, 2006).

———. *The Spirit of Terrorism: And Requiem for the Twin Towers*. Translated by Chris Turner. New York: Verso, 2002.

Bauman, Zygmunt. *Modernity and Ambivalence*. Ithaca, NY: Cornell University Press, 1991.

Beck, Ulrich, Anthony Giddens, and Scott Lash, eds. *Reflexive Modernity.* Cambridge, England: Polity Press, 1994.

Behne, Klaus-Ernst. "Mythen der Inspiration aus den Gründerjahren der Neuen Musik: Hans Pfitzner, Arnold Schönberg und Thomas Mann." In *Vom Einfall zum Kunstwerk: Der Kompositionsprozess in der Musik des 20. Jahrhunderts*, edited by Hermann Danuser and Günter Katzenberger, 331–42. Laaber: Laaber-Verlag, 1993.

Behrendt, Bernd. "August Julius Langbehn, der 'Rembrandtdeutsche.' " In *Handbuch zur 'Völkischen Bewegung' 1871–1918*, edited by Uwe Puschner, Walter Schmitz, and Julius H. Ulbricht, 94–113. Munich: K.G. Saur, 1996.

Benjamin, Walter. "The Author as Producer." In *Walter Benjamin: Selected Writings 1927–34*, edited by Howard Eiland, Michael W. Jennings, and Gary Smith, 768–82. Cambridge, MA: The Belknap Press of Harvard University Press, 1999.

———. "Critique of Violence." In *Selected Writings*, edited by Marcus Bullock and Michael W. Jennings, 236–52. Cambridge, MA: Harvard University Press, 1996.

———. "The Destructive Character." Translated by Edmund Jephcott. In *Reflections: Essays, Aphorisms, Autobiographical Writings*, edited by Peter Demetz, 301–03. New York: Schocken, 1986.

———. "Experience and Poverty." Translated by Rodney Livingstone et al. In *Selected Writings*. Vol. 2, edited by Michael Jennings, 731–36. Cambridge, MA: Harvard University Press, 1999.

———. *Gesammelte Schriften*. Edited by Rolf Tiedemann. Vol. 5. Frankfurt: Suhrkamp, 1982.

———. *Illuminations: Essays and Reflections*. Edited by Hannah Arendt. New York: Schocken, 1969.

———. "A Small History of Photography." Translated by Edmund Jephcott and Kingsley Shorter. In *One Way Street and Other Writings*, 240–57. London: NLB, 1979.

Berghahn, Klaus L. *Grenzen der Toleranz. Juden und Christen im Zeitalter der Aufklärung*. Cologne: Böhlau, 2000.

Bergius, Hanne. "Berlin: A City Drawn from the Linear Network to the Contour." In *German Realist Drawings of the 1920s*, edited by Peter Nisbet, 15–30. Ex. cat. Cambridge, MA: Harvard University Art Museums, Busch-Reisinger Museum, 1986.

Bergland, Betty. "Norwegian Immigrants and 'Indianerne' in the Landtaking, 1838–1862." *Norwegian-American Studies* 35 (2000): 319–50.

Berlin Babylon. Dir. Siegert, Hubertus. Germany: S.U.M.O. Films, 2001.

Berman, Art. *Preface to Modernism*. Urbana, IL: University of Illinois Press, 1994.

Berman, Judith. "The Culture as It Appears to the Indian Himself." In *Volkgeist as Method and Ethic: Essays on Boasian Ethnography and the German Anthropological Tradition, History of Anthropology* 8, edited by George W. Stocking, Jr., 215–56. Madison: University of Wisconsin Press, 1996.

Berman, Russell A. *Modern Culture and Critical Theory: Art, Politics, and the Legacy of the Frankfurt School*, 99–117. Madison: University of Wisconsin Press, 1989.

Bloch, Ernst. *Heritage of Our Times*. Translated by Neville Plaice and Stephen Plaice. Berkeley: University of California Press, 1991.

Bobbio, Norbert. *The Future of Democracy: A Defense of the Rules of the Game*. Translated by R. Griffin. Minneapolis: University of Minnesota Press, 1987.

Bollenbeck, Georg. *Bildung und Kultur*. Frankfurt: Suhrkamp, 1994.

Bookchin, Murray. "Excerpt from the Limits of the City." In *The City Cultures Reader*, edited by Malcolm Miles, Tim Hall, and Iain Borden, 48–49. New York: Routledge, 2000.

Boswell, Peter, and Maria Makela. *The Photomontages of Hannah Höch*. Minneapolis: Walker Art Center, 1996.

Brecht, Christine, and Sybilla Nikolow. "Displaying the Invisible: Volkskrankheiten on Exhibition in Imperial Germany." *Studies in History and Philosophy of Biological and Biomedical Sciences* 31, no. 4 (2000): 511–30.

Broberg, Gunnar, and Mattias Tydén. "Eugenics in Sweden: Efficient Care." In *Eugenics and the Welfare State. Sterilization Policy in Denmark, Sweden, Norway, and Finland*, edited by Gunnar Broberg and Nils Roll-Hansen, 77–150. East Lansing, MI: Michigan State University Press, 1996.

———. "När svensk historia blev an värdsnyhet. Steriliseringspolitiken och media." *Tvärsnitt. Humanistisk och Samhällsvetenskaplig forskning* no. 3 (1998): 2–15.

———. *Oönskad i folkhemmet*. Stockholm: Gidlunds, 1991.

Broberg, Gunnar, and Nils Roll-Hansen. *Eugenics and the Welfare State. Sterilization Policy in Denmark, Sweden, Norway, and Finland*. East Lansing, MI: Michigan State University Press, 1996.

Brock Committee. "Report of the Departmental Committee on Sterilization." Minister to Parliament, December 1933. London: 1934.

Bruknapp, Dag O. "Ideene splitter partiet. Rasespørsmålets betydning i NS's utvikling." In *Fra ide til dom: noen trek fra utviklingen av Nasjonal Samling*, edited by Rolf Danielsen and Stein Ugelvik Larsen, 9–43. Bergen: Universitetsforlaget, 1976.

Buchloh, Benjamin H. D. "Figures of Authority, Ciphers of Regression: Notes on the Return of Representation in European Painting." In *Art in Modern Culture. An Anthology of Critical Texts*, edited by Francis Frascina and Jonathan Harris, 222–38. London: Phaidon Press Limited, 1992.

Bull, Francis, ed. *Knut Hamsun, Artikler 1889–1928*. Oslo: Gyldendal, 1939.

Bürger, Peter. *The Decline of Modernism*. Translated by Nicholas Walker. University Park, PA: Penn State University Press, 1992.

———. *Theorie der Avantgarde*. Frankfurt: Suhrkamp, 1974.

———. *Theory of the Avant-Garde*. Translated by Michael Shaw. Minneapolis: University of Minnesota Press, 1984.

Calinescu, Matei. *Five Faces of Modernity*. Durham, NC: Duke University Press, 1987.

Cameron, Dan. *Marcel Odenbach*. New York: New Museum of Contemporary Art, 1998.

Canguilhem, Georges. *The Normal and the Pathological*. New York: Zone Books, 1991.

Carrier, David. *Artwriting*. Amherst: The University of Massachusetts Press, 1987.

Christensen, Olav, and Anne Eriksen. *Hvite løgner: stereotype forestillinger om svarte*. Oslo: Aschehoug & Co (W. Nygaard), 1992.

Clarke, T. J. *Farewell to an Idea: Episodes from a History of Modernism*. New Haven, CT.: Yale University Press, 1999.

Colomina, Beatriz. *Privacy and Publicity: Modern Architecture as Mass Media*. Cambridge, MA: MIT Press, 1996.

Colquhoun, Alan. "On Modern and Postmodern Space." In *Architecture Criticism Ideology*, edited by Joan Ockman. Princeton, NJ: Princeton Architectural Press, 1985.

Conrads, Ulrichs, ed. *Programs and Manifestos on 20th Century Architecture.* Cambridge, MA: The MIT Press, 1970.

Crary, Jonathan. *Techniques of the Observer: On Vision and Modernity in the Nineteenth Century*. Cambridge, MA: MIT Press, 1998.

Crockett, Dennis. *German Post-Expressionism. The Art of the Great Disorder 1918–1924*. University Park, PA: Pennsylvania State University Press, 1999.

Dahlberg, Gunnar. *Race, Reason and Rubbish*. London: Allan & Unwin, 1942.

D'Alessandro, Stephanie. "Ueber alles die Liebe: the History of Sexual Imagery in the Art and Culture of the Weimar Republic." Ph.D. dissertation, University of Chicago, 1997.

Daston, Lorraine. "Objectivity and the Escape from Perspective." In *The Science Studies Reader*, edited by Mario Biagioli, 110–23. New York: Routledge, 1999.

Davies, Tony. *Humanism*. New York: Routledge, 1997.

De la Grange, Henry-Louis. *Mahler. Volume 1*. New York: Doubleday, 1973.

———. *Gustav Mahler. Volume 2. Vienna: The Years of Challenge (1897–1904)*. Oxford: Oxford University Press, 1995.

———. *Gustav Mahler. Volume 3. Vienna: Triumph and Disillusion (1904–1907)*. Oxford: Oxford University Press, 1999.

Derrida, Jacques. "Des Tours de Babel." In *Difference in Translation*, edited by Joseph F. Graham, 165–248. Ithaca, NY: Cornell University Press, 1985.

Dietz, Burkhard. "Technik und Kultur zwischen Kaiserreich und Nationalsozialismus. Über das sozio-kulturelle Profil der 'Zeitschrift des Verbandes deutscher Diplom-Ingenieure." In *Technische Intelligenz und Kulturfaktor Technik: Kulturvorstellungen von Technikern und Ingenieuren zwischen Kaiserreich und früher Bundesrespulik Deutschland*, edited by Burkhard Dietz, Michael Fessner, and Helmut Maier, 105–30. Münster: Waxmann, 1996.

Dimendberg, Edward. "Down These Seen Streets A Man Must Go: Siegfried Kracauer, Hollywood's Terror Films and the Spatiality of Film Noir." *New German Critique* 89 (Spring–Summer 2003): 113–43.

Dingstad, Ståle. *Hamsuns strategier. Realisme, humor og kynisme*. Oslo: Gyldendal, 2003.

Döblin, Alfred. "About Faces, Portraits, and Their Reality." In *Germany. The New Photography 1927–33*, edited by David Mellor, 55–59. London: Arts Council of Great Britain, 1978.

Doerner, Max. *Malmaterial und seine Verwendung im Bilde: nach den Vorträgen an der Akademie der Bildenden Künste in München*. Stuttgart: F. Enke, 1933.

Dreyfus, Hubert L., and Paul Rabinow. "What is Maturity? Habermas and Foucault on 'What Is Enlightenment?' " In *Foucault: A Critical Reader*, edited by David Couzens Hoy, 109–21. Oxford: Basil Blackwell, 1986.

Eisner, Lotte. *The Haunted Screen: Expressionism in the German Cinema & the Influence of Max Reinhardt* (Orig.: *L'Ecran Démonique*. 1952; rev. 1965). Translated by Roger Greaves. Berkeley: University of California Press, 1969.

Elsaesser, Thomas. *Weimar Cinema and After: Germany's Historical Imaginary*. New York: Routledge, 2000.

Emerson, Rupert. *State and Sovereignty in Modern Germany*. New Haven, CT: Yale University Press, 1928.

Ermen, Reinhard. *Musik als Einfall: Hans Pfitzners Position im ästhetischen Diskurs nach Wagner*. Aachen: Rimbaud, 1986.

Etzemüller, Thomas. "Sozialstaat, Eugenik und Normalisierung in skandinavischen Demokratien." *Archiv für Sozialgeschichte* 43 (2003):492–509.

Evang, Karl. *Racepolitikk og Reaksjon*. Oslo: Fram Forlag, 1934.

———. *Sterilisering etter lov av 1. juni 1934 om adgang til sterilisering m.v.* [Pamphlet]. Sarpsborg: Frank Vardings trykkeri, 1955.

Ferguson, Robert. *Enigma*. New York: Farrar, Straus & Giroux, 1987.

Foster, Hal. *The Return of the Real*. Cambridge, MA: MIT University Press, 1996.

———, ed. *Vision and Visuality*. Seattle: Bay Press, 1988.

Foster, Hal, Rosalind Krauss, Annette Michelson, George Baker, Yve-Alain Bois, Benjamin H.D. Buchloh, eds. *Obsolescence*. Special Issue of *October* no. 100 (Spring 2002): 3–228.

Foucault, Michel. *The Birth of the Clinic: An Archaeology of Medical Perception*. New York: Random House, 1975.

———. *The Foucault Reader*. Edited by Paul Rabinow. New York: Pantheon, 1984.

Frame, Lynne. "Gretchen, Girl, Garçonne? Weimar Science and Popular Culture in Search of the Ideal New Woman." In *Woman in the Metropolis. Gender and Modernity in Weimar Culture*, edited by Katharina von Ankum, 12–40. Berkeley: University of California Press, 1997.

Fukuyama, Francis. *The End of History and the Last Man*. New York: Maxwell Macmillan International, 1992.

Fulbrook, Mary. *The Divided Nation. A History of Germany 1918–1990*. Oxford: Oxford University Press, 1992.

"Gelbrand und Kolbenwasserkäfer." *Die Koralle* 2, no. 3 (June 1926): 184.

Gemünden, Gerd. "Brecht in Hollywood: *Hangmen also Die* and the Anti-Nazi Film." *The Drama Review* 43, no. 4 (T164) (Winter 1999–2000): 65–76.

Gemünden, Gerd, and Anton Kaes. "Introduction to Special Issue on 'Film and Exile.' " *New German Critique* 89 (2003): 3–8.

Geuss, Raymond. *History and Illusion in Politics*. Cambridge, England: Cambridge University Press, 2001.

Giæver, Øyvind. "Abortion and Eugenics. The Role of Eugenic Arguments in Norwegian Abortion Debates and Legislation, 1920–1978." *Scandinavian Journal of History* 30 (2005): 267–92.

———. "Marriage and Madness. Expert Advice and the Eugenics Issue in 20th Century Norwegian Marriage Legislation." *Science Studies* 16 (2003): 3–21.

Gilman, Sander. "Das Gesicht wahren. Zur ästhetischen Chirurgie." In *Gesichter der Weimarer Republik*, edited by Claudia Schmölders and Sander Gilman, 96–112. Cologne: DuMont, 2000.

———. *Making the Body Beautiful: A Cultural History of Aesthetic Surgery*. Princeton, NJ: Princeton University Press, 1999.

Giovanni, Joseph. "Commentary." *Architectural Record* 4 (2003): 89–90.

Giskes, Johan, and Ester L. Woudhuysen, eds. *Mahler in Amsterdam van Mengelberg tot Chailly*. Amsterdam: THOTH/Gemeentearchief, 1995.

Gjellerup, Karl. *Germanernes Lærling*. (rpt. of 1st ed. 1888) Copenhagen: Gyldendal/ Nordisk Forlag, 1908.

Goldberger, Paul. "The Sky Line: Slings and Arrows." *The New Yorker*, February 9, 2004, 84–87.

Golson, Blair. "Gehry Tops Danny: Ground Zero Winner Scores Art Center." *The New York Observer*, October 14, 2004, 1.

Gopnik, Adam. "French Follies." *The New Yorker*, May 6, 2002, 49–50.

Goschler, Constantin, and Rudolf Virchow. *Mediziner-Anthropologe-Politiker*. Cologne: Böhlau, 2002.

Gray, Richard T. *About Face. German Physiognomic Thought from Lavater to Auschwitz*. Detroit: Wayne State University Press, 2004.

Greenberg, Clement. *Art and Culture: Critical Essays*. Boston: Beacon Press, 1961.

Grosz, George. "Zu meinen neuen Bildern." *Das Kunstblatt* 5 (1921): 11–14.

Grosz, George, Raoul Hausmann, John Heartfield, and Rudolf Schlichter. "Die Gesetze der Malerei." In *Hannah Höch. Eine Lebenscollage I*, vol. 2, edited by Cornelia Thater-Schulz, 696–98. Berlin: Berlinische Galerie, 1989.

Gunning, Tom. *The Films of Fritz Lang: Allegories of Vision and Modernity*. London: British Film Institute, 2000.

Haave, Per. *Sterilisering av tatere 1934–1977*. Oslo: The Norwegian Research Council, 2000.

Haavie, Siri. 2003. "Sterilization in Norway—A Dark Chapter?" <www.eurozine.com>. (accessed April 15, 2005).

Habermas, Jürgen. "Kant's Idea of Perpetual Peace, with the Benefit of Two Hundred Years' Hindsight." In *Perpetual Peace: Essays on Kant's Cosmopolitan Ideal*, edited by James Bohman and Matthias Lutz-Bachmann, 113–53. Cambridge, MA: MIT Press, 1997.

———. "Modernity—An Incomplete Project." Translated by Seyla Ben-Habib. In *The Anti-Aesthetic: Essays on Postmodern Culture*, edited by Hal Foster, 3–15. Port Townsend: Bay Press, 1983.

———. "Modernity versus Postmodernity." *New German Critique* 22 (Spring 1981): 3–14.

———. "Reply to Symposium Participants." *Cardozo Law Review* 17, no. 4–5 (March 1996): 771–84.

Hake, Sabine. "Expressionism and the Cinema: Reflections on a Phantasmagoria of Film History." In *A Companion to the Literature of German Expressionism*, edited by Neil H. Donahue, 321–41. Rochester, NY: Camden House, 2005.

———. "Faces of Weimar Germany." In *The Image in Dispute. Art and Cinema in the Age of Photography*, edited by Dudley Andrew, 117–47. Austin: University of Texas Press, 1997.

Hamsun, Knut. *Ringen sluttet. Samlede verker*. Oslo: Gyldendal, 1964.

Hansen, Andreas Martin. *Norsk folkepsykologi*. Kristiania: Jacob Dybwads forlag, 1899.

Hard, Mikael. "German Regulation: The Integration of Modern Technology into National Culture." In *The Intellectual Appropriation of Technology. Discourses on Modernity, 1900–1939*, edited by Mikael Hard and Andrew Jamison, 33–67. Cambridge, MA: MIT Press, 1998.

Hardt, Michael, and Antonio Negri. *Empire*. Cambridge, MA: Harvard University Press, 2000.

———. *Multitude: War and Democracy in the Age of Empire*. New York: Penguin Press, 2004.

Hartlaub, Gustav. "Neue Sachlichkeit." In *Deutsche Malerei seit dem Expressionismus. Ex. cat.* Mannheim: Städtische Kunsthalle, 1925.

Hartmann, Kristina, ed. *trotzdem modern: Die wichtigsten Texte zur Architektur in Deutschland 1919–1933*. Braunschweig: Vieweg, 1994.
Hassan, Ihab. "POSTmodernISM." *New Literary History* 3, no. 1 (1971): 5–30.
Hays, K. Michael. *Modernism and the Posthumanist Subject: The Architecture of Hannes Meyer and Ludwig Hilberseimer*. Cambridge, MA: The MIT Press, 1995.
Heartfield, John, and George Grosz. "The Art Scab." In *The Weimar Republic Sourcebook*, edited by Martin Jay, Anton Kaes, and Edward Dimendberg, 483–86. Berkeley: University of California Press, 1994.
Heidegger, Martin. *The Question Concerning Technology and Other Essays*. Translated by W. Lovitt. New York: Harper and Row, 1972.
Hein, Peter Ulrich. *Transformation der Kunst. Ziele und Wirkungen der deutschen Kultur- und Kunsterziehungsbewegung*. Cologne: Böhlau, 1991.
Herf, Jeffrey. *Reactionary Modernism. Technology, Culture, and Politics in Weimar and the Third Reich*. Cambridge, England: Cambridge University Press, 1984.
Hermand, Jost. "Neue Sachlichkeit: Ideology, Lifestyle, or Artistic Movement?" In *Dancing on the Volcano. Essays on the Culture of the Weimar Republic*, edited by Thomas W. Kniesche and Stephen Brockmann, 57–67. Columbia, South Carolina: Camden Press, 1994.
Herzogenrath, Wulf, and Johann-Karl Schmidt, eds. *Otto Dix. Zum 100. Geburtstag 1891–1991*. Ex. cat. Stuttgart: Verlag Gerd Hatje, 1991.
Hilberseimer, Ludwig. *Berliner Architektur der 20er Jahre*. Afterword by H. M. Wingler. Mainz: Florian Kupferberg, 1967.
———. *Entfaltung einer Planungsidee*. Berlin: Ullstein, 1963.
———. *Großstadtarchitektur*. Stuttgart: Julius Hoffmann, 1978.
———. "Der Wille zur Architektur." *Das Kunstblatt* 7 (1923): 139.
Hoffmann, Heinrich. *Hitler wie ihn keiner kennt: 100 Bilddokumente aus dem Leben des Führers*. Berlin: Zeitgeschichte-Verlag, 1941.
Honnef, Klaus. "Reclaiming a Legacy: Photography in Germany and German History." *Aperture* 123 (Spring 1991): 2–9.
Horkheimer, Max, and Theodor W. Adorno. *Dialectic of Enlightenment*. Translated by John Cumming. New York: Seabury Press, 1972.
Houe, Poul. "Begyndelsen på enden: Karl Gjellerups debutroman(er)." In *On the Threshold: New Studies in Nordic Literature*, edited by Janet Garton and Michael Robinson, 144–51. Norwich: Norvik Press, 2002.
———. "Karl Gjellerup." In *Dictionary of Literary Biography: Danish Writers from the Reformation to World War I*, edited by Marianne Stecher-Hansen, 172–83. Detroit: Bruccoli Clark Layman/Thompson Gale, 2004.
Hutcheon, Linda. *The Politics of Postmodernism*. New York: Routledge, 2002.
Hüter, Karl-Heinz. *Architektur in Berlin 1900–1933*. Stuttgart: Kohlhammer, 1988.
Huyssen, Andreas. *After the Great Divide*. Bloomington: Indiana University Press, 1986.
———. *Twilight Memories. Marking Time in a Culture of Amnesia*. New York: Routledge, 1994.
Israel, O. "XI. Das pathologische Museum der Königlichen Friedrich-Wilhelms-Universität zu Berlin." *Berliner klinische Wochenschrift* 41, no. 14 (October 1901): 1047–52.
Jameson, Fredric. *The Cultural Turn: Selected Writings on the Postmodern, 1983–1998*. London: Verso, 1998.

Jameson, Fredric. "Postmodernism and Consumer Society." In *The Anti-Aesthetic: Essays in Postmodern Cultures*, edited by Hal Foster, 111–25. Port Townsend: Bay Press, 1983.

———. *Postmodernism, or, the Cultural Logic of Late Capitalism*. Durham, NC: Duke University Press, 1992.

———. *A Singular Modernity: Essay on the Ontology of the Present*. London: Verso, 2003.

Joachimides, Alex. *Die Museumsreformbewegung in Deutschland und die Entstehung des modernen Museums 1880–1940*. Dresden: Verlag der Kunst, 2001.

Jochens, Jenny. "Race and Ethnicity." *Viator* 30 (1999): 79–103.

Kaes, Anton. *M*. London: British Film Institute, 2001.

Kaiser, Georg. *Georg Kaiser in Sachen Georg Kaiser: Briefe 1916–1933*. Edited by Gesa M. Valk. Leipzig: Gustav Kiepenheuer, 1989.

Kallmann, Franz. "The Genetic Theory of Schizophrenia: An Analysis of 691 Schizophrenic Twin Index Families." *American Journal of Psychiatry* 151 (suppl.) (1946): 188–98.

———. *Heredity in Health and Mental Disorders: Principles of Psychiatric Genetics in the Light of Comparative Twin Studies*. New York: W.W.Norton, 1953.

Kater, Michael H. *Composers of the Nazi Era: Eight Portraits*. New York: Oxford University Press, 2000.

Kemp, Tage. "Genetic-Hygienic Experiences in Denmark in Recent Years." *The Eugenics Review* 44 (1957): 11–18.

Kemperink, Mary. *Het verloren paradijs. De literatuur en cultuur van het Nederlandse fin de siècle*. Amsterdam: Amsterdam University Press, 2001.

Kent, Neil. *The Soul of the North*. London: Reaktion Books, 2001.

Kervégan, Jean-François. "Ami ou ennemi?" In *La Guerre des dieux*. Special issue of *Le Nouvel Observateur* 46 (January 2002): 34–37.

Kevles, Daniel. *In the Name of Eugenics*. New York: Alfred A. Knopf, 1995.

Kittang, Atle. *Luft, vind, ingenting. Hamsuns desillusjonsromaner frå Sult til Ringen sluttet*. Oslo: Gyldendal, 1984.

Koch, Lene. *Racehygiejne i Danmark 1920–1956*. Copenhagen: Gyldendal, 1996.

———. *Tvangssterilisation i Danmark 1929–67*. Copenhagen: Gyldendal, 2000.

Koepnick, Lutz. *The Dark Mirror: German Cinema between Hitler and Hollywood*. Berkeley: University of California Press, 2002.

Koolhaas, Rem. *Delirious New York: A Retroactive Manifesto for Manhattan*. New York: The Monacelli Press, 1994.

Köstering, Susanne. *Natur zum Anschauen: Das Naturkundemuseum des deutschen Kaiserreichs 1871–1914*. Cologne: Böhlau, 2003.

Kracauer, Siegfried. *Die Angestellten 1929–30. Schriften 1*, 205–304. Frankfurt: Suhrkamp, 1971.

———. *From Caligari to Hitler. A Psychological History of the German Film*. Princeton, NJ: Princeton University Press, 1947.

———. "Zertrümmerung und Aufbau." *Frankfurter Zeitung* 75, no. 30 (January 12, 1931).

Krietsch, Peter, and Manfred Dietel. *Pathologisch-Anatomisch Cabinet: vom Virchow-Museum zum Berliner Medizinhistorischen Museum in der Charité*. Berlin: Blackwell Wissenschafts-Verlag, 1996.

Kringlen, Einar. *Schizophrenia in male monozygotic twins*. Copenhagen: Munksgaard, 1964.

———. "Schizophrenia in Twins: An Epidemiological-Clinical Study." *Psychiatry* 29 (1966): 172–84.

Kropfinger, Klaus. "Gerettete Herausforderung: Mahlers 4. Symphonie—Mengelbergs Interpretation." In *Mahler-Interpretation: Aspekte zum Werk und Wirken von Gustav Mahler*, edited by Rudolf Stephan, 111–75. Mainz: Schott, 1985.

Kuspit, Donald B. *Clement Greenberg: Art Critic*. Madison: University of Wisconsin Press, 1979.

Kyllingstad, Jon Røyne. *Kortskaller og longskaller. Fysisk antropologi i Norge og striden om det nordiske herremennesket*. Oslo: Scandinavian Academic Press/Spartacus Forlag, 2004.

Langbehn, Julius. *Rembrandt als Erzieher. Von einem Deutschen*. 40th ed. Leipzig: C.L. Hirschfeld, 1892.

Lavater, J[ohann] C[aspar]. *Physiognomische Fragmente*. Leipzig: Weidmann, Reich, Steiner, 1775–1778.

Lavin, Maud. *Cut with a Kitchen Knife: The Weimar Photomontages of Hannah Höch*. New Haven, CT: Yale University Press, 1993.

Le Corbusier. *Précisions sur un état présent de l'architetcure et de l'urbanism*. Paris: Vincent, 1930.

Leiser, Erwin. *Nazi Cinema*. Translated by G. Mander and D. Wilson. New York: Macmillan, 1974.

Lenoir, Timothy. *Instituting Science: The Cultural Production of Scientific Disciplines*. Stanford: Stanford University Press, 1997.

———. *The Strategy of Life: Teleology and Mechanics in Nineteenth-Century German Biology*. Boston: Reidel, 1982.

Lethen, Helmut. *Cool Conduct. The Culture of Distance in Weimar Germany*. Translated by Don Reneau. Berkeley: University of California Press, 2002.

———. *Neue Sachlichkeit, 1924–1932*. Stuttgart: Metzler, 1970.

———. *Verhaltenslehren der Kälte. Lebensversuche zwischen den Kriegen*. Frankfurt: Suhrkamp, 1994.

Levi, Primo. *Survival in Auschwitz. The Nazi Assault on Humanity*. New York: Touchstone/Simon & Schuster, 1995.

Levin, Gail. "Kandinsky and Abstract Expressionism." In *Theme & Improvisation: Kandinsky & the American Avant-Garde, 1912–1950*, edited by Gail Levin and Marianne Lorenz, 192–221. Boston: Little, Brown and Company, 1992.

Lindner, Martin. *Leben in der Krise: Zeitromane der neuen Sachlichkeit und die intellektuelle Mentalität der klassischen Moderne*. Stuttgart: Metzler, 1994.

Locke, John. *Two Treatises of Government*. Edited by Peter Laslett. Student Edition ed. Cambridge, England: Cambridge University Press, 1988.

Lucchesi, Joachim, and Ronald Shull. *Musik bei Brecht*. Frankfurt: Suhrkamp, 1988.

Lukács, George. "Expressionism: Its Significance and Decline." Translated by David Ferbach. In *Essays on Realism*, edited by Rodney Livingstone, 76–113. Cambridge, MA: MIT Press, 1981.

Lyotard, Jean François. *The Postmodern Condition: A Report on Knowledge*. Translated by Régi Durand. Minneapolis: University of Minnesota Press, 1984.

Magner, Lois N. *A History of the Life Sciences*. 2nd ed. New York: Marcel Dekker, 1994.

Mahler-Werfel, Alma. *Mein Leben*. Frankfurt: Fischer, 1963.

Makela, Maria. " 'A Clear and Simple Style': Tradition and Typology in New Objectivity." *Negotiating History: German Art and the Past*, edited by Jay Clarke. Special issue of *The Art Institute of Chicago Museum Studies* 28, no. 1 (2002): 38–51.

———. "Modern art and the Grotesque." In *Grotesque Bodies: Weimar-era Medicine and the Photomontages of Hannah Höch*, edited by Frances Connelly, 193–219. Cambridge, England: Cambridge University Press, 2003.

Makholm, Kristin. "Film, Portraiture, and Primitivism in the Photomontages of Hannah Höch." Ph.D. Diss., University of Minnesota, 1999.

Manovich, Lev. *The Language of New Media*. Cambridge, MA: MIT Press, 2001.

Massin, Benoit. "From Virchow to Fischer: Physical Anthropology and 'Modern Race Theories' in Wilhelmine Germany." In *Volkgeist as Method and Ethic: Essays on Boasian Ethnography and the German Anthropological Tradition, History of Anthropology* 8, edited by George W. Stocking, Jr., 79–154. Madison: University of Madison Press, 1996.

Matyssek, Angela. *Das Pathologische Museum. Geschichte einer wissenschaftlichen Sammlung um 1900*. Darmstadt: Steinkopff, 2002.

May, Lary. *The Big Tomorrow: Hollywood and the Politics of the American Way*. Chicago: University of Chicago Press, 2000.

McClintock, Anne. *Imperial Leather: Race, Gender, and Sexuality in the Colonial Contest*. New York: Routledge, 1995.

McCormick, Richard W. *Gender and Sexuality in Weimar Modernity: Film, Literature, and "New Objectivity."* New York: Palgrave, 2001.

Mendelsohn, Erich. *Amerika. Bilderbuch eines Architekten*. 1925. New York: Da Capo Press, 1976.

Metken, Günter. "Eine demokratische Kunst: Das Porträt der Neuen Sachlichkeit." In *Realismus: Zwischen Revolution und Reaktion 1919–1939*, edited by Günter Metken, 106–19. Ex. cat. Munich: Prestel-Verlag, 1981.

Micheels, Pauline. "Gustav Mahler in Amsterdam (1903–1909)." In *Mahler in Amsterdam*, edited by Johan Giskes and Ester L. Woudhuysen, 24–36. Amsterdam: Gemeentearchief Amsterdam, 1995.

———. " 'Sterben werd' ich um zu leben!' (1910–1919)." In *Mahler in Amsterdam*, edited by Johan Giskes and Ester L. Woudhuysen, 37–41. Amsterdam: Gemeentearchief, 1995.

Michel, Andreas. "Culture and the Engineer: German Discourse on Technology in the Weimar Republic." *Humanities & Technology Review* 20 (2001): 1–21.

Mitchell, Donald, and Andrew Nicholson, eds. *The Mahler Companion*. Oxford: Oxford University Press, 1999.

Mjøen, Jon Alfred. *Racehygiene*. Kristiania: Jacob Dybwad, 1914.

Mouffe, Chantal. *The Democratic Paradox*. London: Verso, 2000.

———. "The End of Politics and the Rise of Right-wing Populism." In *Populism and the Mirror of Democracy*, edited by Francisco Panizza, 50–71. London: Verso, 2005.

———. *The Return of the Political*. London: Verso, 1993.

Müller, Karl-Josef. *Mahler. Leben—Werke—Dokumente*. Munich: Schott/Piper, 1988.

Munby, Jonathan. "Screening Crime in the U.S.A., 1929–1958: From Hays Code to HUAC; From Little Caesar to Touch of Evil." Ph.D. Diss., University of Minnesota, 1995. See also his book: *Public Enemies, Public Heroes: Screening the Gangster from Little Caesar to Touch of Evil.* Chicago, University of Chicago Press, 1999.

Murphy, Richard. *Theorizing the Avant-Garde: Modernism, Expressionism, and the Problem of Postmodernity.* Cambridge, England: Cambridge University Press, 1999.

Muschamp, Herbert. "Filling the Void: A Chance to Soar." *The New York Times,* September 30, 2001, AR1, AR37.

The Musical Quarterly 85, no. 1 (Spring 2001). Special issue dedicated to Hans Pfitzner.

Musil, Robert. *Tagebücher.* Edited by Adolf Frisé. Reinbek: Rowohlt, 1976.

———. *Tagebücher: Anmerkungen, Anhang, und Register.* Edited by Adolf Frisé. Reinbek: Rowohlt, 1976.

Myers, Fred R. "Introduction-Around and about Modernity: Some Comments on Themes of Primitivism and Modernism." In *Antimodernism and Artistic Experience: Policing the Boundaries of Modernity,* edited by Lynda Jessup, 13–25. Toronto: University of Toronto Press, 2001.

Næss, Harald. *Knut Hamsun.* Boston: Twayne Publishers, 1984.

———, ed. *Knut Hamsuns brev: 1934–1950.* Vol. VI. Oslo: Gyldendal, 2000.

———. "Ringen sluttet: In Defense of Abel Brodersen." In *Facets of European Modernism,* edited by Janet Garton, 309–22. Norwich: University of East Anglia Press, 1985.

Natorp, Paul. [untitled preface]. In *Adam. Ein Vorspiel. Hyppolytos. Tragödie,* edited by Siegfried Lipiner, 3–13. Stuttgart: W. Spemann, 1913.

"Neue Wege der Charakterforschung. Was die Beinhaltung enthüllt." *Berliner Illustrierte Zeitung* 38 (1929): 517.

Neumann, Dietrich. "Das 'Hochhausfieber' der zwanziger Jahre in Deutschland." In *Centrum. Jahrbuch Architektur und Stadt,* edited by Peter Neitzke and Carl Steckeweh, 38–51. Braunschweig: Vieweg, 1992.

Nietzsche, Friedrich. *Sämtliche Werke.* Edited by Giorgio Colli and Mazzino Montinari. Munich: Deutscher Taschenbuch Verlag/de Gruyter, 1980.

Nikkels, Eveline. "Mahler and Holland." In *The Mahler Companion,* edited by Donald Mitchell and Andrew Nicholson, 326–37. Oxford: Oxford University Press, 1999.

Norton, Robert E. *Secret Germany: Stefan George and His Circle.* Ithaca, NY: Cornell University Press, 2002.

Nybo, Olaf C. *Karl Gjellerup—ein literarischer Grenzgänger des Fin-de-siècle.* Hamburg: Verlag Dr. Kovac, 2002.

Nyhart, Lynn K. *Biology Takes Form: Animal Morphology and the German Universities, 1800–1900.* Chicago: University of Chicago Press, 1995.

O'Brian, John, ed. *Clement Greenberg, The Collected Essays and Criticism.* 4 vols. Chicago: The University of Chicago Press, 1986–1993.

Ødegård, Ørnulf, H.Sæthre, and A. Brinchmann. *Mentalhygiene.* Oslo: Gyldendal, 1941.

Osthoff, Wolfgang. "Einfall und Komposition bei Hans Pfitzner: Das Cellokonzert in G-Dur op. 42 (1935)." In *Vom Einfall zum Kunstwerk: der Kompositionsprozess in der Musik des 20. Jahrhunderts,* 139–60. Laaber: Laaber-Verlag, 1993.

Painter, Karen. "The Aesthetics of Mass Culture: Mahler's Eighth Symphony and Its Legacy." In *Mahler and his World,* edited by Karen Painter, 127–56. Princeton, NJ: Princeton University Press, 2002.

Pan, David. *Primitive Renaissance: Rethinking German Expressionism*. Lincoln: University of Nebraska Press, 2001.

Paul, Fritz. "Gjellerup und die Aufwertung des Jugendstils." *Danske Studier* 66 (1971): 81–90.

Penny, H. Glenn. *Objects of Culture: Ethnology and Ethnographic Museums in Imperial Germany*. Chapel Hill: University of North Carolina Press, 2002.

Peters, Emil. *Menschengestalt und Character. Lehrbuch der praktischen Menschen-Kenntnis*. Constance: Volkskraft-Verlag, 1922.

Peters, Olaf. "Eine demokratische Kunst?-Aspekte der Neuen Sachlichkeit seit 1930." In *Zeitnah Weltfern. Bilder der Neuen Sachlichkeit*, edited by Anke Brakhage and Beate Reese, 21–28. Ex. cat. Würzburg: Städtische Galerie, 1998.

———. "Die Malerei der Neuen Sachlichkeit und das dritte Reich. Bruch-Kontinuität-Transformation." In "*Der stärkste Ausdruck unserer Tage.*" *Neue Sachlichkeit in Hannover*, edited by Christian Fuhrmeister, 83–91. Ex. cat. Hildesheim: Georg Olms Verlag, 2001.

———. *Neue Sachlichkeit und Nationalsozialismus. Affirmation und Kritik 1931–1947*. Berlin: Dietrich Reimer Verlag, 1998.

———. "Rudolf Schlichters Blinde Macht. Zur Genese einer Bildfindung 1932–1936." In *Ueberbrückt. Aesthetische Moderne und Nationalsozialismus*, edited by Eugen Blume and Dieter Scholz, 168–78. Cologne: Walther König, 1999.

Petro, Patrice. *Joyless Streets: Women and Melodramatic Representation in Weimar Germany*. Princeton, NJ: Princeton University Press, 1989.

Pfitzner, Hans. *Bühnentradition, Gesammelte Schriften*. Vol. 1: 1–184. Augsburg: Benno Filser, 1929.

———. *Futuristengefahr, Gesammelte Schriften*. Vol. 1.2: 185–223. Augsburg: Benno Filser, 1929.

———. *Die neue Ästhetik der musikalischen Impotenz, Gesammelte Schriften*. Vol. 2.2: 99–282. Augsburg: Benno Filser, 1929.

———. *Palestrina: Musikalische Legende in drei Akten*. Mainz: B. Schott's Söhne, 1951.

———. *Palestrina: Musikalische Legende von Hans Pfitzner. Klavier Auszug mit Text von Felix Wolfes*. Berlin: Adolph Fürstner, 1916.

———. *Werk und Wiedergabe, Gesammelte Schriften*. Vol. 3. Augsburg: Benno Filser, 1929.

Pollan, Sonja. *Vi selv og de andre: Raseteorier i Norge for hundre år siden*. Oslo: Universitetsforlaget, 1978.

Pommer, Richard. " 'More a Necropolis than a Metropolis.' Ludwig Hilberseimer's Highrise City and Modern City Planning." In *In the Shadow of Mies: Ludwig Hilberseimer. Architect, Educator, and Urban Planner*, edited by Richard Pommer, David Spaeth, and Kevin Harrington, 16–53. Chicago: The Art Institute of Chicago and Rizzoli, 1988.

Proctor, Robert. "From Anthropologie to Rassenkunde in the German Anthropological Tradition." In *Bones, Bodies, Behavior: Essays on Biological Anthropology, History of Anthropology* 5, edited by George W. Stocking, Jr., 138–79. Madison: University of Wisconsin Press, 1988.

Protech, Max, ed. *A New World Trade Center. Design Proposals from Leading Architects Worldwide*. New York: Regan Books/Harper Collins, 2002.

Puschner, Uwe. *Die völkische Bewegung im wilhelminischen Kaiserreich. Sprache—Rasse—Religion*. Darmstadt: Wissenschaftliche Buchgesellschaft, 2001.

Rawls, John. *The Law of Peoples: With, the Idea of Public Reason Revisited.* Cambridge, MA: Harvard University Press, 1999.

Reeser, Eduard. "Die Mahler-Rezeption in Holland, 1903–1911." In *Mahler-Interpretation*, edited by Rudolf Stephan, 81–103. Mainz: Schott's Söhne, 1985.

———. *Gustav Mahler und Holand. Briefe.* Vienna: Universal Edition, 1980.

"Das Rembrandt-Buch über das Judentum." *Deutsch-Soziale Blätter. Organ der deutsch-sozialen Partei* 6, no. 169 (November 8, 1891): 529–31.

Revers, Peter. "The Seventh Symphony." In *The Mahler Companion*, edited by Donald Mitchell and Andrew Nicholson, 376–99. Oxford: Oxford University Press, 1999.

Richardson, Annie. "The Nazification of Women in Art." In *The Nazification of Art: Art, Design, Music, Architecture and Film in the Third Reich*, edited by Brandon Taylor and Wilfried van der Wil, 53–79. Winchester, Hampshire: The Winchester Press, 1990.

Ringer, Fritz. *The Decline of the German Mandarins.* Cambridge, England: Cambridge University Press, 1969.

Roh, Franz. *Nach-Expressionismus, Magischer Realismus: Probleme der neuesten europäischen Malerei.* Leipzig: Klinkhardt & Biermann, 1925.

Roll-Hansen, Nils. "Eugenics before World War II: The Case of Norway." *History and Philosophy of the Life Sciences* 2 (1980): 269–98.

———. "Norwegian Eugenics: Sterilization as Social Reform." In *Eugenics and the Welfare State. Sterilization Policy in Denmark, Sweden, Norway, and Finland*, edited by Gunnar Broberg and Nils Roll-Hansen, 151–94. East Lansing, MI: Michigan State University Press, 1996.

Rosenberg, Alfred. *Der Mythos des 20. Jahrhunderts.* Munich: Hoheneichen Verlag, 1930.

Rosenberg, Wolf. "Mahler und die Avantgarde: Kompositionstechnisches Vorbild oder geistige Sympathie?" In *Gustav Mahler: Sinfonie und Wirklichkeit*, edited by Otto Kolleritsch, 81–92. Graz: Universal Edition, 1977.

Rossel, Sven H. "The Image of the United States in Danish Literature: A Survey with Scandinavian Perspectives." In *Images of America in Scandinavia*, edited by Poul Houe and Sven Rossel, 1–23. Amsterdam: Rodopi, 1998.

Runcis, Maja. *Steriliseringar i Folkhemmet.* Stockholm: Ordfront, 1998.

Schaffing, Ferdinand, Ernst Baumann, and Heinrich Hoffmann. *Der Obersalzberg: Brennpunkt der Zeitgeschichte.* Munich: Langen Müller, 1985.

Scheerbart, Paul. *The Gray Cloth.* Translated by John A. Stuart. Cambridge, MA: MIT Press, 2001.

Schlichter, Rudolf. *Das widerspenstige Fleisch.* Berlin: Ernst Rowohlt Verlag, 1932.

Schmied, Wieland. *Neue Sachlichkeit und Magsicher Realismus in Deutschland 1918–1933.* Hannover: Fackelträger-Verlag, 1969.

Schmitt, Carl. *The Concept of the Political.* New Brunswick, NJ: Rutgers University Press, 1976.

———. "Die Einheit der Welt." *Merkur* 6, no. 1 (1952): 1–11.

———. *Der Nomos der Erde im Völkerrecht des jus publicum Europaeum.* Cologne: Greven, 1950.

———. *Political Theology: Four Chapters on the Concept of Sovereignty.* Translated by George Schwab. Cambridge, MA: MIT Press, 1985.

———. *Positionen und Begriffe: im Kampf mit Weimar—Genf—Versailles; 1923–1939.* Berlin: Duncker & Humblot, 1988.

Schmitt, Carl. *Theorie des Partisanen: Zwischenbemerkung zum Begriff des Politischen.* Berlin: Dunker & Humbolt, 1963.

Schmölders, Claudia, and Sander Gilman, eds. *Gesichter der Weimarer Republik.* Cologne: DuMont, 2000.

Schnitzler, Arthur. *Tagebuch 1913–1916.* Edited by Werner Welzig. Vienna: Osterreichische Akademie der Wissenschaften, 1983.

Scholz, Georg. "Die Elemente zur Erzielung der Wirkung im Bilde." *Das Kunstblatt* 8 (1924): 77–80.

Schwartz, Frederic J. "Form Follows Fetish: Adolf Behne and the Problem of Sachlichkeit." *Oxford Art Journal* 21, no. 2 (1998): 45–77.

Schwarz, Birgit. " 'Otto Hans Baldung Dix' malt die Großstadt. Zur Rezeption der altdeutschen Malerei." In *Otto Dix. Zum 100. Geburtstag 1891–1991*, edited by Wulf Herzogenrath and Johann-Karl Schmidt, 229–38. Ex. cat. Stuttgart: Verlag Gerd Hatje, 1991.

Sheppard, Richard. *Modernism, Dada, Postmodernism.* Evanston, IL: Northwestern University Press, 2000.

Simonsen, Konrad. *Den moderne Mennesketype.* Kristiania: Aschehoug, 1917.

———. *Georg Brandes (jødisk aand i Danmark).* Copenhagen: Nationale forfatteres forlag, 1914.

Simmel, Georg. "Die Großstädte und das Geistesleben." *Gesamtausgabe. Aufsätze und Abhandlungen 1901–1908.* Vol. 7, edited by Rüdiger Kramme, Angela Rammstedt, and Otthein Rammstedt, 116–32. Frankfurt: Suhrkamp, 1995.

Simpson, Allan. "Hamsun's Anti-Semitism." *Edda* 5 (1977): 273–93.

Skouenborg, Ulrik. *Von Wagner zu Pfitzner: Stoff und Form der Musik.* Tutzing: Schneider, 1983.

Sloterdijk, Peter. "Die Klausur in der Mutter: Zur Grundlegung einer negativen Gynäkologie." In *Sphären I: Blasen*, 275–327. Frankfurt: Suhrkamp, 2000.

———. "Poetik der Entbindung." In *Zur Welt kommen-zur Sprache kommen: Frankfurter Vorlesungen*, 99–143. Frankfurt: Suhrkamp, 1988.

———. "Das Sirenen-Stadium: Von der ersten sonosphärischen Allianz." In *Sphären I: Blasen*, 487–531. Frankfurt: Suhrkamp, 2000.

———. "Die sokratische Maieutik und die Geburtsvergessenheit der Philosophie." In *Zur Welt kommen-zur Sprache kommen: Frankfurter Vorlesungen*, 60–98. Frankfurt: Suhrkamp, 1988.

———. "Wo sind wir, wenn wir Musik hören?" In *Weltfremdheit*, 294–325. Frankfurt: Suhrkamp, 1993.

Sloterdijk, Peter, and Hans-Juergen Heinrichs. *Die Sonne und der Tod: Dialogische Untersuchungen.* Frankfurt: Suhrkamp, 2001.

Speer, Albert. *Inside the Third Reich.* Translated by Richard Winston and Clara Winston. New York: MacMillan, 1970.

Spektorokowski, Alberto. "The Eugenic Temptation in Socialism: Sweden, Germany, and the Soviet Union." *Comparative Studies in Society and History* 46 (2004): 84–106.

Staten, Henry. *Wittgenstein and Derrida.* Oxford: Basil Blackwell, 1985.

Steinhauer, Jennifer. "A Symbol of Faith Marks a City's Hallowed Ground." *The New York Times*, October 5, 2001, B12.

Stepan, Nancy. "Biological Degeneration, Races and Proper Places." In *Degeneration*, edited by J. Edward Chamberlin and Sander L. Gilman, 97–120. New York: Columbia University Press, 1985.

Stern, Fritz. *The Politics of Cultural Despair: A Study in the Rise of the Germanic Ideology*. Garden City, NJ: Doubleday & Co, 1965.

Stjernfelt, Frederik. "Hvad blir vi som ikke blir noget?" *Norskrift* 57 (1989): 20–60.

Subotnik, Rose Rosengard. *Developing Variations: Style and Ideology in Western Music*. Minneapolis: University of Minnesota Press, 1991.

Tafuri, Manfredo. *Architecture and Utopia: Design and Capitalist Development*. Translated by Barbara Luigia La Penta. Cambridge, MA: MIT Press, 1976.

———. *The Sphere and the Labyrinth. Avant-Gardes and Architecture from Piranesi to the 1970s*. Translated by Pellegrino d'Acierno and Robert Connolly. Cambridge, MA: MIT Press, 1990.

Taut, Bruno. *Alpine Architektur*. Hagen: Folkwang-Verlag G.M.B.H., 1919.

———. *Der Weltbaumeister. Architekturschauspiel für symphonische Musik*. Hagen: Folkwang-Verlag, 1920.

———. *Stadtkrone*. Jena: Eugen Diederichs, 1919.

Taylor, Brandon. "Post-Modernism in the Third Reich." In *The Nazification of Art: Art, Design, Music, Architecture and Film in the Third Reich*, edited by Brandon Taylor and Wilfried van der Wil. Winchester, Hampshire: The Winchester Press, 1990.

Theweleit, Klaus. *Male Fantasies*. Translated by Stephan Conway. Minneapolis: University of Minnesota Press, 1987.

Thomas, Calvin. "A Knowledge that Would Not Be Power: Adorno, Nostalgia, and the History of the Musical Subject." *New German Critique* 48 (Autumn 1989): 155–75.

Thyssen, Ole. *Påfuglens øjne: Efter postmodernismen*. Copenhagen: Rosinante, 1987.

Tienari, R. "Psychiatric Illnesses in Identical Twins" *Acta Psychiatrica Scandinavia. Supplement* 171, no. 39 (1963): 9–195.

Toller, Owen. *Pfitzner's Palestrina: The 'Musical Legend' and Its Background*. Exeter: Toccata Press, 1997.

Torgovnick, Marianna. *Gone Primitive: Savage Intellects, Modern Lives*. Chicago: The University of Chicago Press, 1990.

Tydén, Mattias. *Från Politik till Praktik. De svenska steriliseringslagarna 1935–1975*. Stockholm: Almqvist og Wiksell International, 2002.

van Pelt, Robert Jan. *Architectural Principles in the Age of Historicism*. New Haven, CT: Yale University Press, 1991.

Venzmer, Gerhard. *Sieh Dir die Menschen an! Was die biologische Verwandtschaft zwischen Körperformen und Wesenskern des Menschen verrät*. Stuttgart: Franch, 1930.

van Amerongen, Martin, and Philo Bregstein. *Willem Mengelberg tussen licht en donker*. Baarn: de Prom, 2001.

Vidler, Anthony. "A City Transformed: Designing 'Defensible Space.'" *The New York Times*, September 23, 2001, WK6.

———. "Fresh Air." *National Public Radio*, September 29, 2001.

Virchow, Rudolf. *Die Eröffnung des Pathologischen Museums der Königl. FriedrichWilhelms-Universität zu Berlin am 27. Juni 1899, Berlin 1899*. Berlin: August Hirschwald, 1899.

Virchow, "The Founding of the Berlin University and the Transition from thePhilosophic to the Scientific Age." In *The Smithsonian Report for 1894*, 681–95. Washington: Government Printing Office, 1896.

———. *The Freedom of Science in the Modern State: A Discourse Delivered at the Third General Meeting of the Fiftieth Conference of the German Association of Naturalists and Physicians at Munich on the 22nd of September, 1877*. London: John Murray, 1878.

———. *Die Freiheit der Wissenschaft im modernen Staat*. Berlin: Verlag von Weigandt, Hempel & Parey, 1877.

Vogel, Johann Peter. *Hans Pfitzner mit Selbstzeugnissen und Bilddokumenten*. Reinbek: Rowohlt, 1989.

von Hofsten, Nils. "De arvsbiologiska verkningarna av sterilisering." *Hygiea. Medicinsk tidskrift utgiven av Svenska Läkaresellskapet* 106 (1944): 177–82.

———. *Steriliseringar i Sverige 1941–1953 Socialmedicinsk Tidskrifts skriftserie*. Vol. 28, Uppsala: Almquist & Wiksell, 1963.

Walter, Bruno. *Gustav Mahler. Ein Porträt*. Berlin: S. Fischer, 1957.

Ward, Janet. *Weimar Surfaces. Urban Visual Culture in 1920s Germany*. Berkeley: University of California Press, 2001.

Weber, Max. *Political Writings*. Cambridge, England: Cambridge University Press, 1994.

Weihe, Carl. "Die kulturellen Aufgaben des Ingenieurs." *Technik und Kultur* 15 (1924): 45–49.

Weiner, Marc A. *Undertones of Insurrection: Music, Politics, and the Social Sphere in the Modern German Narrative*. Lincoln: University of Nebraska Press, 1993.

———. "Urwaldmusik and the Borders of German Identity: Jazz in Literature of the Weimar Republic." *The German Quarterly* 64, no. 4 (Fall 1991): 475–87.

Weingart, Peter. "Science and Political Culture: Eugenics in Comparative Perspective." *Scandinavian Journal of History* 24 (1999): 163–77.

Weingart, Peter, Jürgen Kroll, and Kurt Bayertz. *Rasse, Blut und Gene. Geschichte der Eugenik und Rassenhygiene in Deutschland*. Frankfurt: Suhrkamp Verlag, 1988.

Weinstein, J., and N. Stehr. "The Power of Knowledge: Race Science, Race Policy, and the Holocaust." *Social Epistemology* 13 (2000): 1–36.

Weitz, Ulrich. "Kriegskrüppel, Kapp-Putsch und Kunstlump-Debatte." In *Otto Dix. Zum 100. Geburtstag 1891–1991*, edited by Wulf Herzogenrath and Johann-Karl Schmidt, 95–100. Stuttgart: Verlag Gerd Hatje, 1991.

Westheim, Paul. "Ein neuer Naturalismus?? Eine Rundfrage des Kunstblatts." *Das Kunstblatt* 6 (September 1922): 369–414.

White, Iain Boyd, ed. *The Crystal Chain Letters: Architectural Fantasies by Bruno Taut and His Circle*. Cambridge, MA: MIT Press, 1985.

Widdig, Bernd. *Culture and Inflation in Weimar Germany*. Berkeley: University of California Press, 2001.

Willeke, Stefan. "Die Technokratiebewegung zwischen den Weltkriegen und der Kulturfaktor Technik." In *Technische Intelligenz und Kulturfaktor Technik: Kulturvorstellungen von Technikern und Ingenieuren zwischen Kaiserreich und früher Bundesrespulik Deutschland*, edited by Burkhard Dietz, Michael Fessner, and Helmut Maier. 203–20. Munster: Waxmann, 1996.

Williams, C. E. *The Broken Eagle: The Politics of Austrian Literature from Empire to Anschluss*. New York: Barnes & Noble, 1974.

Williamson, John. *The Music of Hans Pfitzner*. Oxford: Clarendon, 1992.

Wolpert, Klaus. *Die Nackten und die Toten: Folgen einer politischen Geschichte des Körpers in der Plastik des deutschen Faschismus*. Giessen: Anabas, 1982.

Wouthuysen, Ester L. "Het beeld van Mahler door Rodin. Een veelbelovende geste aan het Concertgebouw." In *Mahler in Amsterdam*, edited by Johan Giskes and Ester L. Woudhuysen, 108–13. Amsterdam: Gemeentearchief Amsterdam, 1995.

Žagar, Monika. "Imagining the Red-Skinned Other. Hamsun's Article 'Fra en Indianerleir' (1885)." *Edda* 4 (2001): 385–95.

———. "Knut Hamsun's Black Man or Lament for Paternalist Society: A Reading of Hamsun's Play Livet ivold through Fra det moderne Amerikas Aandsliv." *Edda* 4 (1997): 364–79.

Zeitgenossen. August Sander und die Kunstszene der 20er Jahre im Rheinland. Ex. cat. Göttingen: Steidl Verlag, 2000.

Zimmerman, Andrew. *Anthropology and Antihumanism in Imperial Germany*. Chicago: University of Chicago Press, 2001.

———. "Looking Beyond History: The Optics of German Anthropology and the Critique of Humanism." *Studies in History and Philosophy of Biology and Biomedical Sciences* 32, no. 3 (2001): 385–411.

Zimmermann, Michael E. *Heidegger's Confrontation with Modernity. Technology, Politics, Art*. Bloomington, IN: Indiana University Press, 1990.

Zwart, Frits. *Willem Mengelberg 1871–1951. Een biografie 1871–1920*. Vol. 1. Amsterdam: Prometheus, 1999.

Zylberman, Patric. "Les damnes de la democratie puritaine: sterilisations en Scandinavie, 1929–1977." *Le Mouvement Social* 187 (April–June 1999): 99–125.

Index